THE INVISIBLE HAND OF POWER:
AN ECONOMIC THEORY OF GATE KEEPING

Modern Heterodox Economics

Series Editor: *Carol M. Connell*

THE INVISIBLE HAND OF POWER:
AN ECONOMIC THEORY OF GATE KEEPING

BY

Anton N. Oleinik

Routledge
Taylor & Francis Group
LONDON AND NEW YORK

First published 2015 by Pickering & Chatto (Publishers) Limited

2 Park Square, Milton Park, Abingdon, Oxfordshire OX14 4RN
52 Vanderbilt Avenue, New York, NY 10017

Routledge is an imprint of the Taylor & Francis Group, an informa business

First issued in paperback 2020

BRITISH LIBRARY CATALOGUING IN PUBLICATION DATA

Oleinik, Anton N., author.
The invisible hand of power: an economic theory of gate keeping. – (Modern
heterodox economics)
1. Power (Social sciences) – Economic aspects. 2. North America – Foreign
economic relations. 3. Russia (Federation) – Foreign economic relations.
I. Title II. Series
337-dc23

ISBN-13: 978-1-84893-524-2 (hbk)
ISBN-13: 978-0-367-66909-6 (pbk)

Typeset by Pickering & Chatto (Publishers) Limited

CONTENTS

To Olga, with gratitude for her devotion

ACKNOWLEDGEMENTS

I am grateful to both Commissioning Editors of Pickering & Chatto involved in this publishing project. Philip Good encouraged me to write the present book after reading a draft of what would later become one of its chapters. Sophie Rudland provided valuable assistance at the final stage of my work and showed a willingness to adjust to my changing schedule. Pickering & Chatto's reviewers, including Professor Carol Connell, the series editor, made a number of comments and suggestions that helped me to determine the book's final structure and line of reasoning. I would also like to thank Professor Herbert Gintis, External Professor at Santa Fe Institute, and Professor of Economics at the Central European University, for his reading of an early draft of Chapter 2 and comments that he made. Professor Christopher Brown, the editor of the *Journal of Economic Issues*, helped fix a few problems in an earlier version of two sections in Chapter 3 that were published as a stand-alone article in this journal (A. Oleinik, 'The 2008 Financial Crisis Through the Lens of Power Relationships', *Journal of Economic Issues*, 47:2 (2013), pp. 465–74). An earlier version of two sections in Chapter 5 was also published in the same journal ('Access to Justice as a Form of Inequality', *Journal of Economic Issues*, 48:2 (2014), pp. 405–12). The previously published material is reprinted with permission from the publisher, M. E. Sharpe. Sheryl Curtis of *Les Communications WriteTouch* (Montréal) as usual did a great job with the style editing.

LIST OF FIGURES AND TABLES

1 VISIBLE AND INVISIBLE HANDS OF POWER: THEORETICAL PRELIMINARIES

Power is one of those things without which our lives would be unthinkable. Power in its various forms structures our interactions with children at home, students or instructors in classrooms, superiors and subordinates at work, and public servants in government offices. It would be difficult to find any social relationship that is absolutely free of power. Finding situations in which power turns out to be irrelevant involves thinking counterfactually, i.e. pretending that things are different from the way we know they are. It is no coincidence that counterfactual thinking represents an important analytical tool used by scholars studying power.[1]

Despite its importance and omnipresence, our knowledge about power is limited, especially when comparing it with progress in generating knowledge about the other determinants of human behaviour. Scientists have managed to decode the complete DNA sequence of a single human being, but they still know little about the mechanics of power and its possible forms. The list of the possible explanations for this relative ignorance includes the contested character of the concept of power and the lack of commonly accepted taxonomies.

Scholars studying power acknowledge the 'essentially contested' character of this concept.[2] This means that many alternative definitions of power coexist and no theoretical criterion is available for settling disputes as to how to define this phenomenon. In this book, I use a definition of power inspired by Max Weber. He connects power to one's capacity to carry out one's will: '"power" is the probability that one actor within a social relationship will be in a position to carry out his own will despite resistance, regardless of the basis on which this probability rests'.[3] I define power as one's capacity to achieve one's preferable outcomes regardless of the circumstances, however unfavourable they may be. The eventual material obstacles and resistance on the part of the other people involved do not prevent the power holder from getting what she[4] wants. In more general terms, power refers to one's capacity to go one's own way all the time, to have the upper hand in all relationships, including those with the material environment.

As in the case of the plurality of definitions, taxonomies of power also abound. There is no universally acceptable one, no analogue to the periodic table of the chemical elements in the studies of power, however. As a result, the existing taxonomies serve to address specific issues without covering all possible forms of power.[5] If disagreements as to how power should be defined undermine building a general theory, the multiplicity of the taxonomies of power complicates empirical studies. Randall Collins shows that the focus on empirical discovery represents a necessary component in the progress of scientific knowledge.[6] The empirical data on power tend to be scarce. Furthermore, these data refer to discrepant elements that do not form a coherent picture. We know something about some elements of power, but little about power as a whole.

For instance, scholars have collected a significant amount of empirical data on a particular dimension of power, power distance, in various managerial cultures. Power distance refers to 'the extent to which the less powerful members of institutions and organizations within a country expect and accept that power is distributed unequally'.[7] This information does not shed light on power outside of the context of corporate governance, however.[8] Power distance varies across countries, but it also supposedly varies according to the level at which an activity takes place: macro (government), meso (organization) or micro (family). Harry Eckstein developed a theory in this regard, namely the congruency theory: 'governments will be unstable ... if the governmental authority pattern is isolated ... from those of other social segments'.[9] This theory remains largely unverified due to the scarcity of relevant empirical data at the macro and especially micro levels.[10]

This book is intended to be a small building block in our fragmented knowledge about power. More specifically, it contributes to unveiling invisible forms of power and discusses the situations in which power takes the least obvious forms. The metaphor of power as an upper, guiding hand can be made more nuanced. The guiding hand either helps individuals to better achieve their private and public interests or, on the contrary, undermines their chances of doing so. The former hand is benevolent; the latter hand is unkind and antagonistic. If individuals are aware of the guidance, they see the hand and understand its effects on their behaviour. They may also be ignorant of the existence of the guiding hand because of its invisible character.

Adam Smith's famous arguments on the benefits of the self-interested behaviour illustrate the idea of a benevolent invisible hand:[11]

> As every individual, therefore, endeavours as much as he can both to employ his capital in the support of domestic industry, and so to direct that industry that its produce may be of the greatest value; every individual necessarily labours to render the annual revenue of the society as great as he can. He generally, indeed, neither intends to promote the public interest, nor knows how much he is promoting it. By preferring the support of domestic to that of foreign industry, he intends only his own security; and by directing that industry in such a manner as its produce may be of the greatest value, he intends only his own gain, and he is in this, as in many other cases, led by an invisible

hand to promote an end which was no part of his intention. Nor is it always the worse for the society that it was no part of it. By pursuing his own interest he frequently promotes that of the society more effectually than when he really intends to promote it.

In this passage Smith speaks of a particular type of power, the power embedded in the perfectly competitive market. This power is diffused among the parties in market transactions instead of being concentrated in the hands of a single individual, which also explains its low visibility. Nevertheless, the invisible hand of the market involves exercising power because its existence enables the parties in market transactions to better realize their private and public interests. Smith thus argues that this power has a benevolent, helping nature.

Mancur Olson further develops this line of reasoning and claims that the power embedded in monopolistic structures, namely the power of an autocratic government, leads to similar outcomes. His argument refers to the beneficial effects of encompassing interests. When the autocrat's private interest tends to be broad and encompassing, it essentially coincides with social interest. Olson counterintuitively argues that the autocrat, an apparently powerful individual, is nevertheless subject to an invisible form of power that guides her actions in a benevolent manner:[12]

There is a shift from destructive to constructive use of power – as when Hobbes's 'war of all against all' is replaced by order provided by an autocratic government – is due to another invisible hand. This invisible hand – shall we call it the invisible hand on the left? – that guides encompassing interests to use the power, at least to some degree, in accord with the social interest, even with serving the public good, was not part of the intention. This second invisible hand is as unfamiliar and perhaps counterintuitive as the first hidden hand was in Adam Smith's time, but that does not mean it is less important.

This book's intended contribution to the existing body of knowledge on power refers to its specific focus on the invisible hand, or rather hands, of power. Such emphasis has several rationales. The approach developed in this monograph serves to unveil the presence of power in situations in which an untrained eye does not normally see it. The thesis on the omnipresence and universality of power appears to be confirmed as a result.

The monograph can be read not only out of pure academic interest, however. The knowledge of invisible aspects in the operation of power enables the individual, who is subject to it, to better resist. Smith and Olson discuss benevolent invisible hands. Resistance appears to be superficial in these circumstances. When the individual is subject to antagonistic forms of power, she has the interest and right to resist. 'The word "dissidence" is exactly suited for these forms of resistance that concern, set their sights on, and have as their objective and adversary power that assumes the task of conducting men in their life and daily existence'.[13] This book places primary emphasis on antagonistic invisible hands – on the exercise of power in an *invisible* and *adversarial* manner.

This first chapter serves as a general introduction to the book. It has four sections. Section 1 provides an overview of various forms of power. Particular attention is devoted to domination as the exercise of power in an adversarial manner. Section 2 differentiates the structural and strategic components of power. The theories of power embedded in structures developed by Karl Marx and Michel Foucault serve as two major reference points. In contrast to Smith's and Olson's beliefs in the benevolence of the invisible hands of the market, Marx and Foucault consider the antagonistic invisible hands embedded in economic structures. The concept of a repertoire of techniques for imposing will is introduced in Section 3. Some of them take visible forms; the application of the others usually goes unnoticed. Section 4 contains brief descriptions of the remaining book chapters. It highlights a connecting link between them, a particular invisible technique for imposing will embedded in market structures, namely domination by virtue of a constellation of interests in the market.

1. Power as a Coordination Device and its Forms

The definition of power as one's capacity to achieve one's preferable outcomes regardless of the circumstances does not differentiate between two kinds of obstacles that may eventually complicate the realization of the individual's interests. The skills and know-how necessary to overcome material obstacles differ from the skills required for solving problems in human interactions. Let us compare two situations with a similar outcome, namely, my failure to find some highly specific information on the internet. In the first case, I lack the technical expertise necessary to perform sophisticated searches. In order to solve the problem, I need to learn how to narrow down the search terms. In the second case, I have this expertise, but some agent, a government official, restricts my access to the internet. The required solution is different in this case: I need to get the restrictions removed either by taking legal action against the government official or by voting for someone else at the next elections.

Scholars studying power introduce a distinction between 'power to' and 'power over' that helps one to better understand the particularities of the two sets of skills.

> Explanation in terms of 'power to' concentrates on an actor's ability to achieve *a desired result*, whereas explanation in terms of 'power over' emphasizes an actor's ability to achieve *a submission (compliance) of another actor* which, in turn, can bring the desired result.[14]

Returning to the example of the internet search, the government official's restrictions invalidate my power to perform sophisticated searches. Thus, in order to find the information that I am looking for (i.e. to achieve my preferable outcome), I must reassert my power over the government official, thereby making her respect freedom of access to the internet. It follows that 'power to' refers to technical skills whereas 'power over' involves social skills.

'Power over' always exists in the context of social interactions: at least two parties must be involved. 'Power to' may or may not have a social dimension. The former happens if the agent gets someone else to produce a desired outcome for her. For instance, if I cannot express myself in Chinese, I can hire a translator to get the job done.

The social dimension of power suggests that power tends to be ubiquitous everywhere there is a need for coordinating individual actions.[15] Power represents a solution to coordination problems.[16] When individual actors disagree as to how to act together, one party may eventually assume power by taking the initiative and guiding the others. Mann speaks of 'compulsory cooperation' in this regard.[17] The benevolent guiding hand of power enhances agents' capacity 'to act in concert',[18] to use an apt expression from Hannah Arendt.

By placing emphasis on 'power to', one highlights the positive effects of power, the benevolent character of the guiding hand. The concept of 'power to' directs our attention to what is achieved, to the manner in which power extends the scope of the possible in human action. Emphasis on 'power over', on the other hand, involves mostly negative connotations. Seen in this light, the guiding hand of power has adversarial effects because it produces conflicts and increases tensions. The use of the concept of 'power over' makes us think of how the gains of actions in concert are divided among the parties involved. 'Power to may involve cooperation; power over seems to involve conflict'.[19] Probably for this reason Arendt reserves the word 'power' for the former case. She associates 'power over' with violence.[20]

Because the present monograph intends to study the adversarial effects of power, 'power over' deserves additional discussion. An individual exercises power over another individual either in the latter's interests or contrary to the latter's interests. No conflict emerges in the first case, for example, in relationships between parents and their child. Thomas Wartenberg describes this configuration of power relationships in terms of transformative power:[21]

> In a transformative use of power a dominant agent ... exercises power over a subordinate agent for the latter's benefit. In doing so, the dominant agent's aim is not simply to act for the benefit of the subordinate agent; rather, the dominant agent attempts to exercise his power in such a way that the subordinate agent learns certain skills that undercut the power differential between her and the dominant agent.

Transformative power represents a rare occurrence. Only in a perfect world will all power holders turn out to be so benevolent. In real life situations, the power over a subordinate agent is most commonly exercised against her interests. The term 'domination' applies in this case. Domination involves 'an imposition or constraint working against the interests of those subject to it'.[22] Everyday language attaches a similar meaning to the word 'domination', which allows us to avoid using such awkward equivalent expressions as 'power over used against the subordinate's interests'.

The concept of domination also has solid theoretical foundations. Frank Lovett summarizes them in the form of a theory of domination. According to Lovett, domination requires that three conditions are met, two necessary and one sufficient.[23] First, the parties in a relationship must possess unequal power. Second, one party has to be dependent on the other. Third, the party with more power exercises it in an arbitrary manner. The third, sufficient, condition enables the dominant agent to exercise power without taking into consideration the subordinate's interests and eventually contrary to her interests.

The dominant agent's discretion as the sufficient condition of domination prompts the question as to her objectives. If the subordinate's interests do not count, what does? Scholars studying power acknowledge that power plays the role of either a means or an end. Power used in an instrumental manner helps advance particular individual or common interests. Namely, domination involves the advancement of the dominant agent's interests at the expense of the subordinate's interests. These interests refer to something other than power itself, for instance, the dominant agent's wealth or health. 'Because the tool is not itself an end it lacks the relative independence that the end implies, either as an absolute value or as something that will produce an effect upon us'.[24]

Power represents one of the most universal means, along with money. Dennis Wrong argues that the degree of its universality varies. The universality of power as a means in traditional societies exceeds that of money, whereas in modern societies the situation tends to be opposite. 'Power may be a medium, but a not very generalized medium ... considerably less so than money'.[25]

Similarly to money, power as a means may eventually become an end. Georg Simmel studies this transformation in the case of money. According to Simmel, money is 'the outstanding and most perfect example of the psychological raising of means to ends'.[26] It happens if one values the possession of money more than what it can buy. Likewise, power becomes an end in itself if one values its possession more than what can be achieved with its help. Domination is then valuable not because the dominant agent has a chance for advancing her interests, but because of the control over the subordinate that it allows.

Power as an end in itself has no in-built constraints. The model of rational choice does not explain its value for the power holder either. The case of power becoming an end in itself sheds light on a number of important phenomena; Russian power, or the model of power historically prevailing in the Russian institutional environment, is one.[27]

The omnipresence of power leaves it outside of the focus of attention of scholars representing specialized knowledge. Several disciplines study power

– analytical philosophy, political sociology, political science and economic sciences – but none of them specializes in studying it. This fact shall be added to the list of possible explanations for our limited knowledge about power.

Economists deal with manifestations of power in a particular sphere of human activity, the economy. Power remains on the periphery of mainstream economists' professional attention, however. The term does not appear among index entries of the most introductory and advanced textbooks in economics. An article on power was added to the most authoritative economic dictionary, *The New Palgrave*, only in its recent, second, edition. The authors, Samuel Bowles and Herbert Gintis, enumerate references to power that can be found in economists' works: purchasing power, market power and bargaining power.[28] Purchasing power is the power to buy goods and services; it depends on one's budget. Market power also has features of 'power to'. This form of power enables the economic agent to change the price at will. Bargaining power lies closer to 'power over': it refers to one's ability to capture the joint surplus generated in a transaction. In the three cases considered by mainstream economists, power has an instrumental, as opposed to terminal, value: power is deemed to be a means, not an end.

Analytical philosophers, economic and political sociologists study power more systematically. Their works contain several valuable approaches and insights that may be of interest for those economists who are dissatisfied with their profession's ignorance of the issues of power. The concept of a power dyad developed in analytical philosophy is one. The power dyad represents an elementary power relationship. Two parties constitute the power dyad, *A* (power holder) and *B* (the agent subject to power). *A* achieves her preferable outcomes by imposing her will on *B*. Transactions between *A* and *B* are structured in such a manner that the former commands and the latter obeys.

This concept paves the way for formalizing and modelling power relationships, as we will see in Chapter 2. Theorizing power in terms of the power dyad also serves to find a common language with some heterodox economists, namely institutionalists. In contrast to mainstream economists, institutionalist economists consider power as an important topic in their studies.[29] Institutionalists use the transaction as the unit of analysis:[30]

> These individual actions are really *trans*-actions instead of either individual behavior or the 'exchange' of commodities. It is this shift from commodities and individuals to transactions and working rules of collective action that marks the transition from the classical and hedonic schools to the institutional schools of economic thinking.

The power dyad may then be considered a particular type of transaction. Transactions between *A* and *B* constitute a power dyad if *A* manages to achieve her preferable outcomes whereas *B* fails to do the same.

2. Power Embedded in Structures

The power dyad shows who rules and who obeys but this concept does not explain why it happens. Was *A* born to rule and *B* – to obey? The distinction between the structural and strategic components of power helps one to better understand the process of assignment to the particular roles within the power dyad. Structural components of power provide some agents with objective advantages over the others. A card player with all trump and top cards in her hands has perfect chances of winning the game. The strategic components of power refer to the agent's strategies for gaining the upper hand in the transaction. A card player with no trump or top cards in her hands still has chances of winning, provided that she proves to be a good strategist.

Keith Dowding describes structural components of power in terms of luck. 'Luck ... enables some to get what they want without trying'.[31] According to him, agents enjoying structural advantages in their relationships with the others are simply lucky. The downgrading of agents enjoying structural advantages to the category of lucky people (as opposed to truly powerful people), does not alter the fact that they have better chances for playing the role of *A* in the power dyads than people without such advantages, however.

The situation of bargaining highlights the strategic components of power. In order to achieve her preferred outcome, i.e. to capture a larger share of the surplus generated by the transaction, the agent has to elaborate and successfully implement a strategy or a set of strategies. Among the other options, she may pre-commit herself to a particular course of action, keep her true preferences hidden, make an offer to the other party, issue a threat against the other party or even disrupt communication at a well-chosen moment.[32]

The outcomes of bargaining in the conditions of bilateral monopoly depend only on the agents' strategic capacities. An experiment involving dividing $100 between two individuals approximates this situation. In experimental economics, two participants are invited to divide a certain amount of money, say $100, between themselves. If they disagree with respect to the proportions in which they divide it, then no one gets anything. In order to increase her share, the participant has to play strategically. The factor of structural disparities and inequalities is completely eliminated here:[33]

> The outcome must fall between what may be called the two parties' concession limits, which are defined by each party's refusal to accept any agreement that would make him actually worse off than he would be in the conflict situation. But the two arguments in themselves say nothing about where the two parties' agreement point will actually lie between these two limits.

The two monopolists' strategic bargaining skills determine the exact position of the agreement point within the interval of possible values. The one with the better strategic skills will move the agreement point closer to the other's concession limit.

Marx and Foucault probably offer the two most influential conceptualizations of the structural components of power. More specifically, they discuss the power embedded in economic structures leaving its strategic components outside of their analyses as irrelevant. Marxism comes first in historical and epistemological terms.

2.1 Marxism

Smith characterizes the hand of the market as invisible and benevolent. Marx agrees with the first characteristic but rejects the second. His version of the invisible hand of the market highlights its adversarial nature. The invisibility of the guiding hand is due to its embeddedness in market structures. Marxism studies the depersonalized, diffused power that 'spreads in a more spontaneous, unconscious, decentered way throughout a population, resulting in similar social practices that embody power relations but are not explicitly commanded'.[34]

No one explicitly orders the worker to sell her labour. The worker chooses to do so out of free will. The worker also maintains a formal independence from the capitalist, despite her compliance with the latter's command. At first sight, the transaction between the capitalist and the worker excludes power. The labour hires the capital much in the same way as the capital hires the labour:[35]

> The sphere of circulation or commodity exchange, within whose boundaries the sale and purchase of labour-power goes on, is in fact a very Eden of the innate rights of man. It is the exclusive realm of Freedom, Equality, Property and Bentham. Freedom, because both buyer and seller of a commodity ... are determined by their own free will ... Equality, because each ... exchange equivalent for equivalent ... Property, because each disposes only of what is his own. And Bentham, because each looks only to his own advantage.

If despite freedom, equality and the utilitarian orientation the capitalist gains the upper hand in her relationships with the worker, this happens due to structural disparities that systematically favour the former. The process of the accumulation of capital produces a relative surplus population or 'industrial reserve army'. The existence of unemployment in the labour market weakens the positions of labour and correspondingly strengthens the positions of capital.

A particular system of the division of labour necessitates the capitalist's command of the process of production. 'A capitalist should command in the field of production is now as indispensable as that a great general should command on the field of battle'.[36] Returning to the metaphor of the card game, the capitalist has more trump and top cards than the worker. 'The structure of capitalist society makes capitalists systematically lucky'.[37]

The trump and top cards do not make the capitalist's life happier, however. Marx suggests that even when the capitalist exercises her discretion by selecting one applicant for a job out of many and secures the latter's obedience to her orders in the process of production, she does not do it in an arbitrary manner. Similarly to the worker, the capitalist must follow the laws of accumulation of capital as well. Namely, the capitalist has to prioritize savings and investments over her personal consumption and other small pleasures of life. In Marx's opinion, the capitalist represents nothing other than 'capital personified':[38]

> Except as capital personified, the capitalist has no historical value, and no right to [the] historical existence. In so far as he is capital personified, his motivating force is not the acquisition and enjoyment of use-values, but the acquisition and augmentation of exchange-values ... He ruthlessly forces the human race to produce for production's sake ... Only as a personification of capital is the capitalist respectable ... His actions are a mere function of capital.

At the end of the day, the two seemingly free and equal agents, the capitalist and the worker, turn out to be equally unfree. No one dominates because even the capitalist cannot exercise her discretionary powers in an arbitrary manner. The system dominates both of them. According to Marx, they both personify the logic of accumulation of capital. The invisible hand of the market allows no one to fully enjoy 'Freedom, Equality, Property and Bentham'.

2.2 Foucault's Theory of Security

Foucault also considers the invisible and adversarial hand of the market. However, his demonstration of the invisible and adversarial nature of the power embedded in the market does not involve references to the process of capitalist accumulation. Instead, he emphasizes the standardizing and homogenizing effects of the market. Being subject to the invisible hand of the market, people with their multiple and diverse interests are transformed into a 'population' with a limited range of highly uniform interests.

Foucault differentiates two major systems that serve to make human behaviour more standardized and conformed to the norm, namely discipline and security. Discipline refers to the visible hand of power whereas security is an outcome of its invisible hand. According to Foucault, discipline prevails at the early stages of historical development. An ideal-typical representation of discipline can be found in the institution of prison.[39] Its major function consists in localizing and correcting deviant behaviour by the restriction of freedom. All deviant, rebel and otherwise non-conformist individuals end up being sent to prison and to other disciplinary institutions (mental hospitals, asylums and so forth). There is no easy escape from these disciplinary institutions because of severe exit control measures:[40]

> Discipline is essentially centripetal ... Discipline concentrates, focuses, and encloses. The first action of discipline is in fact to circumscribe a space in which its power and the mechanisms of its power will function fully and without limit.

Security involves the other set of measures as to how to make human behaviour more uniform. Individuals are granted the freedom to pursue their interests. Namely, security minimizes interference in naturally occurring transactions. 'Security ... tries to work within reality, by getting the components of reality to work in relation to each other, thanks to and through a series of analyses and specific arrangements'.[41]

Not all interests have the opportunity to be realized, however. The existing institutions support the pursuit of only a limited range of interests. For instance, the invisible hand of the market serves to prioritize pecuniary interests. In other words, individuals have the freedom to realize their interests with no restrictions as long as these interests are embedded in and supported by the existing institutions. Provided that the institutions promoting the desirable patterns of behaviour are in place, 'it will be necessary to arouse, to facilitate, and to *laisser faire*, in other words to manage and no longer to control through rules and regulations'.[42]

For Foucault as well as for Marx, power does not have a human face since it is embedded in structures. According to some interpretations of Foucault's thought, 'structures themselves, and not social actors, actually have power'.[43] There is very limited, if any, room for the strategic components of power under these circumstances. One of the lines of criticism addressed to both Foucault and Marx refers to their presumed neglect of the strategic components of power. Structural determinism in studies of power excludes the existence of individuals and groups vested in power.

2.3 Combining Structural and Strategic Components of Power

Attempts to combine the structural (Marx, Foucault) and strategic (Dowding) components of power offer a promising theoretical and practical alternative. Steven Lukes speaks of '*combining* a '"faced" with a "de-faced" account of power's mechanisms'[44] in this connection. Human agency can be introduced into the structural analysis of power by inquiring into the origins of structural disparities: agents may create and mobilize them for their benefit. The power holders – members of the power elite[45] – still rely on the invisible hand of the market. But they do not take its existence for granted. Instead, they engineer the invisible hand and maintain its operation.[46]

The market generates incentives that guide people in the same direction. In Foucault's words, the invisible hand of the market serves to transform individuals into a population. The population's behaviour turns out to be uniform and conformist. Who may be interested in the substitution of an aggregate of unruly individuals for the population? The agent, who values order and finds in main-taining order a raison d'être for her own existence, is the primary beneficiary.

Weber observes that order can be maintained either by an entire social group, community ('convention') or by a 'specialized staff' ('law').[47] The second case is of particular interest here. Since it is the primary beneficiary of the operation of the market, the specialized staff may be motivated to design and implement this new institution. This observation is particularly relevant in the emerging market economies, i.e. the countries with discontinued or absent market traditions. One of the emerging market economies is considered in Chapter 4. However, even in the countries with the fully fledged market economies, the proposed line of reasoning leads to interesting insights, as shown in Chapter 3. Applied retro-spectively, this approach tends to support Karl Polanyi's thesis that only local markets emerged spontaneously; the creation of national and international mar-kets required human design and input on the part of the specialized staff (State) even in England, the first capitalist country.[48]

If the market has structural disparities and imbalances, then in addition to the state representatives, a new group of agents interested in its operation emerges, namely economic agents profiting from the conditions of restricted competi-tion. Because they benefit from the existence of 'the bias of the system', to use Lukes's expression,[49] they have all reasons for creating or mobilizing, recreating and reinforcing it. At the initial stage, when no disparities exist, economic agents profiting from the conditions of restricted competition have several options as to their subsequent actions.[50] They may opt for maintaining the status quo (perfect competition) or may attempt to mobilize the bias of the system, which would restrict competition in the market. Should they choose the latter course of action, both the structural and strategic components of power would be present.

Joseph Nye's taxonomy of power represents a similar attempt to combine the structural and strategic components of power. Nye differentiates three forms of power: hard, soft and smart. Hard power refers to the resources at A's dis-posal, including physical and economic constraints through which A controls B's behaviour. Soft power involves persuasion and other strategies indented to motivate B toward achieving A's preferred outcomes. The agent has smart power if she is able to use her hard and soft power in the most optimal manner and to further enhance them. Hard power represents a structural component of A's power; soft and especially smart power represent strategic components. Nye also acknowledges that the strategic components of power can eventually be con-verted into structural components in the manner outline above. 'A key aspect of hard economic power behaviour is efforts by actors to structure markets and thus increase their relative position.'[51]

Instead of considering market and other structural disparities as exogenous, this monograph shows how they can be made endogenous to a theory of power.

The endogenization of structural disparities is achieved with the help of shifting the focus of the analysis from their outcomes to how and why they eventually emerge beforehand. If Polanyi is correct and perfectly competitive markets rarely emerge in a spontaneous manner, the same applies to the case of markets with restricted competition, arguably.

The book focuses on a particular strategy for creating, mobilizing, recreating and reinforcing structural disparities beneficial for the power holders, namely gate keeping. Chapter 2 outlines a theory of gate keeping as a way of combining the structural and strategic components of power. With the help of gate keeping, the agent may eventually create structural disparities when they are initially absent. The agent then uses the structural disparities to further strengthen her positions as a gate keeper and, thus, her ability to continue implementing the strategy of gate keeping in the future.

3. Repertoire of Techniques for Imposing Will

The strategy of gate keeping has not attracted sufficient attention on the part of scholars studying power. An overview of strategies commonly discussed in the literature on the strategic components of power highlights the underexplored character of this concept.

Some scholars describe power holders' strategies in terms of techniques or technologies for imposing will. For instance, Foucault prioritizes the study of techniques for imposing will over inquiries into the other dimensions of power. He believes that scholars studying power should free themselves

> from any would-be general Theory of Power ... or from explanations in terms of Domination in general, when analyzing the normativity of behavior, and [should try] instead to bring out the history and analysis of procedures and technologies of governmentality.[52]

A set of techniques for imposing will that is available in a particular country (or in a lower-level institutional context such as region or local community) at a specific moment in time constitutes their repertoire. The term 'repertoire' was initially introduced by scholars studying the history of social movements and collective action in other forms. 'The word *repertoire* identifies a limited set of routines that are learned, shared, and acted out though a relatively deliberate process of choice'.[53] Namely, a repertoire of collective action is a set of routines and strategies that make collective action possible. Likewise, a repertoire of techniques for imposing will contains a set of routines and strategies that *A* can use for the purpose of imposing and enhancing her domination over *B*. The repertoire of techniques for imposing will can be compared with a toolbox available to the power holder. *A* has a range of options for securing *B*'s obedience to her orders: from the most visible strategies (e.g. the application of brute force) to the least visible ones (e.g. gate keeping).

There are several taxonomies of power constructed using the technique for imposing will as a differentiating variable. Depending on the underlying technique for imposing will, Amitai Etzioni distinguishes three forms of power: coercive, remunerative and normative power.[54] Coercive power rests on the application, or the threat of the application, of physical sanctions. A dominates B by applying or threatening to apply physical punishments. Remunerative power is based on control over material resources and rewards. B receives a pecuniary compensation for her obedience to A's orders. Normative power rests on the allocation and manipulation of symbolic rewards and deprivations. A provides B with non-pecuniary arguments for accepting her power.

Several authors develop more detailed taxonomies.[55] They discuss particular techniques of coercive, remunerative and normative power. For instance, Wrong considers two techniques of coercive power, force and coercion in the narrow sense. Force as a technique for imposing will involves 'the creation of physical obstacles restricting the freedom of another, the infliction of bodily pain or injury including the destruction of life itself and the frustration of basic biological needs'.[56] Coercion in the narrow sense does not rule out the application of physical force. A gives B a choice, however. Either B obeys and no physical obstacles are created or B disobeys and A applies physical force.

At least two techniques for imposing will tend to be associated with normative power: persuasion and manipulation. Persuasion requires that A respects B's integrity and freedom of choice. 'A presents arguments, appeals or exhortations to B, and B, after independently evaluating their content in light of his own values and goals, accepts A's communication as the basis of his own behavior'.[57] Manipulation refers to A's attempts to mislead B. A provides B with erroneous or incomplete information that gives B an impression that she acts in her own interests whereas in fact she acts in A's interests. In other words, manipulation is an invisible, covert technique of power. Valeri Ledyaev defines manipulation as 'a powerholder's ability to exercise a covert influence on the subject which the latter is unaware of'.[58]

Authority can also be added to the list of the techniques for imposing will associated with normative power. Authority as a technique for imposing will requires shifting emphasis from the content of a communication, as in the case of persuasion, to its source. A's perceived status, resources or personal attributes induces B's compliance.[59] Weber's concepts of rational-legal, traditional and charismatic authority help further operationalize authority as a technique of power.[60]

David Beetham proposes a comprehensive threefold test. He argues that power has a legitimate character and rests on authority if (i) it conforms to established rules (ii) the rules can be justified by reference to beliefs shared by both A and B and (iii) there is evidence of B's consent to the particular power relationship.[61] Only in rare cases does A's strategy meet these criteria. For instance, in order to claim authority, A must not only respect the rule of law (i), but also make the law correspond to B's everyday practices (ii) and provide B with an opportunity to express her opinion through a vote (iii). It also follows that authority requires a high level of visibility and transparency in the exercise of power. In this sense, authority represents one of the most visible hands of power.

Most techniques for imposing will are amenable to rationalization and, hence, to the application of the model of rational choice in some form. By selecting a particular technique for imposing will, A intends to maximize her utility. B also behaves in a rational manner choosing between the options imposed by A. Even coercion involves a choice, however specific it may be. When coerced, B chooses the lesser of two evils, namely submission to A's orders or the physical punishment by A. This rule has an exception, however: it does not apply to the situations in which power becomes an end. The thesis on the possibility of a rational take on power paves the way to theorizing and modelling power relationships using the analytical tools of the economic sciences in general and of heterodox economics in particular. Chapter 2 outlines an original approach as to how this can be achieved in practice.

Similarly to repertoires of collective action, the repertoire of techniques for imposing has a time- and country-specific character. The contents of A's toolbox vary across societies and in time. A secures B's compliance in a European country using a different set of strategies than in an Asian or African country. The set of strategies for imposing will available in the same country now and two centuries ago also tends to be different. For instance, the use of force by the government to prevent deviant behaviour evolved over time. After initially taking the form of torture and corporal punishment, it transformed in most European countries into the deprivation of liberty with the help of prison in the first half of the nineteenth century.[62]

This book has no ambition to study the entire repertoire of techniques for imposing will available to the power elite in a particular country at a specific moment in time. It has a rather narrow focus on one technique for imposing will, gate keeping. In contrast to authority or force, gate keeping represents an *invisible* technique for imposing will. This invisible character explains why gate keeping often remains unnoticed or overlooked both in our everyday experience and in theoretical studies of power. Our ignorance of gate keeping and its effects comes at a price, however. Often, we do not know how to react to gate keeping and how to protect our interests when the power holders use this strategy. Lukes rightly suggests that 'power is at its most effective when least accessible to observation, to actors and observers alike'.[63]

4. Structure of the Book

The theory of gate keeping represents a small building block to be used for the construction of a still missing general theory of power and techniques for imposing will. This book offers an outline of the theory of gate keeping (Chapter 2) and discusses its empirical applications. It shows how gate keeping is used by the power holders in various institutional contexts – in the market (Chapters 3 and 4), in the judicial system (Chapter 5), within organizations (Chapter 6) and in academia (Chapter 7). Instead of focusing on a single country, the book chapters contain case studies of gate keeping practices in several countries, both Western and Eastern: the US, the United Kingdom, Canada and Russia. This decision has a rationale. It serves to explore whether gate keeping as a particular technique for imposing will is becoming modular, i.e. *As* in various countries use gate keeping because of its effectiveness in securing *Bs*' obedience. The modular strategies for imposing will tend to be replicated across various countries and periods of time. I argue that gate keeping is one of those modular strategies that will become widespread in all societies that value formal freedom and the rational pursuit of self-interest.

Chapter 2 discusses an original conceptualization of elementary power relationships, namely the power triad. The theory of the power triad provides an understanding of the nature and operation of domination by virtue of a constellation of interests in the market, a previously neglected and underexplored concept put forward by Weber. The existence of barriers (the structural component) and entry control (the strategic component) is necessary to make this type of domination work. A gate keeper is the key actor within the power triad. The gate keeper restricts access to the field of transactions to some actors and thus creates structural imbalances. The agents who find themselves on the short side of the market are able to capture rents, whereas the agents on the long side of the market overpay for the products in which they are interested. A portion of the captured rents is subsequently seized by the gate keeper. The concept of the power triad is compared with a number of the influential conceptualizations of power in markets; John Commons's concept of goodwill and the theory of contested exchange of Bowles and Gintis are the prime references. The idea of the power triad serves as a guiding framework throughout the book.

The subsequent chapters of the book discuss various applications of this concept. In particular, they show how it provides a better understanding of the US government's response to the 2008 financial crisis (Chapter 3), practices of entry control to the regional markets in Russia (Chapter 4), the problematic character of access to justice in three Western countries, the United Kingdom, the US and Canada (Chapter 5), the operation of internal labour markets as a source of managerial discretion (Chapter 6) and, finally, practices of peer review in academia (Chapter 7). These case studies also serve to better differentiate my original approach from several other theories of power in general and of some relevant techniques for imposing will in particular. The case studies included in this book provide an opportunity for confronting my line of reasoning with the arguments of Marx and Foucault (in this introductory chapter), Commons, Bowles and Gintis (in Chapter 2), public choice theory (in Chapters 3 and 4), Pierre Bourdieu (in Chapter 5), the theory of internal labour markets of Peter B. Doeringer and Michael J. Piore (in Chapter 6), and the new institutional economics (the concept of measurement costs of Douglass C. North) (in Chapter 7).

Chapter 3 focuses on the financial crisis of 2008 as seen through the lens of power relationships, in particular, the opportunities it created for strengthening the positions of the economic and political actors vested in power. I argue that domination by virtue of a constellation of interests in the market serves to provide a better understanding of the internal mechanics of the governmental response to the crisis in the US. Public choice theory, an approach to studying interactions between the government and the business, which is popular among economists, overlooks a constellation of these actors' interests that eventually emerges in the aftermath of the 2008 crisis. The statistical analysis of the data about recipients of stimulus funds made available to the selected businesses under the Recovery and Reinvestment Act (2009) informs the discussion in this chapter.

Chapter 4 continues with the comparison of the theory of gate keeping and public choice theory, confronting them this time with data from an emerging market, namely Russia. It argues that the former theory produces riskier predictions than the latter one. The Popperian criteria for falsification of a theory suggest that the riskier predictions the theory produces, the more confidence we have in the outcomes of its falsification. Theory of public choice predicts that either the government wins and the business loses (the tollbooth hypothesis) or the business wins and the government loses (regulatory capture theory). The theory of gate keeping predicts that both the government and the business win. Furthermore, the third agent's (the population's) pecuniary interests are also supposedly associated with interests of the first two agents. A series of econometric tests using sub-national data from Russia show that the gate keeper's interests are indeed positively associated with the interests of the businesses that manage to get admitted to the field of transactions. The population's interests also turn out to be correlated with interests of the gate keeper and the business. The gains of the three agents tend to be unequally distributed, however. The market system in Russia ultimately works in the interests of state representatives who assume the gate keeper's role and to a lesser extent in interests of the selected businesses.

Chapter 5 compares three approaches to the issue of access to justice, namely neoclassical economic theory, critical sociology and the concept of the power triad developed in this book. Economic approaches highlight the most visible aspect of the problem, namely, inflated legal fees. Critical sociology focuses on the symbolic power of labelling. The concept of the power triad serves to explain the problematic access to justice in terms of gate keeping. The theoretical discourse of access to justice is confronted with the public discourse. A total of 642 texts published in three major newspapers, the *Times*, the *New York Times* and the *Globe and Mail* in the period from July 1985 to March 2013 were content-analysed using both qualitative and quantitative techniques. The outcomes of the content analysis confirm the lack of public acknowledgement that there is a serious problem with access to justice, especially as far as the most invisible techniques of domination are concerned.

Chapter 6 places the concept of gate keeping within the context of organization theories and the functioning of the organization. The theory of internal labour markets differentiates its two segments, internal and external, as well as connecting links (the ports of entry). Advocates of this theory do not pay particular attention to benefits of controlling the ports of entry and, thus, access to the internal labour market. The theory of gate keeping serves to bridge this gap. It is argued that gate keeping in the organization first and foremost involves determining the ratio of permanent and temporary positions. Permanent employees gain access to the internal labour market, whereas temporary workers remain outside the organization, in the external labour market. Permanent employees might support the segmentation of the labour market and the boss's gate keeping because this arrangement guarantees them employment stability and a privileged status within the organization. Temporary workers prefer having unstable employments to being unemployed. In other words, the power triad might emerge in the dual labour market. The case study of four universities, two North American and two Russian, suggests that, on one hand, the academic labour market does indeed have a dual character and, on the other hand, the opportunities for gate keeping are seized by the university administration in at least one of these universities.

An application of the theory of gate keeping to the study of the process of peer review in academia is offered in Chapter 7. It continues the analysis of the academic labour market started in Chapter 6. A finer distinction between two positions in the internal labour market, tenured and tenure-track, serves to unveil a power triad that emerges in the peer review of tenure applications. Several assessors, who hold both superior and equal ranks in the hierarchy, keep the gate leading to tenure, i.e. a permanent position in the internal labour market. The existence of boundaries – legal protection of tenure – enables the assessors to use gate keeping strategies as a means to enhance their status in academia by promoting particular theories or networks or by complementing the manager's visible hand with an invisible hand. The character of the assessment of one's contribution to the body of knowledge as a public good creates incentives for gate keeping. Assessors agree to contribute to quality control in exchange for some private good (such as enhanced status). This chapter extends the case study of the four North American and Russian universities by comparing their procedures for peer reviewing applications for permanent positions.

A similar situation is observed in academic publishing where a power triad also emerges. The power triad in academic publishing include reviewers and editors, authors of manuscripts accepted for publication and readers. Editors and reviewers of manuscripts eventually become gate keepers. Gate keeping allows them to eventually promote their particularistic agendas.

2 DOMINATION BY VIRTUE OF A CONSTELLATION OF INTERESTS: BENEFITS OF GATE KEEPING

This chapter lays down the key points that guide the discussion in the rest of the book. Namely, it outlines a theory of domination by virtue of a constellation of interests in the market. The concept of domination by virtue of a constellation of interests was initially proposed by Max Weber. He used this concept in opposition to domination by virtue of authority. The notion of authority is relatively well researched. It would not be an exaggeration to say that the theory of authority represents one of the major contributions made by Weber to the studies of power. However, he did not elaborate on domination by virtue of a constellation of interests to the same extent. He simply suggested that

> because of the very absence of rules, domination which originates in the market or other interest constellations may be felt to be much more oppressive than an authority in which the duties of obedience are set out clearly and expressly.[1]

Subsequent developments did not turn out to be particularly enlightening either. Few scholars have attempted to shed more light on the second form of domination, whereas references to various forms of authority can be found in virtually any textbook on sociology or political science. John Scott's synopsis of power is the exception that confirms the rule. The author mentions domination by virtue of a constellation of interests as a rare combination of such opposite techniques of power as coercion and inducement.[2] Coercion is a technique of coercive power, whereas inducement derives from the logic of remunerative or compensatory power.[3] He also notes that the control of A (power holder) over the actions of B (subordinate) does not take manifest forms in this case,[4] which makes this form of domination particularly relevant for our discussion of the *invisible* hand of power.

This book intends to argue that the concept of domination by virtue of a constellation of interests has been neglected without just cause. This concept offers a rich potential for theoretical and empirical research that has been unexplored and undervalued so far. The concept of domination by virtue of a constellation of interests serves to avoid a false opposition between power and the market. The market is commonly believed to be a liberating force, a constraint limiting the need for power as a coordination device. Actually existing markets tend to be deeply permeated by power relationships. The fusion of power and the market takes on particularly manifest forms in countries such as China[5] or Russia,[6] where administrative barriers erected by state officials allow them to extract rents and strengthen their power. Chapter 3 suggests, however, that even the developed markets, for instance, the North American market, are not immune to being embedded in power.

The concept of domination by virtue of a constellation of interests in the market is not the only analytical tool available to economists for theorizing the fusion of power and the market. The theory of contested exchange developed by Samuel Bowles and Herbert Gintis since the 1980s offers an alternative explanation for the phenomenon in question. This theory shows that power is in no way exogenous to the market. The scope of power exceeds the boundaries of the firm or other organizations. 'Power may be exercised in the absence of firms or indeed any organizational structure whatsoever. Short-side power is exercised *in* markets, not simply outside markets or despite markets.'[7] Restricted competition characterizes the short side of the market, whereas no restrictions exist on the long side.

The theory of contested exchange also highlights the fact that power in the market involves a constellation of interests of *A* and *B*. Both parties involved in contested exchange gain something, even if the gain is distributed unequally. 'Short-side power is not a zero-sum game'.[8] The power emerging in the context of contested exchange also has structural and strategic components.[9] Structural imbalances (a structural component) may exist, but remain unused or underexploited by the party located on the short side of the market. In other words, a strategic component may be missing.[10]

Neither the idea of a constellation of interests as a precondition of domination nor the thesis on the necessity of both structural and strategic components of power is elaborated in the theory of contested exchange to a sufficient extent. For instance, this theory takes into account only manifest forms of a constellation of interests in the market, such as *A* pays *B* a bonus in addition to the equilibrium wage. Keeping in mind the focus on *invisible* techniques of power, there is a need for the further development of the concept of domination by virtue of a constellation of interests that would use some insights of the theory of contested exchange but go beyond its premises. The objective of this chapter is to show how domination by virtue of a constellation of interests can be theorized. It uses Bowles's and Gintis's approach as a major point of reference.

This chapter has five main sections along with the introduction and conclusion. Section 1 compares two types of dyads: power dyads within an organization, including the firm, and dyads in the market environment. The theory of contested exchange is discussed in Section 2. This theory serves to highlight the transformation that the dyad undergoes in the context of a contested exchange. Section 3 further extends the typology of transactions and discusses tetrads and squads, as suggested by John Commons. Section 4 outlines an original model of market transaction – the power triad. The power triad represents an analytical tool that helps unveil *invisible* forms of domination by virtue of a constellation of interests in the market. I will refer to the model of the power triad in all other chapters of the book. Section 5 discusses how interactions within the power triad reshape the choice sets of the parties involved. It does this by showing how some options are excluded from the menu of choices of *A* and *B*. The division of labour between the three parties constituting a power triad (*A, B* and a gate keeper, *C*), is recapped in the conclusion. The figure of a dissident is also taken into consideration.

1. Configurations of Business Transactions: Dyads

Studies of power relationships do not necessarily require the assumption of rational choice. Depending on a particular configuration of power,[11] the parties involved may or may not be expected to behave in a rational manner. For instance, authority (normative or conditioned power) requires that *A* justifies her control over *B*. Rational considerations do not suffice for the existence of this kind of power.

Domination by virtue of a constellation of interests, as the name suggests, requires putting the rational pursuit of interest ahead of other considerations. It should be noted that Weber used this form of domination in opposition to domination by virtue of authority. The latter necessarily has a moral dimension, whereas the former may be based solely on rational calculations. Thus, the assumptions of neoclassical economics may be retained for the study of domination by virtue of a constellation of interests. The list includes the premises that people have rational preferences among outcomes and that individual actors maximize utility and firms maximize profits.[12]

Transactions in a perfectly competitive market take the form of dyads. Two actors constitute a market dyad. The fact that the perfectly competitive market achieves equilibrium and clears leaves no place for third parties. Bowles and Gintis offer a demonstration with the help of a thought experiment. They consider what would happen in the clearing market if *B*'s bid for a contract with *A* could have been contested by a third bidder.

> There would be some third agent, *C*, currently occupying a position with the same value as *B*'s next best alternative and who would benefit from occupying *B*'s current position. Agent *C* could thus have offered *A* a contract superior to that offered by *B*, blocking *B*'s exchange with *A*. Since this did not occur, no such *C* exists.[13]

In other words, *A* and *B* transact because *A* offers the best deal to *B* and vice versa.

The conditions of perfect competition place the transacting parties on an equal footing. The neoclassical market dyad does not exclude the emergence of power, nevertheless. Conflicts about the distribution of gains from trade lie at the origin of power relationships within the market dyad. Neoclassical economists assume that the market transaction is a 'win-win' strategy for both A and B. But this does not necessarily mean an equal distribution of gains from trade. The exact ratio of the distribution of gains from trade depends on A's and B's relative bargaining power.[14] 'Who wins or loses from the exchange relationship must depend on the balance of power between both parties'.[15] If both parties try to maximize their shares in the gain from trade, as neoclassical economists assume, then they may actually fail to conclude an otherwise beneficial deal.[16] A and B will simply struggle over who gets what. Bargaining power penetrates even the most ideal-typical market transaction.

Power takes more manifest forms within the organization, namely the firm. Since Ronald Coase's work on the nature of the economic organization[17] neoclassical economists have admitted that power structures relationships inside a firm. They place the concepts of the market as a place of presumably free exchanges and the firm as a hierarchical structure in opposition. This dual model requires the introduction of a second type of dyad, the organizational dyad. In contrast to the market dyad, the parties constituting the dyad within the organization have unequal standings. Organizations set their own rules, change and enforce them through A's 'visible hand'.[18] In this sense, the organizational dyad is qualitatively different from the market dyad. The organizational dyad has the key features of the power dyad discussed in Chapter 1, Section 1: A, the principal, and B, the agent, are involved in asymmetrical relationships in which A commands and B obeys. A has power, B does not.

Neoclassical economics offer several models of employment relationship.[19] For instance, Joseph Stiglitz argues that transactions between A and B must satisfy the system of equations [1]. A hires B to perform some productive tasks: the firm presumably intends to generate income as opposed to redistributing it. The privilege of having an upper hand in the transaction allows A to maximize her utility. B is satisfied with any value of her expected utility that exceeds the income from the second-best alternative (an alternative employment or unemployment benefits). A cannot directly observe B's level of efforts and thus needs to design an incentive scheme that will help A to counter B's tendency to shirk in the presence of incomplete information.

$$\begin{cases} \max EU_A\,(Y, Q, E, S) \\ EU_B\,(Y, E, S) \geq \bar{U} \\ Y = \varphi(Y) \end{cases} \quad\quad [1]$$

where EU refers to the expected utility; $\bar{U}$ refers to B's reservation wage; Q is a set of output variables; E is a set of inputs (actions) by B and a production function connects E with Q; S stands for a set of state variables (like weather) that can be observed but not controlled; Y is a compensation scheme; and φ refers to a function connecting the agent's compensation with the output.

B supposedly obeys A's orders in exchange for a monetary compensation (Y). In addition to monetary incentives, this obedience also pays in terms of organizational incentives: promotions, group motivations and so on.[20] Bowles and Gintis, however, rightly pointed out that in the clearing market B's compensation cannot exceed her reservation wage ($\bar{U}$). In the Walras–Arrow–Debreu model of general equilibrium 'workers would be indifferent between holding their current job and the next-best alternative'.[21] This means that B receives next to nothing for giving up her freedom. Why work for A if B can simply stay home and receive unemployment benefits? This means that the market either does not achieve equilibrium or does, but this takes place at the price of leaving B with no incentive for accepting A's power.

2. Dyad in the Context of Contested Exchange

Bowles and Gintis claim to have bridged the theoretical gap identified above. Their theory of contested exchange does not involve differentiating between the market dyad and the organizational dyad. Instead, they offer a more general model of the dyad that encompasses transactions both in the market and within the firm. They place the dyad in the context of contested exchange that, according to Bowles and Gintis, prevails in the economy. Exchange has a contested character if information and, consequently, contracts are incomplete. The labour market, the credit market and even the market for consumer goods have these features. As we will see, the study of contested exchange requires taking into consideration a third party who actually wanted to transact with A in B's place, but failed to do so. The dyad transforms into a triad as a result.

Let us consider the labour market and its constitutive element, the employment contract, in depth. The starting point in Bowles's and Gintis's reasoning refers to the completeness of information. If information was complete, it would be possible to foresee any contingencies and to draw a contract covering all of them. Under conditions of complete information, the market would clear without simultaneously creating a need for additional incentives for fulfilling contract obligations. Should A or B choose to dishonour their contract obligations, the contract would be declared void by means of exogenous enforcement (by a court of law, for instance) and someone else would be willing to accept the contract under the same conditions because competition in this imaginable market would be perfect as well.

The slightest departure from the assumption of complete information undermines the system of checks and balances in the relationship between A and B. The incompleteness of information creates a need for endogenous enforcement and makes contract obligations contestable. B's attempts to shirk may well remain undetected and/or unpunished by A. In the same way, A may pay less than promised, referring to some state variables S beyond her control.[22] The impact of these variables cannot be adequately assessed by B. Bowles and Gintis argue that incomplete contracts prevail in actual markets:[23]

> Exogenous enforcement will generally be absent and exchanges will be contested when there is no relevant third party (as when A and B are sovereign states), when the contested attribute can be measured only imperfectly or at considerable cost (work effort, for example, or the degree of risk assumed by a firm's management), when the relevant evidence is not admissible in a court of law (such as an agent's eye witness but unsubstantiated experience) when there is no possible means of redress (for example, when the liable party is bankrupt), or when the number of contingencies concerning future states of the world relevant to the exchange preclude writing a fully specified contract.

The incompleteness of contracts along with the lack of exogenous enforcement leads A to think of other means for securing B's compliance with her orders. And A finds one of them in the procedure of contingent contract renewal. A offers B a compensation that exceeds B's reservation wage[24] but simultaneously imposes an additional condition: the perspectives for the contract renewal depend on B's satisfactory performance and on her compliance with A's orders. 'Contingent renewal obtains when A elicits performance from B by promising to renew the contract in future periods if satisfied and to terminate the contract if not.'[25] Now B has incentives for giving up her freedom: she trades it for a bonus that she would not otherwise be able to get.

B's compensation equals her reservation wage plus the bonus that Bowles and Gintis call enforcement rent. '*Enforcement rents* ... arise in all cases of competitively determined contested exchange under conditions of contingent renewal.'[26] This bonus solves a microeconomic problem, namely the creation of incentives for B, at the price of undermining the perspectives for achieving equilibrium at the macro level. The market does not clear as a result. The fact that there are more people willing to work for such high compensation means that some of them remain unemployed.

A third agent, C, remains behind the scenes but her presence has an impact on the overall dynamics of the interactions between A and B. C fails to make a transaction with A and chooses a suboptimal option. In C's presence, B has an incentive to work harder than in C's absence, nevertheless. 'If B enjoys an employment rent, then there must be another otherwise identical agent, C, who would be willing to fill B's position at the going, or even a lower, wage.'[27] B knows that if she loses her current job, she may not be able to secure a similarly well-paid offer. 'The employee excluded from access to *her current employer's asset* may not find access to *any asset* even in a competitive economy in which transaction-specific assets are absent.'[28]

C and *B* compete for the same job. Taken together, they constitute the long side of the labour market. Because *A* does not face competition from similar agents (i.e. the agents who hire labour), she finds herself on the short side of the same market. The position on the short side of the market enables *A* to have power over *B*. 'Agents on the short side of the market will have power over agents on the long side with whom they transact'.[29]

Using the concepts introduced in Chapter 1, Section 2, we can say that *A*'s position on the short side of the market refers to a structural component of her power. In order to have power, *A* also has to act strategically: she must be able to exploit opportunities provided by the structural imbalances by paying as little in excess of *B*'s reservation wage as possible. The strategic aspect of power, however, attracted little attention on the part of those advocating the theory of contested exchange.

A's power over *B* benefits both parties. *B* receives a bonus for her compliance with *A*'s orders. *A* maximizes her utility with *B*'s assistance. 'The employer profits in this case by paying to exercise power over the employee'.[30] The fact that *B* receives a rent does not confer power on *B*. *A* can easily find an alternative to *B*, *C*, whereas *B* has no capacity to make threats or to use sanctions against *A*. This asymmetry in the relationship between *A* and *B* does not exclude the constellation of their interests. 'Despite the clear disparity in the positions of *A* and *B* in this case, both parties gain from *A*'s exercise of power over *B*'.[31]

The model of the labour market as a non-clearing market with contested exchanges can be generalized to a number of other key markets. Bowles and Gintis applied it to the credit market and the consumer goods market. Exchanges on the credit market have a contested nature because 'the borrower's promise to remain solvent is no more amenable to exogenous enforcement than is the employee's promise to supply a particular quality of work'.[32] The borrower, *B*, tends to take excessive risks as a result. The creditor, *A*, solves the problem by charging a lower interest rate than the equilibrium interest rate and by using the strategy of contingent contract renewal.

As for the consumer goods market, the consumer, *A*, presumably pays a price in excess of the marginal costs (the equilibrium price equals the marginal costs) and implicitly threatens to switch suppliers if the quality of *B*'s product fails to meet *A*'s expectations.[33] *A*'s reason for paying a rent to *B* refers to difficulties with measuring the quality of *B*'s product. This quality has several dimensions not all of which can be assessed before the purchase. Lettuce in a supermarket may look fine despite the fact that it is contaminated by Escherichia coli (E. coli). Douglass North argues that attempts to minimize the transaction costs of measuring quality account for the evolution of economic institutions and organizations throughout human history.[34] The theory of contested exchange offers a potentially more universal solution.

The theory of contested exchange provides an important step toward a better understanding of domination by virtue of a constellation of interests in the market. *A* dominates *B* but both benefit from transacting. This theory leaves several issues unaddressed, however.

First, it tends to overemphasize the structural aspects of power and correspondingly to overlook strategic components. The assignment of an economic agent either to the short or to the long side of the market depends on her initial endowment. This endowment can be further enhanced by transactions on the credit market: a wealthier borrower is able to offer better collateral and, thus, to secure a still lower interest rate from the creditor. 'Ownership of wealth confers power on agents by allocating them to short-side positions in contested exchange markets'.[35] Specific strategies implemented by economic agents have little bearing on their opportunities for domination.

Second, domination in the non-clearing market usually takes manifest forms. The discovery that the boss has power over the employee or the lender has power over the borrower comes as no surprise for anyone. *A*'s power catches an observer's eye and sophisticated techniques are not required to unveil it. It should be noted that this book is intended to shed more light on power techniques that are barely detectable, namely *invisible*.

3. Triads, Tetrads and Quads

The figure of a third party, *C*, has remained in the background so far. A closer look at the parties who act behind the scenes is needed for exploring *invisible* techniques of power. In this section, I will consider three attempts to bring the third party or parties to the focus of the analysis.[36] They are heterogeneous in nature: their only common element refers to an explicit account of the role that the third party or parties play in transactions between *A* and *B*.

The first approach refers to a theory of power 'which works through "triadic" relationships'[37] outlined by Kaushik Basu. Gintis and Bowles find a third party in the same market as *A* and *B*. Together with *B*, the third party constitutes the long side of this particular market. Basu sees a relevant third party elsewhere in the other market. He considers interactions between a landlord, *A*, and a tenant, *B*, and shows how *A* may make *B* accept an offer that falls short of *B*'s reservation wage.

A manages to do so by threatening to use her influence on a merchant *C* who sells goods to both *A* and *B*. *A* and *B* transact on the labour market; *A*, *B* and *C* transact on a product market. *A* essentially tells *B* that should *B* reject *A*'s proposal to work hard for less, *A* will ask *C* not to transact with *B*.

> It is possible that a landlord in offering a package (*E*, *Y*), gives – along with it – the threat that if he does not accept the package the landlord will ensure that a third person *C* will refuse to trade with him.[38]

This case of using B's trade with C as a lever for securing B's compliance with A's commands may be interesting, but it involves a constellation of their interests in a solely negative sense. B simply wants to avoid the worst by choosing the lesser of two evils.[39] A's power over B benefits A; B does not gain from it.

Kurt Rothschild considers a triad at the macro level[40] and its transformation into a tetrad (a group of four interconnected agents). Three agents constitute a triad at the macro level: a business sector (the group of owners of capital, As), a labour force (the group of owners of labour force, Bs) and a state sector (bureaucrats working in government and public bodies).[41] The state deserves particular attention because of its role as a third party, C. The state establishes and enforces the rules of the game, including a particular regime of property rights. 'The state is [also] important because it can support the national enterprises through protection, subsidies and the provision of a business-friendly taxation and infrastructure'.[42]

A more complex configuration emerges as a result of the increasing heterogeneity of the business sector. Rothschild sees it splitting into two subsectors: transnational companies and small businesses. The triad then transforms into a tetrad. The transnational companies have the upper hand in the new configuration of transactions.[43] The small businesses, on the other hand, are relegated to a subaltern position similar to that of the labour force. Rothschild's approach highlights the mutual dependence of the economic agents, whereas our primary interest refers to a constellation of their interests and to its uses as a technique of power.

Commons proposes another conceptualization of the tetrad. He considers transactions at the micro level and argues that 'the minimum number of persons necessary to constitute a transaction is four parties, two buyers and two sellers, namely, the actual buyer and seller, and the next best alternative for each'.[44] This definition suggests that the alternative offer is not as attractive as Bowles and Gintis suppose. The buyer has two offers: the first best from the seller with whom the buyer will actually transact and the second best from the seller's competitor. Likewise, the seller considers the buyer's offer as the first-best option and an offer from the buyer's competitor as the second-best one. The market achieves equilibrium, but no party dominates under these circumstances. The relationships have a symmetrical character.

Some asymmetry emerges as a result of introducing the institution of goodwill that plays a key role in Commons's work. Goodwill refers to a voluntary restriction on the number of offers made to an economic agent. The voluntary nature of the restrictions must be specifically emphasized. An economic agent that makes an offer to the other agent persuades her competitor(s) not to come up with alternative offers in exchange for some monetary compensation. 'A third party, the possible trespasser or competitor, is burdened ... by a duty of avoidance. Up to a certain point he must not intrude between the first and second parties to the potential bargain.'[45]

Goodwill introduces us to the idea of entry control that will be discussed in the next section in more detail. The party that makes the offer restricts the third party's access to the transaction. The former agent negotiates the conditions under which the third party assumes the duty not to intrude between the parties to the potential bargain. The third party would otherwise prefer to make the alternative offer, which leads us to acknowledge that the party that makes the offer exercises power over the third party. This power has more strategic than structural elements: goodwill results from negotiations between the economic agents. Goodwill also implies that the interests of the economic agents constellate. The transacting parties increase their utility by trading a good or service. The excluded parties receive compensation paid by the transacting parties out of benefits that increase as a result of restricted competition.

Commons further argues that, although the interests constellate, conflicts may still emerge. Namely, the economic agents may contest the exact division of the surplus generated by the transaction. A fifth party to the transaction, 'namely a judge, priest, chieftain, paterfamilias, arbitrator',[46] may then help. A quad (a group of five interconnected agents) supersedes the tetrad. In the final account, five parties are involved in a business transaction:

> the first party who claims the right; the second party with whom the transaction occurs; the 'third' parties, of whom one is the rival or competitor of the first party, the other is the rival or competitor of the second party; and the fifth party who lays down the rules of the concern of which each is an authorized member.[47]

The approach developed by Commons serves to make several important break-throughs. First, it shows how power and domination emerge out of a constellation of interests in the market. Each party gains something from the transaction, even the excluded one, if the exclusion has a voluntarily character. Second, it introduces us to the idea of entry control. Once again, however, domination by virtue of a constellation of interests is supposed to take mainly manifest forms. Goodwill refers to a formal contract that may be enforced in the courts. Goodwill also lacks universality: this institution exists in selected legal systems only, namely in common law. In other words, we still need to consider a form of domination by virtue of a constellation of interests that would be more universal and more suitable for unveiling the *invisible* techniques of power.

4. Power Triad: Benefits of Entry Control

When discussing barriers to entry and barriers to exit, neoclassical economists focus on the fact that both types of barriers restrict competition and create unequal conditions for incumbent firms and new entrants. For instance, they define barriers to entry as 'the set of structural, institutional and behavioural conditions that allow incumbent firms to earn economic profits for a significant length of time'.[48] Barriers to entry and barriers to exit may underpin different techniques for imposing will, however.

A test for the existence of power requires that the agent subject to it would prefer to act differently if she had a choice. 'What would have happened if *A* did not act?'[49] When applied to barriers to entry and barriers to exit, this approach raises the question about what the economic agent would do in their absence. If barriers to entry were absent, the economic agent would prefer to enter the market. Her best interests lead her to make the transaction in the market. If barriers to exit were absent, the economic agent would prefer to exit the market. Her preferred choice is to stop transacting in the market.

Exit control means that *B* is prevented from leaving the group of interconnected agents, the dyad, the triad, the tetrad or the quad. Let us consider the smallest group, the dyad. A parallel can be drawn between exit control and prison.[50] A prison guard, *A*, has power over a prisoner, *B*. *A* imposes restrictions on *B*'s personal freedom (*A* applies force) as a means for securing *B*'s compliance with her orders. If escape were less costly, *B* would not accept *A*'s power and would stop interacting with her.

Entry control has *B*'s goodwill to transact with *A* as a point of departure. *B*'s involvement may be subject to additional conditions, however. *B* may be allowed to make the transaction that she is interested in if *B* agrees to assume a subordinate role in their relationship. For instance, *B* accepts a smaller share of the surplus generated by the transaction, whereas *A* captures the rest. Commons considers the case when a party receives compensation for not interfering with the transaction between *A* and *B*. Here, *B* actually pays for making the transaction with *A*.

Why do restrictions on *B*'s involvement exist beforehand? Why can *B* not make *A* pay for accessing the transaction? Several requirements have to be met for imposing entry control. First, a field of transactions must be clearly differentiated and separated.[51] Boundaries separate the field from the other transactions. The boundaries can have different natures: informal institutional (ethnic groups, clans and other 'us versus them' divisions), formal institutional (legal restrictions), spatial (an area or a territory), financial (entrance fees or membership dues) or symbolic (professional jurisdictions and credentials).[52] If the field includes two agents, then it is a dyad. A triad with boundaries constitutes a larger field, and so on.

Second, there must be disparities in the conditions of *A* and *B*, no matter how minor they may be. Disparities refer either to structural or to strategic components of power. A smaller structural advantage enables *A* to impose additional conditions on *B*. If no party has a structural advantage, then their strategic capacities enter into play. In a card game in which both parties do not have a single trump or top card (or have an equal number of trump and top cards), the outcome will depend on the players' memory and capacity to make rational decisions. One player's capacity to cheat on the other player may help too: opportunism deified as 'seeking self-interest with guile'[53] should not be *a priori* excluded from the menu of possible strategies. A situation in which both A and B turn out to be perfectly similar in terms of the structural and strategic components of power cannot be ruled out. This situation is highly unlikely, however.

Structural disparities can also result from the actions of a third party, C, if she assumes the role of a gate keeper in charge of entry control. The third party's involvements allow the parties to profit from the division of labour, which is a standard neoclassical argument. Thus, the third precondition for imposing entry control refers to gate keeping. Gate keeping represents a particular strategic component of power. It can be used in the absence of structural components. Gate keeping serves to create structural disparities when they did not exist.

The gate keeper decides who will be admitted to the field and under which conditions. If the gate keeper does not restrict the access of B-type agents, they find themselves on the long side of the market. If the gate keeper restricts the access of A-type agents, they find themselves on the short side of the market. A and A' (see Figure 2.1) want to make an offer to B, but A' fails to transact with B because of C's entry control. A, B and C constitute a specific type of triad, the power triad. The concept of the power triad was initially developed in my previous work.[54] This book is intended to show its subsequent developments and the areas of eventual application to empirical research.

For the sake of clarity, it should be noted that the role of C in the theory of contested exchange and her role in the power triad differ. C has no power in the first case as she does not have any power in Basu's model.[55] C dominates over A and B in the power triad. By limiting the access of A-type agents, C creates structural disparities favourable to A, who is admitted. A has to pay for her admission, however. A shares the monopoly profits generated as a result of restricted competition in the market with C. The exact ratio in which the profits are divided depends on A and C's relative bargaining power (their capacity to act strategically), along with structural factors (whether A can get access to the other field of her interest).

A and C benefit because they share the monopoly profit. B gains because she has an interest in transacting with A, for instance, she needs a good or service that is offered by A. B's consumer surplus shrinks, but remains positive. The three parties constituting the power triad gain something, however unequal their shares may be. The interests of A, B and C form a constellation despite the fact that their power is unequal. C dominates over A and B, A dominates over B.

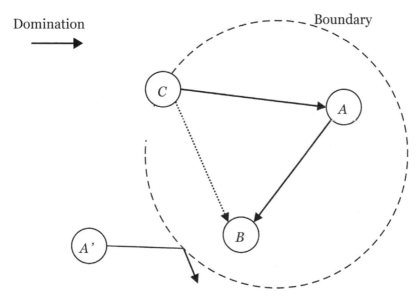

Figure 2.1: Power triad.

Compared with the conceptualvizations of elementary power relationships discussed in the two preceding sections, the power triad has several advantages. One advantage consists in unveiling an *invisible* technique of power. *C*'s domination does not need to take manifest forms. Because *C* does not restrict the entry of *B*-type agents to the field, *B* may even not be aware of *C*'s role. *C* interacts solely with *A*, *A* transacts with *B*. Thus, *C* dominates over *B* in an indirect manner, from behind the scenes.[56]

Furthermore, *C* instructs neither *A* nor *B* to act in a particular manner. All *C* does is decide the ratio of the number of *A*-type agents to the number of *B*-type agents. By doing so, *C* creates structural disparities in the market. The market turns out to be split into two sides, short and long. *A* finds herself on the short side whereas *B* finds herself on the long side of this market. The particular position in the two-side market determines the range of possible options for both *A* and *B*.

A parallel with parental control through restricting access to specific areas and objects seems relevant.[57] The child does whatever she wants with toys and objects that she finds in 'her' area of the home. Objects and materials in the other parts of the home remain outside of her reach. Activities that one can undertake with the help of the latter objects may be deemed undesirable for the child by her parents. The key point is that the parents do not need to explicitly tell the child what to do and what not to do. They instead control entry to some areas of the home and backyard and keep some objects locked.

In other words, *A* and *B* are free to choose any course of action after being admitted to the field. For instance, *A* may apply any pricing strategy for increasing her monopoly profits of her choice.[58] *B* has a limited range of options because of her position on the long side of the market. *C*'s domination thus meets the requirement for domination exercised by the natural course of things discussed in Chapter 1, Subsection 2.2. Entry control refers to 'a regulation based upon and in accordance with the course of things themselves'.[59] The natural course of things just needs to be corrected beforehand in a manner that will subsequently benefit particular actors, namely *C* and *A*.

The other advantage consists in explaining the eventual conversion of political power into economic power and vice versa. Economists have been puzzled by this issue for a long time. '"Pure" economic monopolies are logically possible, but seem rare and unstable ... [whereas] monopolies based on political and economic power are common and stable'.[60] How can the synergistic effect resulting from the combination of political and economic power be explained?

Economic power has multiple dimensions,[61] but in the present context it suffices to define it as the agent's capacity to set a price above the marginal cost. The equilibrium price in the perfectly competitive market is equal to the marginal cost. When defining political power, Weber connects it to a territory. He calls a 'state' 'a compulsory political (*i.e. with a territorial basis*) organization with continuous operations ... insofar as its administrative staff successfully upholds the claim to the monopoly of the legitimate use of physical force in the enforcement of its order'.[62] It follows that political power necessarily has a spatial, territorial dimension.

The territorial embeddedness of political power enables the agents, who have it, to exercise entry control. Within the power triad, *C* has political power and, consequently, the privilege of entry control. As a result of *C*'s entry control, *A* gains economic power. *C*'s political power and *A*'s economic power do not exist independently from one another. They create and reinforce each other. *C* may charge *A* some entrance fees for being admitted to the field. *C* may also impose taxes on *A* for being allowed to continue transacting within the field. *A* pays these charges out of the monopoly profits that she receives due to restricted competition. The gate keeper's revenues may be subsequently reinvested in erecting even better barriers and applying even more sophisticated gate keeping strategies. Political power creates structural disparities favourable for the emergence of economic power. Economic power generates resources necessary for strengthening political power.

Last, but not least, the proposed conceptualization of elementary power relationships is compatible with a number of influential approaches for studying power. This is in keeping with Bowles's and Gintis's suggestion that there is no qualitative difference between power exercised in the market and power exercised within the firm or any other organization. The character of the boundaries delimiting the field and strategies for entry control may differ. But the organization necessarily has boundaries and they are established by the power holder. 'The *boundaries* of "integrated" organizations are determined by decision-making power'.[63] We will explore the particularities of entry control in the organization in Chapter 6 using the concept of the internal labour market as a point of departure.

The concept of the power triad is also compatible with the three-dimensional view of power proposed by Steven Lukes.[64] The first dimension refers to observable behaviour: what changes in *B*'s behaviour do *A*'s commands produce? The second dimension of power emerges when *A* prevents some issues from being included in the agenda for decision making. *A* has power if she manages to exclude the issues that she considers as going against *A*'s interests from *B*'s consideration. The third dimension of power involves changes in *B*'s preferences and wants under *A*'s influence. '[*A*] also exercises power over [*B*] by influencing, shaping or determining [*B*'s] very wants'.[65] The power triad provides a better understanding of the two last dimensions of power. Because of *A*, *B* and *C*'s involvement in the transactions structured in the form of the power triad, the ranges of options available to them change. We will discuss this aspect of the power triad in the next section.

5. Choice Sets

The issue of how the range of options from which the economic agent makes her choice has not been researched thoroughly. Using a common metaphor, economists have much to say about choosing between apples and oranges. They pay less attention, however, to the question about why one chooses between these fruits while setting aside many other equally relevant options: pineapples, bananas or passion fruits, to cite just a few.

The assumption of exogenous and stable preferences represents a starting point in the neoclassical economists' reasoning on this matter. 'The homo economicus model assumes preferences are exogenous: they are determined outside of, and substantially unaffected by, the structure of strategic interaction or any other substantive aspect of the economy'.[66] The agent's exogenous and stable preferences are then applied to choice sets. How are these choice sets populated?

The simplest answer involves drawing a parallel with shopping at a supermarket. The agent takes a basket and looks at what is available on the shelves. The use of the term 'market basket' clearly suggests such a shopping environment. The agent's task is to decide the optimal combination of various goods placed in the basket in keeping with her preferences and budget constraints.[67] As in the case of preferences, the selection of goods on the shelves – the agent's set of choices – is deemed to be exogenous. The agent applies her exogenous preferences to the exogenous choice set.

Subsequent developments in the choice set model[68] introduce restrictions on their scope. Non-zero information costs (a type of transaction cost) account for the agent's ignorance of some of the relevant products in the market.[69] To return to the fruit metaphor, not all shoppers may know enough about passion fruit or pomegranates. If, in addition to the scarcity of information, we consider the agent's limited cognitive capacities,[70] then the agent's bounded rationality emerges as a new restriction on her choice set. The agent's subjective perceptions make a difference too. In his theory of situated rationality Tony Lawson invites economists to consider the agent's selective perception of available choices in the context of her socialization.

> Not only are individuals' choices of actions conditioned by the situated options which they perceive, but also the individuals themselves, their expressions of their needs and motives, the manner in which their capacities and capabilities have been moulded, their values and interests and so forth, are conditioned by the context of their birth and development.[71]

The acknowledgment that the agent's subjective choice set tends to be smaller than the objective choice opens the way for research in several directions. The assessment of the value of the options in the agent's choice set represents one such direction. Some economists argue that the agent values a menu 'as much as she values the best option it contains'.[72] The size of the choice set, i.e. the number of options that it contains, does not matter in this case. Another approach assumes that having a choice is valuable in itself. Georg Simmel discusses the value of money in these terms: 'the value of a given amount of money is equal to the value of any object for which it might be exchanged plus the value of free choice between innumerable other objects'.[73] Thus, any restrictions on the choice set have a monetary expression: the narrower the choice, the less value the agent attaches to it.

Another line of research refers to the attempts to place changes in the choice sets in the context of power relationships. These studies appear to be particularly relevant for the discussion of the power triad, as they help connect the last two dimensions of power, according to Lukes, to the issue of choice studied by economists. The agent's choice set may be changed by the power holder either by excluding some relevant options (the second dimension) or by influencing the agent's perception of particular options (the third dimension).

Changes in decision sets under the influence of power relationships have been studied both theoretically and empirically. Original institutionalists made important theoretical contributions to a better understanding of this issue. They called for endogenizing changes in the system of constraints under which the agent makes a choice in general and for studying factors that influence the scope of the choice set in particular. One possible theoretical solution involves highlighting the role of power. 'The analysis of the mechanisms through which social interaction modifies constraints on individuals and produces economic results leads to discuss the problem of economic power'.[74]

A system of conditional welfare implemented in several Western countries in the framework of neoliberal policies provides an illustration. The agent gains access to welfare if she modifies her behaviour in the manner required by the government: improves her professional skills, enrolls in professional development programmes and so on. The government exercises its power by imposing conditions on the access to welfare and, thus, modifying the agent's choice set. The government tries 'to shape the actions of individuals by establishing the conditions under which choice is made'.[75] Some choices become available only after the agent changes her behaviour in the manner dictated by the power holder; they are simply excluded from the initial choice set.

John Galbraith's analysis of advertising also helps connect changes in the agent's choice set to the exercise of power by the other agent. He argues that some options are included in the decision set solely under the influence of advertising. A consumer buying a product after seeing an advertisement would otherwise neither be aware of its existence nor willing to consume it.[76] The producer's priorities influence the consumer's choice by including and highlighting a new option in the latter's choice set.

Marketing research produces empirical evidence supporting the assumption that advertising has an effect on the choice set. Experiments show that advertising does indeed lead to increased product differentiation that in turn decreases perceived substitutability between perceived alternatives.[77] In other words, some options become more salient as a result of advertising. Only salient options constitute the subjective choice set. 'The consumer's attention is drawn to the salient attributes, which are then overweighted in his choice'.[78] By changing the level of salience of particular goods and their attributes, one manipulates the agent's choice.

Now let us return to the power triad. Each party involved in the power triad, *A*, *B* and *C*, has a particular choice set. The three choice sets change compared with the situation in which no power triad exists. The involvement in the power triad affects *A*, *B* and *C*'s choice sets in a different manner, however. Let us assume that *A* is a producer who sells her products to *B* (if *A* and *B* assume the other roles, some minor corrections have to be made in the reasoning below).

B participates in the transactions as long as her expected utility exceeds her reservation utility. Compared to the dyad, *B* does not necessarily operate solely in the labour market (in this case, the reservation utility is equal to the reservation wage). The power triad may exist in various markets and within organizations. Here, we are considering the case of *B* performing the role of a consumer.

C maximizes her expected utility. The role of a gate keeper enables *C* to select the mode of transactions. She can vary the intensity of competition in the field of transactions: from perfect competition (if all interested *A*-type agents are admitted) to monopoly (if only one *A*-type agent enters the field). Consequently, *C*'s choice set expands.

Compared with the power dyad discussed in the first section of this chapter, *A*'s choice set also changes. Now *A* fails to maximize her expected utility. She minimizes her missed opportunities instead.[79] *A*, namely, chooses between accepting *C*'s domination and staying outside the field. The former option is accompanied by compensation for *A*'s obedience. *A* captures some rent (a portion of the monopoly profits generated as a result of restricted competition). It follows that *A* is either involved in a productive activity and rent-seeking or is satisfied with the productive activity. In both cases, *A*'s expected utility has positive values.[80] Yet *A* does not obtain the maximum in either case. *A* misses some opportunities when accepting *C*'s upper hand (entrance fees and taxes levied by *C*) and when staying out of the field (monopoly profits). In these circumstances, *A* minimizes her missed opportunities instead of maximizing her expected utility. In more formal terms, the interactions between *C* and *A* satisfy the system of equations [2].

$$
\begin{cases}
\max EU_C\,(Z, R, T, S) \\
\min (U' - \bar{U}') \\
U' = EU_A\,(Z, E, S) \\
\bar{U}' = EU_A\,(E, S) \\
U' > \bar{U}' > 0 \\
Z = \omega(R) \\
R = \varphi(T)
\end{cases}
\qquad [2]
$$

$\bar{U}'$ refers to *A*'s expected utility if she refuses to carry out the transaction with *C*, U' stands for *A*'s expected utility when she enters the field on *C*'s conditions, *R* is the rent captured by *C*, *Z* denotes the rent captured by *A* (the function connects *Z* to *R*), *E* refers to the level of *A*'s efforts devoted to production, *S* stands for a set of state variables and *T* designates the costs related to entry control (because they represent an 'input' necessary to extract the rent, a particular 'production' function[81] φ connects *Z* to *R*).

Now *B*'s choices can be taken into account. *B* obtains the reservation utility, $\bar{U}$, as she chooses not to buy *A*'s products. If *A* sells her product outside of the field of the transaction, she charges the price *P*. If *A* sells her product under conditions of restricted competition, within the power triad, she charges the price *P**. Returning to the metaphor of the choice of a supermarket shopper, the selection of the products that *B* sees on the shelves and their prices are determined by *C*'s decisions regarding entry control.[82] Both *B*'s and *A*'s choices are endogenous to the model: they are explained in terms of C's decisions. The interactions within the power triad satisfy the system of equations [3].[83]

$$\begin{cases} \max EU_C\,(Z, R, T, S) \\ \min\,(U^\flat - \bar{U}^\flat) \\ U^\flat = EU_A\,(Z, E, S, P^*) \\ \bar{U}^\flat = EU_A\,(E, S, P) \\ U^\flat > \bar{U}^\flat > 0 \\ Z = \omega(R, P^*) \\ R = \varphi(T) \\ EU_B\,(P) > EU_B\,(P^*) > \bar{U}^\flat \\ P^* > P \end{cases} \qquad [3]$$

The first equation in the system of equations [3] describes the choice set of the gate keeper, C. She maximizes her expected utility by picking T. Structural and strategic factors (the structural disparities and strategies used by A and C in the process of bargaining) determine the ratio in which the rent R is divided between them. The second through the fourth equations describe A's choice set. A chooses between a purely productive activity and a combination of the productive activity and rent-seeking. If A chooses not to enter the field, her expected utility depends on E, S and the competitive price P. If A enters the field, she charges a higher price for her products, P^*, and consequently captures a rent. In both cases, A maintains an independent status regarding C, which sharply contrasts with the employment contract specified by the system of equations [1]. Finally, the eighth equation describes B's choice set. She also obtains a positive expected utility from transacting within the field.

It should be noted that opportunities for transacting outside of the field may turn out to be limited for A and B. This happens if the field emerges at a focal point, i.e. a natural meeting place for A and B.[84] C then restricts access to the natural meeting place (a historical market place, for instance) on the part of A-type agents. This means that A-type and B-type agents may not be able to find each other outside of the field and, consequently, the choice sets would contain only two options for them: to transact in the field or not.[85]

A numerical example shows how the choice sets may appear within the power triad. Despite its simplicity, it illustrates the need for making changes in choice sets endogenous. Let us consider the market for natural gas, C being an institutional regulator, A – a natural gas producer and B – a consumer of natural gas. C decides the exchange regime: a competitive one if neither A's access nor B's access is restricted and one with restricted competition if A's access is limited. A can receive approximately \$10 per 1MMBtu[86] if selling natural gas in the competitive market and about \$20 per 1MMBtu if selling it under conditions of imperfect competition. In the latter case, there are some natural gas producers who will fail to transact because they are denied access to the market.

Under these circumstances B's choice set is {0, $10, $20}, where 0 refers to her failure to transact because of her decision not to consume natural gas, $10 refers to making the transaction on the competitive market and $20 stands for transacting in the market with restricted competition. A's choice set is {0, $10, $20-$R$}. C's choice set is {0, Z}. $Z + R =$ $10 per 1MMBtu ($20-$10). If C chooses Z, which would be a rational decision for her, then A and B's choice sets change: {0, $20-$R$} for A and {0, $20} for B. In the end, A and B's choice sets are shaped by C's decision.

6. Conclusions

The power triad involves a particular configuration of power relationships. The parties involved divide their labour in the following manner. C performs the role of a gate keeper which enables her to have an upper hand in the relationships. C erects barriers delimiting the field of transactions and determines the ratio of the number of A-type agents to the number of B-type agents. The access of A-type agents may be restricted; those admitted to the field have a competitive advantage in this case. They find themselves on the short side of the market and capture rents. These rents are subsequently shared by A and C. In order to increase her share of the rent, C may use a modified form of two-part tariff (A pays both for entering and staying in the field),[87] among other strategies. The B-type agents operate on the long side of the market and overpay for goods or services that they are interested in buying.

By exercising entry control, C obliges A to choose between a productive activity and a combination of a productive activity with rent-seeking. As a result of narrowing down her choice set, A clearly prefers combining the productive activity with rent-seeking to the alternative option (exclusion from the field and the resulting failure to make any transaction). A's option of investing only in the productive activity disappears. Within the power triad, it does not matter who initiates bribes, C or A. Both may take the first step in this direction. Who actually takes this step does eventually have an impact on the division of the monopoly rent (if the chosen strategy implies a first-mover advantage).

The division of labour within the triad can also be described using the typology of transactions proposed by Commons. This exercise further confirms the compatibility of the proposed conceptualization with some widely recognized approaches. Commons differentiates three types of transactions: bargaining, managerial and rationing.[88] Exchanges in the market take the form of bargaining transactions. Managerial transactions refer to relationships between a superior and an inferior within the firm. Rationing transactions are activities related to setting and enforcing the rules of the game (norms that underpin interactions). The relationships between A and B within the power triad have the features of bargaining transactions. Because *C* sets and enforces rules regulating access to the field, the relationships of *C*, *A* and *B* have the features of rationing transactions. The employment contract specified by the system of equations [1] illustrates the idea of managerial transactions.

The parties involved in the power triad maintain their formal independence. No one hires anyone else. They also have unequal choice sets. *C* maximizes her expected utility. *A* minimizes missed opportunities. We can assert that the power triad creates an environment favourable for the minimization of missed opportunities that contrasts with the perfectly competitive market as the environment favouring the utility maximization. *B* obtains a utility that marginally exceeds her reservation utility. No one loses, however. *C*, *A* and *B* obtain positive utilities. Their interests form constellations.

In this sense, the concept of the power triad provides a better understanding of the mechanics of domination by virtue of the constellation of interests in the market. The existence of barriers (the structural component) and entry control (the strategic component) is necessary to make this type of domination operational. *C* dominates over *A* and *B* and does so in an *invisible* manner. *B* may never enter in contact with *C* whereas *A* does not receive any explicit command from *C*. As a result, all of them want the power triad to continue operating. Thus, a source of changes, if it exists at all, may eventually be located outside the power triad.

So far, the *A*-type agent that is excluded from the field, *A'*, has remained outside the focus of our analysis. Can this excluded agent be considered a 'dissident', a possible force for driving changes in an otherwise internally stable system? Upon closer inspection, it appears that *A'* is poorly suited for such a role. *A'* just turns out to be less fortunate than *A*, who was actually admitted to the field. *A'* would behave in the same way as *A* does, if *A'* were given a chance.

An agent who does not want to be involved in the power triad *independently* of her chances to be admitted would be a better candidate for the role of a dissident. Michel Foucault calls such agents 'people' in contrast to the 'population'.

> The people comprise those who conduct themselves in relations to the management of the population, at the level of the population, as if they were not part of the population as a collective subject-object, as if they put themselves outside of it, and consequently the people are those who, refusing to be the population, disrupt the system.[89]

Instead of trying to negotiate admission into the power triad, the 'people' question its existence and especially the rationale underpinning its operation, namely domination by virtue of a constellation of interests.

3 THE 2008 FINANCIAL CRISIS THROUGH THE LENS OF POWER RELATIONSHIPS

The 2008 financial crisis and its aftermath provide a good opportunity for testing the concept of the power triad outlined in Chapter 2 one more time and for highlighting its difference from the approach of public choice theory, an influential branch of neoclassical economics. The label 'second Great Depression' may seem somewhat exaggerated. However, the 2008 crisis led to a drop in the US GDP that has had no match since the end of the Great Depression in the late 1930s (Figure 3.1).[1] The crisis originated in the US but affected the world economy as a whole. In 2009, the US economy contracted by 3.1 per cent,[2] the European Union economy – by 4.3 per cent, the OECD economies – by 3.7 per cent and the world economy – by 2.1 per cent.[3]

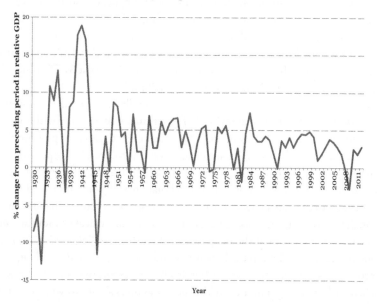

Figure 3.1: Real GDP growth rates, the USA, 1930–2012, annual percentage. Source: The US Bureau of Economic Analysis, at http://www.bea.gov/iTable/index_nipa.cfm [accessed 24 November 2013].

The formation of a bubble in the housing market preceded the crisis. Real estate assets not only tended to be overpriced, but households and other economic agents conventionally believed that the prices would continue to rise indefinitely. In the words of John Maynard Keynes, 'the essence of this convention ... lies in assuming that the existing state of affairs will continue indefinitely, except in so far as we have specific reasons to expect a change'.[4] Very few, if any, actors expected any change in the circumstances.

The institution of mortgage connects the housing market to the financial sector.[5] Real estate prices affect the amount of credits and loans available, as well as interest rates. Credits underpin the demand for products of the real sector of the economy (industry, agriculture, research and development, and so forth). The availability of affordable loans is also a prerequisite for growth in the real sector. The bursting of the housing bubble in 2007 naturally created a chain reaction leading to a financial crisis and to a general slowdown in economic activity, namely a recession.

In contrast to the late 1920s, the US government was quick to respond. Both the conservative administration of President George W. Bush (in office until 19 January 2009) and the democratic administration of his successor, President Barack Obama, initiated several large-scale state interventions in the housing and financial markets, as well as in the industry. These interventions took various forms: from the 'bailouts', i.e. the purchase of 'toxic' mortgages which had fallen significantly in value from the insurers and other financial institutions, to textbook Keynesian policies such as public spending. The total amount of bailout funds is estimated at $700 billion, whereas the total amount of stimulus funds is estimated at $800 billion.[6] If one adds to these figures the $250 billion in public debt increased by ad hoc tax cuts, then state interventions cost $1.75 trillion,[7] or 12 per cent of the US GDP in 2008 ($14.72 trillion).

State interventions on such a large scale naturally attracted the attention of neoclassical economists who are critical of government interference with the market. During the Great Depression, only the lack of state capacity prevented the implementation of large-scale planning and the emergence of a corporatist state in the US, as per initial design of the National Industrial Recovery Act signed into law in 1933.[8] Public choice theory scholars have a comparative advantage under these circumstances because they study taxation and public spending using the analytical tools of neoclassical economics. For neoclassical economists, nevertheless, power remains at the periphery of their theories. '"Power" is a concept frequently employed by political scientists and sociologists, and totally ignored by economists and practitioners of public choice'.[9] Neoclassical economists are satisfied with reducing power to market power as one's ability to set prices above marginal cost observed in the 'deviant' cases of imperfect competition only (monopoly, monopsony, and oligopoly). Advocates of the new institutionalism have extended the scope of power in the economy by recognizing its role in structuring relationships within the firm[10] and 'relational contracting'.[11] Yet, they continue to view the market as an exact opposite of power.

The scholars of original institutionalism also enjoy a comparative advantage in studying the 2008 crisis and its aftermath, but for another set of reasons. Original institutionalism represents one of the few economic approaches that explicitly takes power into account and studies its forms and effects. For institutionalists, 'the economy is a system of power'.[12] Institutionalists acknowledge the existence of power in all types of economic relationships, including between producers and consumers, government and businesses, and employers and employees.

This chapter compares two views on the 2008 crisis: a public choice view and an institutionalist view. The former uses the concept of rent-seeking to explain the behaviour of government officials and businesses profiting from bailout and stimulus funds. The latter places the 2008 crisis in the context of power relationships. In particular, what opportunities does it create for strengthening the positions of the actors vested in power? In the process, I add a new item to the institutionalists' toolbox for studying power. Namely, I apply the concept of the power triad outlined in Chapter 2. The underlying theory of domination by virtue of a constellation of interests in the market helps to overcome, among other things, the false opposition between the market and power.

I divide this chapter into four sections. Section 1 discusses what public choice theory has to say about economic power, political power and their eventual connection. In Section 2, I summarize the writings of public choice theorists about the 2008 crisis. Two articles specifically commissioned by the editors of *Public Choice*, a flagship scholarly journal in this field, appear particularly relevant.[13] In Section 3, I briefly outline the institutionalists' contributions to studies of power. In Section 4, I discuss how the 2008 crisis created new opportunities for strengthening the power of government in its relationships with businesses and the broader population. I argue that, in the context of the crisis and subsequent recovery, a power triad has emerged. In it, government dominates over businesses and the broader population; selected businesses (e.g. those with privileged access to bailout and stimulus funds) dominate over the remainder of businesses and population by virtue of a constellation of their interests in the market. Thus, the power triad represents a combination of power and the market. Power structures the market in such a manner that the latter becomes a pillar of the former.

1. Power: A Public Choice View

Since it is an essentially contested concept,[14] power does not have a single and commonly accepted definition. Nevertheless, Dennis Mueller is correct when acknowledging the lack of interest in the concept of power on the part of public choice theorists. He invites them to consider a broad definition of power, initially proposed by Max Weber.[15] He also shows how Weber's approach could be adapted to the subject matter of public choice theory: 'Political power means inducing someone to do something that he did not want to do, as when A gets a committee to choose x when all but A favour feasible alternative y'.[16] Legislative committee deliberations regarding budget allocation attract public choice theorists' particular attention.

Mueller links power to uncertainty. In a world with perfect information (zero transaction costs) no party could decide the outcomes of a transaction in a discretionary manner even if one party is superior, whereas the other plays a subordinate role. The subordinate would know about the rewards corresponding to each level of effort that the subordinate applies for meeting the objectives set by the superior. By choosing a particular level of effort, the subordinate would secure a specific reward regardless of the superior's wishes. Recalling Frank Knight's idea that profit represents a reward for risk taking,[17] Mueller concludes that 'both profit and power exist owing to uncertainty; both accrue to the possessors of information'.[18]

Public choice theory considers four types of actors: voters (they pay taxes and elect legislators), legislators (they allocate budgets and oversee bureaus), bureaucrats (their bureaus supply government services and other public goods) and businesses (they are either regulated by the bureaus or depend on government subventions). All of them supposedly maximize utility, but in a different manner. Voters want public goods at a price that minimizes their tax burden. Legislators maximize political power.[19] Bureaucrats maximize the budgets of their bureaus or, as an option, 'discretionary' budgets. The discretionary budget refers to the difference between the bureau's total budget and the minimum cost of producing the expected output.[20] Businesses seek rents. In contrast to rent creation, rent-seeking involves the redistribution of income. Income is produced in the first case and redistributed by means of 'getting a monopoly or getting some other government favour'.[21]

Public choice theory does not consider interactions between the four types of actors. Instead, its advocates focus on bilateral transactions, for instance, between voters and legislators, legislators and bureaucrats and so on. Let us consider some of these pairs in more detail.[22] Interactions between voters and legislators lie at the origin of logrolling, or vote trading. Legislators attempt to tax the entire population of a country for a rather small amount per capita in order to spend large amounts in specific areas where their constituency lives.[23]

To do so, they need to form coalitions with legislators representing the other jurisdictions. Today, members of such a coalition vote for preferences for one jurisdiction, tomorrow – for preferences for the other.

Rent-seeking leads to both static and dynamic losses in interactions between voters (tax payers and also customers) and businesses. A static loss results from setting prices above the equilibrium level. The triangle ABC in Figure 3.2 shows the static loss, or the net loss. It is sometimes called Harberger's triangle. Neither party appropriates the revenue ABC. The quadrangle DECA (Tullock's quadrangle), on the other hand, refers to a dynamic loss, the cost of creating a monopoly.[24] The revenue DECA involves the redistribution of income from the voter to the business or from one business to another:[25] the latter captures what the former loses. The revenue captured by the business (or at least a significant part of it) is subsequently spent on bribing bureaucrats and legislators and on transferring resources to them in other forms, however.

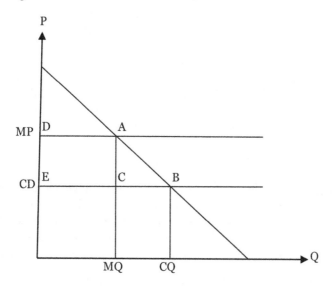

Figure 3.2: Static and dynamic losses as a result of a monopoly. Legend: P refers to price, Q to quantity, MP to a monopolistic price, CD to a competitive demand, MQ to a monopolistic quantity and CQ to a competitive quantity. Adapted from Tullock, *Public Goods, Redistribution and Rent Seeking*, p. 93.

Interactions between businesses and bureaucrats or legislators who regulate particular industries lead to two outcomes. In the first case businesses 'are able to acquire regulations that create rents for themselves'.[26] This situation is studied by a version of public choice theory, namely regulatory capture theory.[27] In the second case, 'politicians use regulation both to create rents and to extract them through campaign contributions, votes and bribes'.[28] In contrast to the capture of the regulator by businesses, in this case the regulator captures them. From the viewpoint of public choice theory, both parties, the business and the regulator, cannot win simultaneously. Either one 'gets' the other, or vice versa. This excludes a win-win outcome, however unequally the rent generated by the transaction might be distributed between the parties involved.

Regulatory capture and business capture theories do not account for unexplained eventual connections between economic and political power. On the one hand, these two versions of public choice theory suggest the interconnectedness of economic and political power. A monopolist is better off with a regulator's assistance when erecting barriers and restricting competition on a particular market. The involvement of a monopolist allows a regulator to capture a rent. On the other hand, public choice theorists acknowledge that 'the pursuit of profits is not the perceived legitimate goal of public bureaus, and thus it is ... difficult for public bureaucrats to convert the power they have into income'.[29]

Seen from the perspective of public choice theory, political power and economic power do not form a coherent whole. Either political power prevails over economic power (the situation of business capture) or vice versa (the situation of regulatory capture). This comes as no surprise because the imputed interests of the voter, the legislator, the bureaucrat and the business tend to diverge rather than to constellate. For instance, the legislator can achieve outcome x of a committee vote without any input on the part of the business.

2. Crisis as an Outlier Event

According to public choice theorists, the 2008 crisis represents an unfortunate event that calls, however, neither for extraordinary policy responses nor for theoretical re-evaluations and breakthroughs. Roger Congleton insists that the scope of the problem was simply exaggerated. The owners of 'toxic' assets had an interest in prompting large-scale state interventions as a way to cover their losses.

> A good deal of the initial talk of 'crisis' was induced by the financial sector, because many of its firms (and employees) were in a state of crisis and stood to profit if a major intervention by the Federal government could be induced.[30]

A closer look at texts of the annual presidential addresses does not support the hypothesis about the drift into exaggeration. Content analysis of the presidential addresses helps outline an official take on the current situation and policy responses to it. Two countries were considered, the US and Russia. The Russian case adds a comparative dimension to the present discussion. In contrast to the US, Russia's economy was severely affected not only by the 2008 crisis, but also by the

1997 Asian financial crisis. In 1998, Russia's economy contracted by 5.3 per cent.[31] The effect of the 2008 crisis was also more severe in Russia than in the US: Russia's economy shrank by 7.8 per cent in 2009. The talk of crisis tended to be more widespread in the Russian official discourse than in the American official discourse (Figure 3.3).[32] President Obama in his 2009 address was certainly not attempting to underscore the scope of the crisis. Yet he was not exaggerating it either:

> If you haven't been personally affected by this recession, you probably know someone who has: a friend, a neighbor, a member of your family. You don't need to hear another list of statistics to know that our economy is in crisis, because you live it every day. It's the worry you wake up with and the source of sleepless nights. It's the job you thought you'd retire from but now have lost, the business you built your dreams upon that's now hanging by a thread, the college acceptance letter your child had to put back in the envelope. The impact of this recession is real, and it is everywhere.[33]

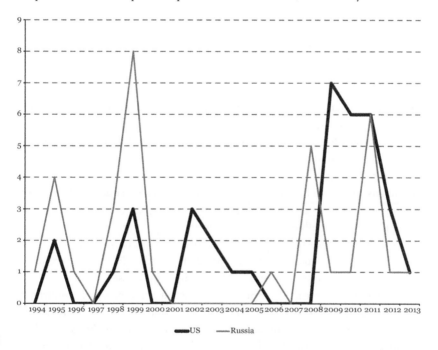

Figure 3.3: Frequency of references to crisis in the presidential addresses, the United States and the Russian Federation, 1994–2013. Legend: the dictionary based on substitution includes the following expressions and their equivalents in Russian: financial_cris* (* refers to any letter or their combination), recession*, global_cris*, great_depression. Source: transcripts of the presidential addresses are available on the American Presidency Project website, at http://www.presidency.ucsb.edu/ws [accessed 5 August 2014] and on the President of Russia's official website, at kremlin.ru [accessed 5 August 2014].

Russian President Boris Yeltsin in his address delivered in early 1999 sounded more alarmist after the Russian government defaulted on domestic debt in late summer 1998:

> The task of strengthening the state capacity cannot be achieved without building the trust of the society in the state. Unfortunately, this trust has significantly eroded today, which has a negative impact on the socio-political atmosphere in the country and its economy. A telling example can be found in the situation of the past summer when citizens' mistrust in the government led to a deepening of the financial crisis and caused the collapse of the entire banking system.[34]

In his attempt to demonstrate the 'normality' of the 2008 crisis, Congleton sees its origin in an excessive yet 'perfectly legal' opportunistic mood that prevailed in the markets before its start.

> Opportunists, unlike optimists, may expect the good times to end at any time, but expect to gain sufficient income during the good times to carry them through the bad times, even if their companies fail. Both optimists and opportunists can offer terms in the short run that more prudent firms cannot.[35]

Opportunist consumers continued to convert rising real estate values into new credits that fuelled overspending. Opportunist insurers and investors continued to decrease their reserves by profiting from low financial delinquency rates and so forth. When doing so, they missed the moment when 'neglected outlier possibilities came to pass'.[36] In other words, the crisis had an 'all too human' nature.

So far, the only significant particularity of the public choice theorists' take on the crisis refers to the presumed (yet not confirmed) tendency of 'perfectly legal opportunists' to exaggerate the negative consequences of their belief that 'the existing state of affairs will continue indefinitely'. Public choice theory also predicts that the government's response to the crisis – increased state interventionalism – would lead either to the capture of businesses by the state regulator or to the capture of the state regulator by regulated businesses.

Congleton claims that these predictions turned out to be largely confirmed. On the one hand, 'many of Treasury's decisions appear to be consistent with regulatory capture theory, because they benefit the recipient firms and their employees far more than they do the taxpayers'.[37] On the other hand, the government re-nationalized – captured – privately held government sponsored enterprises (GSEs) such as Fannie Mac and Freddie Mac (home mortgage insurers). It is worth noting that these two GSEs directly or indirectly insured more than half of the market for mortgage-backed securities.[38]

According to public choice theorists, the crisis did not undermine the essential differences in the interests of voters, legislators, bureaucrats and businesses.

State interventions lobbied for by particular businesses profit the rent-seeking business at the expense of voters-taxpayers, which causes the legislator to manoeuvre between mutually excluding expectations on the part of the rent-seeking business and voters-taxpayers. 'When incumbents vote on special interest legislation, they weigh continued financial support from special interests *against* continued electoral support of (or loss of it from) their constituents.'[39] The interests of voters, legislators and businesses in these circumstances contradict one another instead of constellating. Congleton suggests that voters, who are not directly affected by the crisis, may vote for increasing bailout and stimulus funds out of altruism.[40] The assumption of altruism may well be plausible, but how can it be reconciled with the foundational – for neoclassical economists – assumption of self-interested behaviour?

3. Power: An Institutionalist View

The 2008 financial crisis, and its subsequent developments, caused a revival of institutional economists' interest in the issues of power. For instance, the *Journal of Economic Issues* has published a total of forty-six articles with 'power' as their topic in the five year crisis and post-crisis period (2008–12), which exceeds a similar figure in the previous sixteen years (1992–2007).[41]

A critical and sceptical stance of 'original institutionalists' toward existing institutions leads a number of them[42] to adapt Weber's definition: power refers to one's ability to impose one's will on others, despite their eventual resistance. This ability can be used in various interactions: social, political, and economic. Domination as a particular form of power means that the one in a dominant position imposes her will on those whom she dominates to the detriment of the latter group.[43]

Compared with political power, economic power has several distinctive features. Economic power influences resource allocation,[44] despite the wishes of the 'have-nots'. Political power underpins claims to determine the parameters of an order within a particular territory,[45] despite eventual counter-claims. Techniques for achieving a desired outcome differ accordingly. Physical force is rarely used as a technique of economic power. On the other hand, the monopoly of the use of physical force is quintessential of political power.

It would be an exaggeration to say that there is a coherent institutional theory of economic power. Instead, the relevant literature contains the detached building blocks of what would eventually become a theoretical edifice. Even though a detailed overview is far beyond the scope of this chapter, I will briefly introduce some ideas to prepare the ground for subsequent discussion.

John R. Commons's taxonomy of transactions serves to differentiate bargaining transactions that do not involve power from those that do: managerial transactions and rationing transactions. Managerial transactions take place within the firm and thus appear to be less relevant for bridging the gap between power and the market. 'The rationing transactions differ from managerial transactions in that the superior is a collective superior while the inferiors are individuals.'[46] This distinction paves the way for interpreting relations between government, on one hand, and businesses and population, on the other, in the same terms.

The dependence effect, described by John Kenneth Galbraith,[47] represents another useful concept for theorizing power in the market (and through the market). With respect to the dependence effect, Galbraith means that producers create the demand for their products – i.e. they shape consumers' needs by urging them to buy something that they would not otherwise consider.[48] The dependence effect shows that power relationships structure basic market transactions in accordance to how the market works.

A similar line of reasoning is further developed by Samuel Bowles and Herbert Gintis.[49] They argue that power relationships emerge every time the market does not clear.[50] Economic actors on the short side of the market influence the range of choices available to those on the long side of the market. In other words, actors on the short side of the market are able to define the individual choice (decision-making) sets of their counterparts on the long side of it. Economic power finds its expression in the system of constraints under which actors make their 'free' choices.[51]

Weber juxtaposes domination by virtue of a constellation of interests to domination by virtue of authority (i.e. compliance with rules and norms; see Chapter 2). The key feature of this concept is the idea that the interests of those who are dominated may actually *constellate* with those who dominate, instead of being totally suppressed. The economic actor, dealing with a monopoly, appears to still be better off transacting with the monopoly than if refusing to do so. True, the monopoly appropriates the lion's share of the rent generated by any and all transactions, but those who are dominated still retain a greater share of the rent than when not transacting at all.

Although political and economic powers have their own particularities studied by separate disciplines – political science and institutional economics – they tend to be interconnected. The case of monopolies illustrates this point. Because the exact nature of the links existing between political and economic monopolies remains obscure,[52] this calls for further exploration. The 2008 crisis makes the study of interconnections between political and economic powers more theoretically and practically relevant than ever.

4. Crisis as an Opportunity for Strengthening Power

The crisis, which started in the second half of 2008, created a situation with substantial risk for transforming the market into a weapon in the hands of the power holders. Existing approaches to studying power are arguably insufficient for evaluating all of its emerging configurations. For instance, the effect of conspicuous consumption, attributed by Thorstein Veblen to top income groups (those vested in economic power by virtue of pecuniary wealth),[53] may be a factor explaining the emergence of the US housing bubble.[54] Yet, it hardly explains the situation in the financial market. A rise in government spending – a textbook Keynesian recipe – boosts the relative size and scope of rationing transactions. Bargaining transactions, however, are believed to remain unaffected.[55]

The crisis involves a series of structural biases that create numerous opportunities for profiting from them and converting them into a resource for strengthening the market power of particular businesses. Government interventions, intended to bridge structural gaps, also offer ample opportunities for strengthening power with their help, the power of office holders and that of selected businesses. The crisis has given rise to a power triad consisting of C (government), A (selected businesses) and B (the rest of the population).

The unusually sharp structural biases, occurring during the crisis, have called for government interventions around the world. And current governments, unlike those of the 1930s Great Depression in the US, appear to be better prepared and more willing to intervene in the market by providing financial assistance and through investments. Access control to funds distributed by government may eventually take place, provided that access to subventions, loans and tax exemptions becomes a matter of survival for businesses.

The power triad may emerge as a result of transformation in the distribution of public funds into a particular field of domination with clear boundaries and control of access. Although everyone wants to get into the field, only a few succeed because of the scarcity of funds and the barriers erected by the government (C) before them. At the same time the rest of the population (Bs) would be better off if some businesses survive and provide them with jobs; no one has an interest in a total collapse even if most funds come out of their pockets. C eventually transforms the role of a distributor of public funds into a resource for strengthening its power. As a result, a constellation of the interests of C, A and B – government, businesses and population – emerges.

The key elements of the power triad are: boundaries (they have an institutional nature: to apply for stimulus funds, one must meet several criteria as to the type of business, nationality, etc.) and entry control.[56] The existence of boundaries and entry control allows C to convert political power (the control over a territory) into economic power of A, having a privileged access to stimulus funds and fewer competitors, even though some A-type actors do not manage to gain access (see Figure 2.1 in Chapter 2). A's economic power then becomes a resource for strengthening C's political power by returning part of its profits to C through formal (e.g. political contributions or support for C's initiatives) and informal (kickbacks and other services rendered in exchange) channels.

C, A and B may engage in bargaining, rationing and managerial transactions. On one hand, C, A and B maintain their autonomy and interact in the market. On the other hand, C distributes stimulus funds (rationing transaction) and controls entry to the market (managerial transaction). This unusual combination helps one to better understand that C dominates B and A, while C and A dominate B without using physical force or threats. Instead, domination involves changing the individual choice sets of B and A. They are better off accepting C's power even if they are unable to maximize their utility/profit as a result. Instead, B and A minimize missed opportunities.[57]

Some sections of the Recovery and Reinvestment Act 2009 do not prevent the possible drift into transforming the distribution of public funds into a weapon in the hands of office holders charged with this function. The Act is intended to regulate government spending and tax credits totalling about $800 billion, or approximately 5.5 per cent of the GDP, at the federal level. The authors of this law devote significant attention to issues of accountability and transparency in using public funds. For instance, the Recovery Accountability and Transparency Board was established 'to conduct oversight of covered funds to prevent fraud, waste, and abuse' (Section 1521). An official website, www.recovery.gov, was created in order to help taxpayers track their money spent under the Act 'from below'. This represents 'a first-time government-wide accountability system'.[58] However, the existing transparency safeguards do not extend to all instances of power relationships, especially when power does not take manifest forms.

The provision on the mandatory use of American iron, steel and manufactured goods in all projects benefiting from the funds appropriated under the Act appears particularly controversial (Section 1605, labelled 'Buy American'). This provision facilitates office holders' eventual transformation into gate keepers within the power triad (C). The head of a federal department or agency can waive the 'Buy American' requirement under certain conditions (Subsection 1605b). At least some non-American suppliers (A), on the other hand, are not excluded from being admitted to the national market, characterized by less severe competition (i.e. a structural bias), in exchange for their reinforcing the interests of those who could waive the requirement (C). For their part, taxpayers

(*B*) gain something, as an alternative to nothing (when there is no Act), since some jobs are still created.

To find out whether the power triad emerges as a by-product of the recovery policies, I offer several tentative tests. First, I have to check whether the access to bailout and stimulus funds depends on the economic agent's organizational form and geographical location within the US. If it does, the boundaries and access control probably exist within the US. Content analysis of publications in the mass media confirms that access to the funds, made available under the Act (1) varies across different groups of businesses and (2), in some cases, has a problematic character. *LexisNexis Academic* shows a higher frequency of references to car-makers in the context of 'access to bailout funds', followed by those to banks and insurers. Car-makers were mentioned in 50 per cent of the major US and foreign English-language publications in 2009. Three years later, the frequency of mentioning of banking and financial institutions exceeded that of car-makers.[59]

Not all financial institutions appear equally eligible for funds, however. Only those registered as banks can get access to the funds, which prompted some institutions, such as *Goldman Sachs, Morgan Stanley* (both initially financial firms) and *American Express* (initially a credit- and charge-card company), to change their organizational form. There are also sharp divides between large and small banks, as well as between regional and national ones.[60]

The analysis of the data about recipients of stimulus funds produces rather surprising outcomes. The total value of stimulus funds per state does not depend on the dynamic of their GDP. I found no correlation between, on one hand, the GDP changes in 2008, 2009, 2010 and 2011 and, on the other hand, the total value of awards (grants, contracts and loans), made under the Act, in 2009, 2010, 2011 and 2012.[61]

If the total value of stimulus funds awarded to businesses in a particular state does not depend on the recession's depth (regardless of the temporal lag used), then the impact of a number of other macroeconomic and political variables could also be explored. These include the size of the population (in 2011), the value of the GDP, the number of electors representing the state in the US Electoral College, and a political index that I constructed.[62] The number of electors turned out to be the only significant predictor for the independent variable, the total value of stimulus funds (Table 3.1).[63] This means that the location of a particular business does indeed influence its chances to gain access to stimulus funds. At the national level, the institutional boundaries derive from political, rather than from economic or social, considerations: the larger the number of electors representing a particular state (as opposed to its total population), the easier access to stimulus funds.

Table 3.1: Results of statistical (Method = Forward) multiple regression to predict total value of awards (Y) from population (in 2011), GDP, number of electors and political index, 2009–12

	Total value of awards (LG10)	Number of electors	B	Beta	$SR^2_{incremental}$
Number of electors (LG10)	.922***		1.098***	.922	.85
Not entered:					
Population	.807***	.873***	–	–	–
GDP	.813***	.863***	–	–	–
Political index	.041	–.031	–	–	–
			Intercept=	8.576***	-
Mean	9.566	0.902	R^2=.85		
St. deviation	.372	0.312	R^2_{adj}=.847		
			R=.922		

Legend: *** Significant at the .001 level (2-tailed).

Second, I studied the profile of foreign businesses that gain access to the US stimulus funds. If businesses from particular countries outnumber businesses from the rest of the world, then boundaries and access control probably exist at the international level. At this stage, the data about foreign recipients of US stimulus funds was used with a country as a unit of analysis, excluding the five US insular areas. The dependent variable was the number of awards as a result of significant omissions in the data about the total value of awards received by foreign recipients. The longlist of candidate predictors included standard macroeconomic indicators from the Word Bank's World Development Indicators, the data about the US trade produced by the US Department of Commerce and political indicators, namely, the Freedom House's indexes of political rights and civil liberties. However, after correlational analysis, only four variables were used in regression analysis: the share of a particular country in the total volume of US exports and imports, the Freedom House's composite index (an average of its indexes of political rights and civil liberties), the Gross National Income and the World Bank's Ease of doing business index. The first and second of these candidate variables turned to be the only significant predictors (Table 3.2).[64] This result suggests that the national origin of a particular business influences its chances to get access to the US stimulus funds. At the international level, the institutional boundaries derive from political considerations and priorities in the US trade. The more important a trade partner is and the more developed democracy it has, the more chances exist that the requirements of the Act will be waived.

Table 3.2: Results of statistical (Method = Forward) multiple regression to predict total number of awards (Y) from export–import share, Freedom House composite index, GNI and World Bank's ease of doing business index, 2009–12

	Total number of awards (LG10)	Export–import share	Freedom House composite index	B	Beta	$SR^2_{incremental}$
Export import share (LG10)	.654***			1.012***	.611	.423
Freedom House composite index (1 = full-fledged democracy)	.357***	.146*		.045***	.271	.072
Not entered:						
GNI (LG10)	.459***	.424***	.525***	–	–	–
Ease of doing business index (1 = the most business friendly regulations)	.409***	.338***	.512***	–	–	–
				Intercept=	.197***	
Mean	.138	.0935	3.307	R^2=.495		
St deviation	.32	.193	1.971	R^2_{adj}=.49		
				R=.704		

The case of Canada is revealing. Canadian businesses got more awards (ninety-five) than businesses from any other country. However, this exceptional success is the result of a long and difficult bargaining process, involving the governments of both countries. A bilateral agreement signed with Canada in early February 2010 provides Canadian companies with access to contracts under the US stimulus package in exchange for some preferential treatment of American companies in Canada. The treaty also confirms the reality of case by case exemptions and horse trading.[65] Furthermore, the Canadian government decided in 2012 to implement a similar plan, nicknamed 'Buy Canadian'. This involves spending CAN$240 billion over the next twenty years on military acquisitions, giving priority to domestic suppliers.[66] Access control to these funds will probably be used by the Canadian government as a lever in dealing with its foreign partners. This lever neither needs parliamentary approval, and is not subject to public scrutiny.

5. Conclusion

In conclusion, the insufficient attention paid to issues of access to bailout and stimulus funds can potentially undermine the spirit of public accountability and transparency intended for the recovery policies. This shortcoming does not necessarily result from 'ill will' on the part of office-holders seeking an additional opportunity to strengthen and extend their power. It may also be attributed to an insufficient understanding of the conditions, under which government intervention transforms from a means to restore order into an end-in-itself.

At a more theoretical level, this chapter compares the approach developed in the present book with that of public choice theory. Both theoretical frameworks are intended to be ways of studying the relationships between businesses, government and population. Public choice theory, nevertheless, assumes a divergent character from such interests. What one party gains, the other party loses. The concept of the power triad, on the other hand, suggests that the interests of the parties constellate instead of being divergent and mutually exclusive. Government, businesses and population gain, but to an unequal extent.

When applied to the study of the 2008 crisis, public choice theory views it as an opportunity for creating and capturing rents. Because these rents are captured only by some actors (for instance, businesses in the situation of regulatory capture), the emerging equilibrium tends to be unstable. The idea of a constellation of interests in the market, on the other hand, suggests that rents can be captured by all the parties involved in transactions. This makes the emerging imperfect equilibrium more sustainable. C, A and B might have incentives to sustain the power triad even after the crisis is over.

4 WELCOME TO RUSSIA: BENEFITS OF OBEDIENCE

The discussion of the 2008 financial crisis in the previous chapter resulted in a situation that is common in the social sciences: the same event can be explained in terms of several theories, namely, public choice theory and the theory of gate keeping outlined in this book. The application of public choice theory required the introduction or modification of several assumptions, however. These assumptions were absent from the initial formulation of its premises.

From the point of view of neoclassical economists, the 2008 financial crisis represents an outlier event, a 'black swan' in the population of white swans. In contrast to terrorism, a financial crisis has a non-zero probability that can eventually be assessed in a rational manner.[1] Financial crises of a similar magnitude occur on a regular basis (see Figure 3.1). Rationally minded individuals – the model of rational choice is a core premise of neoclassical economics – should not completely discard the eventuality of a crisis. If they do, their behaviour fails to meet standards of rationality. Rational agents hold enough reserves for covering any eventual losses during a financial crisis.

In order to address this problem, public choice theorists introduce additional assumptions of optimism and opportunism.

> The under-holding of reserves may be regarded as products of optimism and perfectly legal forms of economic opportunism. Optimists will take on more debt and have higher rates of return during good times than more prudent investors, because they hold lower reserves (on which lower rates of return are earned).[2]

Opportunists believe that the extra income gained during good times will help them cope during bad times. The activities of both opportunists and optimists contribute to the deepening of the crisis. Public choice theorists enhance the explanatory power of their theory by adding particular adjectives to rational agents, opportunist and optimist. The theory turns out to be saved at the price of reformulating a statement with which it is eventually inconsistent. Reformulation makes the statement consistent with the theory.

The alternative strategy consists in introducing a new theory based on a new set of assumptions. The new theory is intended to explain the behaviour of individuals when an outlier event occurs without ad hoc reformulations and adjustments. For instance, an alternative to neoclassical economics, Keynesian economics, emerged in response to the Great Depression of the 1930s. Premises of Keynesian economics go beyond the assumption of individual rationality. They also include elements of social economic action. In contrast to economic action, social economic action 'is driven by economic interests *and* oriented to other actors'.[3] John Maynard Keynes argues that a successful investor must predict the behaviour and expectations of the other market players:[4]

> Professional investment may be likened to those newspaper competitions in which the competitors have to pick out the six prettiest faces from a hundred photographs, the prize being awarded to the competitor whose choice most nearly corresponds to the average preferences of the competitors as a whole; so that each competitor has to pick, not those faces which he himself finds prettiest, but those which he thinks likeliest to catch the fancy of the other competitors, all of whom are looking at the problem from the same point of view. It is not a case of choosing those which, to the best of one's judgment, are really the prettiest, nor even those which average opinion genuinely thinks the prettiest.

Keynes also explicitly acknowledges the importance of optimism in economic decisions instead of doing this on an ad hoc basis. He asserts that 'a large proportion of our positive activities depend on spontaneous optimism rather than on a mathematical expectation'.[5] In other words, optimism refers to a rule in Keynesian economics and to an exception to the rule in neoclassical economics. The exception applies mostly to times of crisis.

To further complicate the matter, the assumptions of Keynesian economics are subject to revisions and ad hoc adjustments as well (as reflected in the development of Post-Keynesian economics, for instance). The relative elasticity of premises and the acceptance of adjustments made on an ad hoc basis complicate the task of collecting empirical evidence that confirms or refutes a particular theory. As a result, both neoclassical economists and advocates of Keynesian economics claim that the 2008 crisis can eventually be explained using their theoretical frameworks. It comes as no surprise that economists using competing theories rarely listen to arguments put forward by their opponents.[6] As long as scholars have the freedom to adjust the premises of a particular theory at will, they do not need to consider alternative theories. All theories are believed to be true in all situations.

The tendency to make ad hoc adjustments can be avoided or at least limited by raising standards for the formulation of premises and predicted outcomes of a theory. Premises and predictions have to be specific and precise enough. This chapter is intended to further specify the key assumptions of the theory of gate keeping. It also shows that the theory of gate keeping explains the economic agents' responses to the 2008 financial crisis in North America (as discussed in the previous chapter) and transactions in an apparently very distant situation, in the emerging market in Russia, without ad hoc adjustments. More specifically, this chapter discusses the practices of access control in the regional markets in Russia and offers a new empirical test for the theory of gate keeping. In contrast to the empirical test whose outcomes were reported in Chapter 3, the new test was designed in such a manner as to oppose predictions of public choice theory and the theory of gate keeping.

This chapter has four sections along with this introduction and the conclusion. Section 1 provides a theoretical discussion of falsifiability as a criterion of the validity of a theory. The emphasis on falsifiability is not universal in nature. However, from the outset, economic sciences have been attempting to replicate the model of the natural sciences.[7] Consequently, an *economic* theory shall pass the test of falsifiability however positivist or conventionalist it may otherwise be. Section 2 presents the Russian case. It also provides an overview of some forms that gate keeping takes in this emerging market. Sources of data, key variables and their operationalization, procedures for data screening and robustness checks are explained in Section 3. Section 4 discusses the outcomes of the empirical test. It argues that the interests of the state representatives (C), selected businesses (A) and population (B) form a constellation. Contrary to the predictions of public choice theory, the interests of one actor (C or A) do not tend to suppress the interests of the others.

1. Can the Theory of Gate Keeping be Falsified?

Public choice theory claims to be able to interpret the 2008 financial crisis. The arch-rival of neoclassical economics, Keynesian economics, offers a different take on the crisis, insisting on its unique validity. Paul Krugman argues that 'John Maynard Keynes … is now more relevant than ever'.[8] The theory of gate keeping also claims to provide an explanation for a particular aspect of the crisis, namely the reaction of the state representatives and economic agents to the recession and the wave of bankruptcies in the financial sector. The number of theories making similar claims does not stop here. How is it possible for so many theories using conflicting premises to be valid?

In this respect, Karl Popper recalls his experience with psychoanalysis at the start of the twentieth century in Vienna, the capital of this discipline at that time. He observed that many cases (stories of particular patients or behavioural patterns) could be interpreted 'in the light of [Alfred] Adler's theory or equally of [Sigmund] Freud's',[9] despite the conflicting premises on which these theories are based. The lack of commonly accepted procedures for assessing the validity of competing theories leads to their proliferation. Even today, one century later, psychology suffers from the proliferation of theories. Some psychologists admit that '"theory" accumulation is not a proof for progress, but rather an indicator for the lack of a shared methodology for theory construction and testing in our science'.[10] Arguably, the same observation applies to the economic sciences, even if one approach in economics, the neoclassical one, clearly prevails. The prevalence of neoclassical economics is partly due to the elasticity of its premises and the acceptance of adjustments made on an ad hoc basis.

Popper's solution to the problem of theory accumulation involves requiring that a theory must be falsifiable. 'A theory is falsifiable if the class of its potential falsifiers [basic statements with which it is inconsistent] is not empty'.[11] Two aspects of falsification deserve particular attention. First, falsification involves empirical testing. Popper insists that logical considerations and tests are not sufficient for falsifying a theory. 'Empirical scientific statements or systems of statements are distinguished by being empirically falsifiable'.[12]

Second, empirical tests must be very specific. A simple reference to 'empirical evidence' is not sufficient. A valid test has several possible outcomes only one of which is consistent with a theory's predictions. The more eventual outcomes of a test there are and the more diverse they are, the more powerful confirmation it produces of a theory. Popper insists that falsification requires risky predictions.

> Confirmations should count only if they are the result of *risky predictions*; that is to say, if, unenlightened by the theory in question, we should have expected an event which was incompatible with the theory – an event which would have refuted the theory.[13]

Economic theory deals with several kinds of empirical evidence: econometric tests, experiments,[14] case studies and, far less frequently, qualitative data collected with the help of in-depth interviews or participant observation.[15] Econometric tests represent probably the most commonly used procedure of falsification, at least by neoclassical and Keynesian economists. Very often, however, econometric tests fail to meet the standard of riskiness: the list of independent variables (predictors) tends to be wide open. As the author of the article with the telling title 'I Just Ran Two Million Regressions' admits, 'the problem faced by empirical growth economists is that growth theories are not explicit enough about what variables x_j belong in the "true" regression'.[16] A data-driven approach appears to some economists as a natural (if not unique) solution. They 'tease' data by running 'two million regressions' or more, if it is needed to confirm a theory.

By formulating a theory in a weak, non-specific manner one extends one's room for manoeuvring at the falsification stage. The preference for weakly formulated theories does not solely characterize growth economists. Public choice theorists also avoid making risky predictions when conducting empirical tests. Let me illustrate this point by considering one of the pioneering attempts at falsifying public choice theory, namely the study of the regulation of entry by Simeon Djankov, Rafael La Porta, Florencio Lopez-de-Silanes and Andrei Shleifer.[17] The authors had used a battery of predictors that was subsequently included by World Bank experts in the Ease of Doing Business index: the number of procedures that a start-up must comply with in order to obtain legal status; the time that it takes to obtain legal status; the cost of obtaining legal status; the number of taxes that a start-up has to pay and their volume; and so forth. They run a series of regressions to test a more specific version of public choice theory, namely the tollbooth hypothesis. The tollbooth hypothesis predicts that the regulation of entry benefits regulators: 'politicians use regulation both to create rents and to extract them through campaign contributions, votes and bribes'.[18] The alternative hypothesis, regulatory capture theory, states that regulation benefits the business subject to it.[19]

Two actors are of particular interest: regulators (government officials) and start-up businesses. To test the tollbooth hypothesis, the authors cited formulate a prediction: 'corruption levels and the intensity of entry regulation are positively correlated'.[20] Is this prediction risky as per the Popperian criterion? It is not because, on the one hand, it can be made on the basis of a number of other theories as well and, on the other hand, it takes into consideration the situation of only one actor (regulators). The theory of gate keeping also predicts a positive correlation between the level of perceived corruption and the intensity of entry regulation. Thus, it would eventually be possible to use the results reported by the cited authors as evidence in support of the theory that has little in common with the tollbooth hypothesis.

So formulated, the prediction totally omits the situation of the second actor, start-up businesses. What if start-up businesses benefit from regulation as well as a result of restricted competition? Then a hybrid of the tollbooth hypothesis and regulatory capture theory would be needed. Neoclassical economics fail to make a more specific prediction by differentiating a win-win situation and the situation with a single winner. An explanation for this failure refers to neoclassical economists' exclusive focus on individual decision making as opposed to the transaction as a unit of analysis.[21] The prediction of the win-win outcome appears to be riskier because it increases the number of relevant outcomes (regulator wins, business wins and both win) and simultaneously restricts the number of outcomes consistent with a particular theory.

Andreas Glökner and Tilmann Betsch propose several principles that can help formulate a theory in a stronger manner: specification, empirical content and critical properties.[22] Specification involves stating a finite set of definitions and propositions that constitute a theory. A theory with empirical content predicts that particular states of the world will occur and others will not. Critical properties refer to the empirical observations that would constitute a fundamental violation of a theory. If an economic theory does not meet these Popperian requirements, then it contributes solely to theory accumulation and can be discarded without substantial loss.

Does the theory of gate keeping meet these requirements? The statistical tests whose outcomes were reported in Section 4 of Chapter 3 are not risky enough. These tests have the same flaw as the tests designed by Djankov and the co-authors: they do not serve to discriminate between the theory of gate keeping and the alternative explanations, namely the tollbooth hypothesis. Thus, additional empirical tests are needed. The new test should refer to more specific, riskier predictions made on the basis of the theory of gate keeping, the predictions that the tollbooth hypothesis and regulatory capture theory would rule out.

The theory of gate keeping considers interactions between three actors, the gate keeper, C, the business acting under conditions of restricted competition, A, and the population as the buyer of A's goods and services (or, eventually, as the seller of labour to A). According to this theory, all three economic agents gain, no matter how unequally the gains may be distributed among them.[23] In the case of the interactions of C, A and B in the market, their gains have a monetary expression. C maximizes her expected utility by appropriating a significant part of the rent captured by A under conditions of restricted competition. A minimizes missed opportunities by keeping the remaining part of the rent. B obtains goods and services of interest even if she overpays for them and her consumer surplus may actually decrease, approaching zero asymptotically.

The interactions of C, A and B may eventually produce eight possible states: all three gain; A gains and the others lose; B gains and the others lose; C gains and the others lose; A and B gain and C loses; A and C gain and B loses; B and C gain and A loses; all three lose. Depending on the operationalization of the economic actors' gains, only two states are compatible with the predictions of the theory of gate keeping: (i) all three gain and (ii) A and C gain whereas B loses. Ideally, a theory should predict a unique state of the world. The assessment of B's situation may be difficult because the theory predicts that she loses in relative terms and can still gain something in absolute terms. If empirical observations underpin one of the remaining six states then the theory of gate keeping would be refuted. This theory absolutely excludes the eventuality that A and/or C incur losses.

The application of two criteria for assessing the empirical content of the theories suggested by Glökner and Betsch serves to summarize the discussion of falsification. These criteria refer to:

> their level of universality (Allgemeinheit) and their degree of precision (Bestimmtheit). The former specifies to how many situations the theory can be applied. The latter refers to the precision in prediction, that is, how many 'subclasses' of realizations it allows.[24]

This book is intended to show that the theory of gate keeping is both universal and precise enough. The universality of this theory can be confirmed by applying it to various countries and diverse contexts of interactions. Chapter 3 suggests that the responses of the government and businesses in North America to the 2008 financial crisis can be interpreted in line with the theory of gate keeping. The subsequent sections of this chapter will show that the theory of gate keeping successfully predicts outcomes of transactions in the emerging Russian market as well. As for the degree of precision, the theory of gate keeping produces riskier predictions than, for instance, both versions of public choice theory, namely the tollbooth hypothesis and regulatory capture theory.

It would be a mistake, however, to reduce the theory of gate keeping to purely positivist content. The positivist reading of this theory is offered in order to facilitate exchanges with the representatives of the economic mainstream, neoclassical economics. 'Popper's proposal that scientific theories are distinguishable from non-scientific theories because they are testable has been widely accepted in the social sciences', namely economics.[25] Neoclassical economists commonly refer to the Popperian criteria, even if they often prefer to use these criteria in a weak form that leaves enough room for manoeuvring. The theory of gate keeping also has some constructivist content. The constructivist dimension appears to be a must, taking into consideration the essentially contested character of several key concepts used in this book, starting with the concept of power.[26] Thus, the theory of gate keeping does not rule out empirical tests built upon mixed and qualitative methods (for instance, case studies as illustrated in Chapter 7, and content analysis as exemplified by Chapter 5).

2. Particularities of Gate Keeping in Russia

The country specific repertoire of techniques for imposing will[27] in Russia has been evolving over time.[28] For some, Russia is still associated with the heavy reliance of the power elite on the use of force. The use of force in international affairs requires a strong military;[29] in internal affairs it involves prioritizing the prison institution. There is little doubt about the strength of both components during the Soviet times. For instance, the prison population ratio – the number of prisoners per 100,000 of the national population – in the Soviet Union was one of the highest in the world. In the late 1940s and early 1950s, the power elite kept almost every seventieth citizen behind prison walls (Figure 4.1). Prison has recently lost its privileged status within the Russian repertoire of techniques for imposing will, however. Russia is no longer among the most punitive countries in the world. In 2013, this country ranked tenth in the world prison population list, with the US, St Kittis & Nevis and the Seychelles being the top three countries on the list.[30]

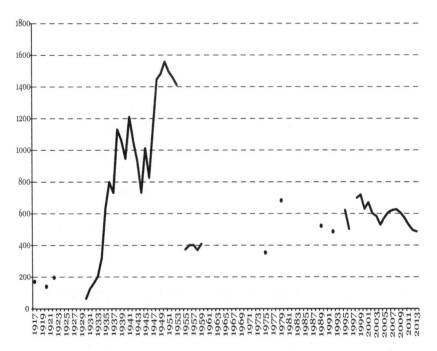

Figure 4.1: Prison population ratio (number of prisoners per 100,000 of national population), the Soviet Union and the Russian Federation, 1917–2014, selected years. Source:
The Federal Penitentiary Service of the Russian Federation, at http://www.fsin.su/statistics
[accessed 5 August 2014] and the Federal State Statistics Service of the Russian Federation,
at http://www.gks.ru/wps/wcm/connect/rosstat_main/rosstat/ru/statistics/population/
demography [accessed 5 August 2014].

Which technique(s) for imposing will has/have recently taken the place of brute
force in the Russian repertoire? The members of the Russian power elite rely on
manipulation by closely controlling the mass media, especially electronic media
(TV and radio). 'Control of the mass media is ... key to control of the virtual
world.'[31] As of 2014, Russia ranks 148th out of 180 countries in the world press freedom list: the mass media in Russia have less freedom than in most other countries.[32]

I argued elsewhere,[33] however, that the market, more specifically the market with restricted access and resulting structural disparities, has become the key
instrument for maintaining and strengthening the dominant positions of the
Russian power elite in the first decade of the twenty-first century. It is highly
unlikely that the members of the Russian elite read Michel Foucault or other
theorists who have written about the invisible hand of power.[34] More plausibly,
they realized the benefits of using the techniques of power based upon and in
accordance with the course of things themselves after the multiple trials and
errors of the 1990s when the market was officially legalized in this country, following the collapse of the centrally planned economy.

Strategies for controlling access to a particular field of transactions work if individuals are interested in entering the field beforehand. Why are economic agents interested in doing business on the Russian market? Russia has a resource-rich economy, one of the best endowed economies in the world. In 2011, total natural resources rents amounted to 22.03 per cent of the Russian GDP.[35] The mean value of total natural resources rents is 9.53 per cent; the standardized Z-value for the Russian economy is 0.83. In other words, fewer than 20 per cent of countries have more natural resources than Russia does. The value of the Mineral Potential Index compiled on the basis of mining company executives' perceptions of the geology (discovered and potential deposits) for this country is 89 out of 100.[36]

Natural resources rent directly and indirectly (through spillover effects) fuelled the Russian economy in the first decade of the twenty-first century. After nine years of recession in the 1990s (the average annual growth rate was -6.2 per cent in 1990–8), Russia experienced ten years of remarkable economic growth interrupted by the 2008 financial crisis (the average growth rate was 6.9 per cent in 1999–2008). The 2009 recession (-7.8 per cent) was followed by a slow recovery (the average growth rate was 3.4 per cent in 2010–13).[37] By 2012, the Russian GDP per capita had fully recovered from the 2008 financial crisis (Figure 4.2). Similar tendencies are observed at the regional level.

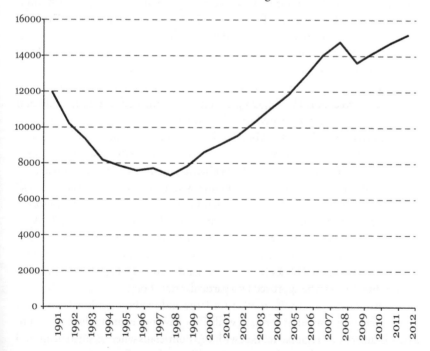

Figure 4.2: GDP per capita, purchasing power parity (PPP), constant 2005 international dollars, the Russian Federation, 1991–2012. Source: World Development Indicators by the World Bank, at http://data.worldbank.org/data-catalog/world-development-indicators [accessed 5 August 2014].

Controlling access to the market makes little sense if growth rates are negative as in the 1990s. However, when growth rates are positive and eventually reach the two digit level, as in 2000, the domination by virtue of a constellation of interests in the market starts to be considered feasible and even desirable by all the actors involved because none of them loses in absolute terms. To control the access to the market C has to erect barriers, namely, administrative barriers. This generic term refers to official and unofficial restrictions of various kinds that have no other purpose than to make access to the market more complicated and restricted. The existence of administrative barriers enables government representatives to perform the role of gate keepers (C) and, consequently, to appropriate a significant share of the monopoly profits captured by A transacting with B under conditions of restricted competition.

World Bank data on the ease of doing business suggest that access to the market tends to be problematic in Russia. As of 2013, this country ranked 111th (out of 189) in the world ease of doing business list.[38] An individual planning to start a business needs to go through eight procedures (7.4 on average for the World Bank sample) spending 18 days (29.6 on average) and 2 per cent of her annual income on fees (33.9 per cent on average). After registering the start-up, the businessperson must be prepared to pay labour taxes and contributions amounting to 41.2 per cent of her profit (16.5 per cent on average). The total tax rate amounts to more than half of the profit, 54.1 per cent (44.1 per cent on average). If the businessperson intends to trade across borders, she should be prepared to file more documents than on average (9 compared to 6.2 in the case of export; 11 compared to 7.3 in the case of import) and to bear higher than average costs to export (US$2,595 per container compared to US$1,473.8) and to import (US$2,780 compared to US$1,769.3).

It should be noted that the World Bank data do not cover all types of businesses. The Doing Business Project looks at domestic small- and medium-sized companies. Large international companies face higher barriers on their way to the Russian market, especially if they want to invest in mining and several other so-called 'strategic' industries. Federal Law 57-FZ 'On Foreign Investments in Economic Enterprises of Strategic Importance for the State Security and Defense' enacted on 29 April 2008 (i.e. before the 2008 financial crisis) restricts access both to natural resources as the key source of wealth in Russia and to the fields of transactions characterized by significant structural biases (for instance, natural monopolies).[39] Investments in these industries must be approved by a particular state body.

Controlling access to the market for large and medium national economic agents takes more manifest forms as well. They have to negotiate their entry into a new industry or a regional market with top politicians whereas small firms deal mostly with low-level state representatives. The authors of an econometric study report that 'large and medium firms are more likely to rely on personal networks with top politicians than small firms are'.[40] In other words, no business in Russia can expect to get free, unrestricted access to the market. Particular barriers differ according to the industry and business type, but they exist everywhere.

In the 1990s, before the strengthening of the 'vertical of power' during the tenure of President Vladimir Putin,[41] the variation of administrative barriers, their forms and height across regions and industries was particularly significant. The Russian economy was stagnant at that time, which did not rule out the eventuality of local growth in some industries and regions. This means that the access to these markets could have been regulated with profit to regulators. State representatives and organized crime (because of the weakness of the state) seized the opportunity by restricting access to the market for certain agricultural products, vodka and other alcoholic beverages. State representatives, for instance, charged regional tariffs on the import or export of certain agricultural products in the regions of Ulyanovsk, Belgorod, Sverdlovsk and Orel. The practice of collecting regional duties on the importation of vodka and other alcoholic beverages was common. '*Arbitrary licensing* of one kind or another is also pervasive, and provincial authorities often create local monopolies by granting single licenses'.[42]

After 1999, the variation of practices for capturing and redistributing rents in the markets decreased. The regional and local governments lost not only the opportunity for charging their own tariffs, collecting additional duties and levying extra taxes, but also their previously tolerated attempts to collect regional and local taxes in a more diligent manner than federal taxes are now subject to discipline. An econometric study of tax administration shows that

> the central government during its periods of strength did not really rely on strategic tax collection; there is no evidence that the regional tax administrations differentiated their attention with respect to federal and to regional taxes, that is, tax arrears accrued on costs of both central and regional budgets.[43]

State representatives have not lost all their discretionary powers with respect to controlling access to the market at the regional and local level, however. They cannot vary the level of their efforts when collecting federal and regional taxes, but they can still enforce various rules and regulations differently, depending on the particularities of their relationships with a specific business. Despite being set in a centralized manner, administrative barriers remain high. Administrative barriers can be lowered or removed altogether on a case by case basis, if the beneficiary manages to 'motivate' the regulator to do so. The tax administration may pay more or less attention to particular taxpayers. The former taxpayer suffers and incurs losses; the latter prospers and enjoys a competitive advantage. The enforcement of health and food security by a state body, the Federal Service for the Supervision of Consumer Rights Protection and Human Welfare, and its branches in the regions also may vary, and so forth.

To get a green light in business endeavours, an economic agent has to secure the removal of administrative barriers from her way. The economic agent must show her willingness to share prospective profits with the gate keeper. A share of the additional income that is captured by A as a result of lowering or removing administrative barriers and subsequently transferred to C, accelerates the wheels of commerce. The arrangement between A and C can be made either informally, on the basis of personalized relationships and connections, or formally, within an institutionalized system of agreements between state bodies and selected businesses. Personal connections play a notoriously important role in the emerging markets. If businesses, namely foreign companies, do not have such connections, they cannot solve problems related to their entry into the market, even when using bribes or other corrupt practices.[44] In this sense, the need for membership in networks of personalized relationships that include state representatives performing the role of gate keepers is itself a barrier delimiting the field of transactions.

The agreement between C and A also takes explicit and institutionalized forms. It is known as the 'agreement of socio-economic cooperation' between a state body and a business in several regions of the Russian Federation.[45] A agrees to pay 'voluntary contributions' to C in exchange for a green light to pursue business projects from C. A makes voluntary contributions in addition to paying regular taxes. A's voluntary contributions are accumulated on specific accounts in C's budget or are spent in C's interests without being accounted for in the budget (for instance, A sponsors a project deemed important by C). Regardless of the manner in which A's voluntary contributions are accounted for, they further C's individual or group interests. A's voluntary contributions are tended to strengthen C's position of power and her capacity to perform gate keeping functions. For instance, if C is an elected official, A's voluntary contributions may be spent on increasing electoral support for C.

A-type economic agents do not try to change the system, however. They do not protest against its existence either. Instead, they maintain the status quo by bribing state representatives. Corruption serves as a means for securing the economic rents captured by A in these circumstances. Bertrand Venard reports on the basis of a survey of Russian managers that 'the greater competition between private firms, the greater corruption'.[46] This finding is consistent with both the regulatory capture theory and the theory of gate keeping, however. A riskier test will help to discriminate between the alternative explanations for the same finding.

3. Sources of Data, Key Variables and their Operationalization

Because of the focus on the emerging market in Russia, the region was used as a unit of analysis in econometric tests. As of the start of 2014, eighty-three subjects constituted the Russian Federation: forty-six regions (*oblast'*), twenty-one republics, nine territories (*krai*), four autonomous districts (*okrug*), one autonomous region and two federal cities.[47] Sub-national data informed a number of relevant econometric studies exploring the relationships between, on the one hand, political regimes and, on the other hand, economic performance,[48] tax administration,[49] foreign direct investments (FDI)[50] and the entry of new firms.[51]

The data are for 2012. The year 2012 was chosen for the following reasons. The 2008 financial crisis caused disruptions in the 'business as usual' scenario of the interactions between *A*, *B* and *C*. Instead of controlling access to the market, *C* started to control *A*'s access to subventions, loans and tax exemptions. Without these funds, *A* would not have been able to survive.[52] During the crisis, fewer firms sought entry to Russia in general and to the Russian regional markets in particular. 'In the period 2008–2011, EU investors established fewer firms in resource-abundant Russian regions than before the crisis.'[53] By 2012, however, the Russian economy had fully recovered from the crisis (Figure 4.2). Consequently, practices of controlling access to the market made sense again for *C* and *A*.

This section and the following sections discuss an econometric study of the factors conditioning the amount of voluntary contributions received by the administrations of the seventy-nine components of the Russian Federation in 2012.[54] The theory of gate keeping suggests that voluntary contributions represent a part of the price for entering the regional markets in Russia and for continuing operations in these markets. This theory considers the pecuniary interests of the three economic agents, *A*, *B* and *C*, and predicts that they form a constellation. The empirical model [1] describes the constellation of interests of *A*, *B* and *C*. To test it, I used official statistical data from Russian government bodies, the Federal State Statistical Service of the Russian Federation, the Ministry of Finance of the Russian Federation and the Russian Federal Treasury.

$$CONTRIBUTIONS_i = \beta_0 + \beta_1 NET\_PROFIT_i + \beta_2 INCOME_i +$$
$$\beta_3 OWNERSHIP_i + \beta_n CONTROL_{ni} + \varepsilon_i [1]$$

where $CONTRIBUTIONS_i$ is the amount of voluntary contributions in a particular Russian region *i* (*i*=1,...,79) in 2012;[55] NET_PROFIT_i refers to net profits (profits minus losses) of the firms operating in the region *i*;[56] $INCOME_i$ to monthly income per capita (PC) in the region *i*;[57] $OWNERSHIP_i$ to the share held by the regional administration in the share capital of the firms operating in the region *i*;[58] and $CONTROLS_i$ to the set of control variables.

The thesis that the interests of *A*, *B* and *C* form a constellation does not necessarily imply the existence of causal relationships between them. Cross-sectional studies are not sufficient for establishing causation in any case: experiments produce more relevant information in this respect. The theory of gate keeping predicts that the interests of *A*, *B* and *C* will be statistically associated, which allows for the use of the cross-sectional econometric model. The language of dependent and independent variables is used in the following discussion for the sake of convention rather than for more substantial reasons.

The task of operationalizing C's interests, the dependent variable in the model [1], represents several challenges. Broadly defined, C's interests consist in maintaining and strengthening their position of power. Monetary and other material resources represent a necessary, but hardly sufficient condition for achieving this outcome. On the one hand, significant material resources may simply be misused if a strategic component of power is missing.[59] Strategic components of power – C's capacity to apply the best strategy furthering her interests given the available resources – can eventually be assessed with the help of expert surveys. Namely, a panel of Russian experts regularly assesses the chances of a particular regional leader, governor, to remain in power.[60] The reliability of experts' assessments tends to be low, unfortunately. For this reason, the use of official statistics represents a better option, even bearing in mind the fact that these data do not cover strategic components of power.

On the other hand, in addition to material resources the power holder also needs non-material ones. For instance, in addition to two kinds of material sources of power, namely military and economic, Michael Mann considers two non-material sources, ideological and political.[61] Ideology as a particular worldview 'influences behaviour and the framework of institutions of a society'.[62] However, in order to be consistent with the premises of neoclassical economics, it is assumed in this case that only C's pecuniary interests count.[63]

The official statistical data contain several indicators that can be used as a proxy for C's pecuniary interests. The number of state servants employed in the region represents one option. This indicator is subject to multiple interpretations, which results in some ambiguity. The number of state servants is indicative of either state capacity or competition inside the state service.[64] The size of the budget which a power holder has the discretion of spending provides a better idea of C's pecuniary interests. Public choice theorists use the term 'discretionary budget' in this regard.[65] 'All the models of bureaucracy [proposed in the public choice literature] suggest that bureau budgets will be too big in some sense because bureaucrats have the discretion to pursue their own goals at the sponsor's (citizen's) expense'.[66]

My previous studies reveal that, in the Russian context, funds accumulated in the account 'Other voluntary contributions' of the regional budgets[67] serve as a proxy for their discretionary part.[68] A transfers the official part of her voluntary contributions to this account and C has discretion for spending these moneys as she sees fit. The account 'Other voluntary contributions' accumulates a relatively minor part of the consolidated regional budgets – 39.5 billion Russian roubles in 2012 (US$1.3 billion), which corresponds to 0.45 per cent of all budget revenues[69] (0.35 per cent in 2007).[70] A plausible explanation consists in *C*'s preference for receiving *A*'s voluntary contributions through unofficial channels, which further extends the scope of *C*'s discretion. *A* rarely if ever uses bank accounts, let alone regional budget accounts, to transfer the unofficial part of voluntary contributions. *A* often pays her unofficial contributions in cash or in kind (by providing *C* with some goods or services). Because monetary flows induced by informal arrangements between *C* and *A* tend to be non-transparent, only monetary flows resulting from formal agreements and arrangements are likely to be analysed in a vigorous manner.

Some parallels may be drawn between the funds accumulated in the account 'Other voluntary contributions' and campaign contributions made in the context of US politics. *A*'s voluntary contributions help *C* to remain in office by being reappointed for the next term. Campaign contributions help a candidate to get elected or re-elected. Businesses interested in having their projects lobbied for by the prospective public official willingly make such contributions. A study of votes cast by US congress members on proposals regarding financial support for various sectors of the US economy affected by the 2008 crisis shows that 'larger campaign contributions from the financial sector increase significantly the probability that the representative voted *yes* on the initial bailout proposal' essentially benefiting banks and some other financial institutions.[71] Most studies of connections between campaign contributions and lobbying reject the eventuality of a constellation of interests of the regulator (the US congress member) and the regulated business explored in this chapter.

Two key dependent variables refer to *A*'s and *B*'s equally pecuniary interests. As per the system of equations [3],[72] *A* minimizes her missed opportunities by capturing a part of the monopoly rent (the other part goes to *C*). *B* buys goods and services of interest from *A*, paying for them more than in a perfectly competitive market. *B*'s consumer surplus tends to zero, remaining positive. The amount of net profits serves as a proxy for *A*'s interests. The population's level of income – monthly income per capita – is a proxy for *B*'s interests. Based on the theory of gate keeping, I make a *risky* prediction that *A***'s, *B***'s and *C***'s interests will be positively correlated**. A slightly weaker form of the prediction is that there is **a positive association between *A*'s and *C*'s interests, whereas *B*'s interests are associated (in a positive *or* negative manner) with the interests of the first two agents.** It should not be forgotten that *B* plays the role of a utility donor in transactions with *A* and *C*. Any other outcome of the econometric test will constitute a fundamental violation of the theory of gate keeping.

The list of control variables includes more than a dozen items. The first of them, the share of the regional administration in the share capital of firms operating in the regional market (Regional_assets), should be singled out. This variable serves to oppose the invisible and the visible hands of power. The first three variables are intended to operationalize the technique for imposing will that underpins the invisible hand of power. Economists conventionally consider state ownership (regional government ownership in this case) to be a measure for the government's *direct* involvement in the economy.[73]

The outcomes of the relevant previous studies account for the selection of the other control variables, namely Gross Regional Product (GRP) per capita,[74] capital funds (the value of fixed assets per capita),[75] the volume of retail trade turnover per capita (RetailPC),[76] the size of population,[77] the stock of human capital (the number of students in the system of higher education per 10,000 of population, StudentsPC),[78] the stock of entrepreneurship as a factor of production (the number of small enterprises per 10,000 of population, Small_businessPC),[79] the volume of foreign direct investments (FDI), foreign portfolio investments (PortfInv) and other foreign investments (OtherInv) largely composed of trade credits and bank deposits,[80] the density of telephone coverage (the number of cell phones per 1,000 of population, Cell_phonesPC),[81] the density of railroads per 10,000 square kilometers of territory and the density of paved roads per 1,000 square kilometers of territory,[82] the distance between the national capital and the regional capital (Distance),[83] the average temperature in January (as a proxy for the severity of climate, WTemperature)[84] and a dummy variable for border regions and regions with sea ports (Border_port).[85]

Taking into consideration the importance of Russia's mining sector, the value of natural resources rents has to be controlled. Russian regions are unequally endowed with natural resources: for instance, only thirty-eight out of the eighty-three Russian regions report non-zero oil and natural gas production.[86] In order to account for the use of the other natural resources (minerals, coal and timber) and also to ensure a more normal distribution of the data, I used the amount of the tax on mining, oil and gas extraction (*Nalog na dobychu poleznykh iskopaemykh, NDPI*) levied in a particular region as a proxy for natural resources rents.[87]

The distribution of all the variables was inspected visually and it turned out that their values were not distributed normally. The application of log, square root or exponential transformation helped significantly improve normality in most cases.[88] Bivariate distributions of each independent/control variable and the dependent variable were also inspected in order to identify eventual outliers. Six regions with zero other voluntary contributions[89] represent a borderline case: they were kept in most econometric models but removed in one. The assumption of the equality of variances was also tested for the sole dummy variable. Levene's F-test suggests the existence of another borderline case. On the one hand, the number of scores in two groups ('1'=border regions and regions with sea ports, '0'=all other regions) is similar. On the other hand, the F ratio is large enough to approach the level of statistical significance.[90] A decision was made to run regressions with and without the dummy variable.

The ordinary least squares (OLS) method was used for running regressions. The variables were entered in groups (method: 'Enter') based on their shared attributes. Model 1 specifies a statistical relationship between the interests of C, A and B in a pure form, i.e. without taking other factors into account. Model 2 introduces the variable of regional government ownership and, consequently, accounts for the impact of the visible hand of power. The volume of retail trade turnover was added in Model 3. This separate treatment serves to assess the predictive value in a more careful manner. The region's resources were entered in Model 4. It turned out that three variables (GRP per capita, Population and Capital funds) had to be dropped because of collinearity issues.[91] Model 5 controls for external resources, namely foreign investments. Models 6 and 7 introduce the variables that operationalize various aspects of the regional infra-structure. Model 6 includes the dummy variable for border regions and regions with sea ports, whereas Model 7 does not. I dropped the density of railroads and paved roads because of their high collinearity with the other variables.

In order to perform robustness checks, I used different operationalizations for a number of variables.[92] In Model 8, A's interests are operationalized as the total amount of the profits of the firms operating in the region i.[93] This opera-tionalization does not account for the amount of losses. The total amount of losses as a proxy for A's interests is entered in Models 9 through 14. This vari-able has a symmetric flaw and does not take into account the amount of profits. The dependent variable has two alternative operationalizations: the number of state servants employed in state bodies at the regional level per capita (Regional_staffPC)[94] and the average assessment of the governor's chances of remaining in office for 2013 (Survival).[95] The use of both indicators in Models 9 through 15, however, made it necessary to make additional assumptions, such as Robert Merton's claim that 'bureaucracy maximizes vocational security'.[96] These claims may be plausible, but they lead us away from our initial assumption of C's pecu-niary motivation.

4. A Constellation of Interests in the Russian Regional Markets

The testing of the basic model (Model 1) shows that the interests of A and C do indeed have a positive association. The higher A's net profits are, the more volun-tary contributions A transfers to C's account. B's interests tend to have a negative association with A's and C's interests, but this relationship fails to reach the level of statistical significance (Table 4.1).

Table 4.1: Results of statistical (Method = Enter) multiple regression to predict other voluntary contributions, lg10 of, (Y) from net profits, income per capita and control variables, standardized (beta) coefficients, 2012

Model	1	2	3	4	5	6	7	8
Net_profit (exp)	0.391*	0.347*	0.371*	0.354*	0.336*	0.313^	0.299^^^	
	(2.39)	(2.19)	(2.65)	(2.36)	(2.2)	(1.93)	(1.82)	
Profit (lg10)								0.826***
								(4.845)
IncomePC (lg10)	-0.138	-0.127	-0.676***	-0.649**	-0.605**	-0.662**	-0.605**	0.390*
	(-0.84)	(-0.81)	(-3.725)	(-3.48)	(-3.12)	(-3.375)	(-3.08)	(2.12)
Regional_ assets (Lg10)		-0.284**	-0.189*	-0.213*	-0.255*	-0.262*	-0.248*	-0.005
		(-2.68)	(-1.97)	(-2.18)	(-2.42)	(-2.47)	(-2.31)	(-0.06)
RetailPC (Lg10)			0.700***	0.692***	0.710***	0.771***	0.717***	-0.523**
			(4.71)	(4.49)	(3.885)	(4.14)	(3.84)	(-2.7)
Natural_ resources (Lg10)				0.082	0.093	0.115	0.096	-0.024
				(0.7)	(0.78)	(0.91)	(0.75)	(-0.19)
StudentsPC				0.085	0.084	0.087	0.086	-0.112
				(0.76)	(0.735)	(0.76)	(0.735)	(-1.25)
Small_ businessPC (entrepreneurs)				-0.142	-0.154	-0.191	-0.190	0.109
				(-1.185)	(-1.22)	(-1.41)	(-1.38)	(1.09)
FDI (Lg10)					-0.201	-0.236	-0.216	0.174
					(-1.28)	(-1.49)	(-1.35)	(1.28)
PortfInv (Lg10)					0.060	0.021	0.057	0.201
					(0.52)	(0.175)	(0.47)	(1.955)
OtherInv (Lg10)					0.101	0.082	0.105	-0.144
					(0.71)	(0.57)	(0.725)	(-1.13)
Cell_ phonesPC (Lg10)						0.124	0.104	-0.201
						(0.85)	(0.7)	(-1.71)
Distance (Lg10)						0.097	0.048	0.050
						(0.76)	(0.38)	(0.47)
Border_port (dummy)						-0.180^^		
						(-1.75)		
C (unstandardized coefficient)	14.749	14.973	-2.669	-4.522	-8.572	-11.262	-10.704	12.734*
	(1.26)	(1.33)	(-0.25)	(0.4)	(-0.67)	(-0.83)	(-0.78)	(2.12)
R^2	0.092	0.171	0.362	0.380	0.399	0.430	0.403	0.623
R^2_{adj}	0.068	0.138	0.328	0.319	0.310	0.316	0.295	0.547
F-statistic	3.834*	5.160**	10.503***	6.226***	4.512***	3.776***	3.718***	8.246***
Obs.	79	79	79	79	79	79	79	73

Legend: ^ significant at p=0.059, ^^ significant at p=0.084, ^^^ significant at p=0.074.

The introduction of Regional_assets in the model does not change the pattern. There is a negative and significant association between C's pecuniary interests and the scope of her direct involvement in the regional economy.[97] This finding suggests that C tends to substitute gate keeping practices for the visible hand of power. The invisible hand of power and the visible hand do not seem to complement one another, at least not in the Russian case. The visible hand requires more resources, namely human resources, than the invisible hand. Regional_staffPC is positively correlated with Regional_assets (Pearson's $r=0.301$ significant at $\alpha=0.01$) and negatively correlated with the amount of voluntary contributions (Pearson's $r=-0.373$ significant at $\alpha=0.001$). C has good reasons for preferring to make the system work for her to employing a large number of lieutenants who assist C in realizing her interests.

In keeping with my previous findings, RetailPC appears not only to be associated with the three previously entered variables, it makes the negative association between B's interests and C's and A's interests statistically significant. In terms of the elaboration paradigm, entering RetailPC serves to achieve an interpretation of the relationships within the power triad. 'Interpretation represents the research outcome in which a test variable [RetailPC in this case] is discovered to be the mediating factor through which an independent variable [IncomePC] has its effect on a dependent variable [Other voluntary contributions]'.[98] C and A rely on retail trade as a mechanism for appropriating B's monetary resources. C and A increase their well-being by making B overpay for goods of interest and thus reducing B's consumer surplus. RetailPC has a positive association with the proxies for A's and C's interests and a negative association with B's interests. The present study confirms my previous conclusion about the important role played by retail trade in securing and strengthening C's position of power in the Russian case.[99] C controls access to the field of retail trade in the same manner as she controls access to the other industries and markets.

The addition of sets of variables referring to the region's internal and external resources does not alter the picture significantly (Models 4 and 5). Beta coefficients significant for the falsification of the theory of gate keeping remain unaffected. Of the three variables specifying the regional infrastructure, only one, namely Border_port, has an impact on the amount of other voluntary contributions that approaches the level of statistical significance (Model 6). The more a regional economy is open to the outside world, the more difficult it is for C to control access to it. It comes as no surprise that this dummy variable has a negative association with the rents appropriated by C. The removal of the dummy variable due to the eventual non-homogeneity of variances does not change the previously described patterns (Model 7).

Model 8 is even more conservative. I substituted the total amount of profits for the amount of net profits as a proxy for A's interests and did not enter the dummy variable. I also removed the regions with zero other voluntary contributions.[100] A's and C's interests continue to have a positive association. More surprisingly, B's interests start to have a positive association with C's and A's interests whereas the beta coefficient for RetailPC changes sign and becomes negative. A possible explanation refers to the difference between total profits and net profits. The latter indicator takes losses of A into account (businesses that did not manage to get administrative barriers removed out of their way) whereas the former does not. Both total profits and total losses increase as a result of gate keeping. Profit and Loss appear to be strongly and positively correlated (Pearson's $r=0.814$ significant at $\alpha=0.001$). As for the negative beta coefficient for RetailPC, it may well be possible that the total losses of small retailers (who find themselves in the position of A' in the field of retail trade) actually exceed the total profits of large retailers (they occupy the position of A in this case). Additional studies focused on the situation in retail trade are needed to falsify this speculation.

Models 9 through 15 represent additional robustness checks to the baseline model (Table 4.2). Models 9–14 produce results that are consistent with the risky predictions of the theory of gate keeping. C's interests are positively correlated with A's interests (because total losses decrease relatively)[101] and B's interests (because B's income increases relatively). These models also confirm that the power holder does not need to use both her hands, visible and invisible, to achieve her interests understood here as C's desire to increase the number of subordinates, lieutenants. A large number of lieutenants are needed for carrying out direct government interventions. When C rules by relying on market forces, namely in retail trade, her army may be much smaller. The fact that B relatively loses in Models 1–7 and relatively gains in Models 8–15 is still consistent with the weak prediction of the theory of gate keeping (B's interests are associated with A's and C's interests). B's income simply does not tap all aspects of her pecuniary gains or losses (namely, the size of her consumer surplus and the range of choices of products of interest).

Table 4.2: Results of statistical (Method = Enter) multiple regression to predict number of state servants employed in state bodies at the regional level per capita, lg10 of, and average assessment of the governor's chances to remain in office (mean of two assessments in 2013) (Y) from net profits, income per capita and control variables, standardized (beta) coefficients, 2012

Model	9	10	11	12	13	14	15
Dependent Variable	Regional_staffPC (lg10)						Survival
Loss (lg10)	-0.835***	-0.787***	-0.512***	-0.509***	-0.442**	-0.430**	-
	(-8.65)	(-8.2)	(-5.09)	(-4.44)	(-3.58)	(-3.19)	
Net_profit (exp)		-		-		-	-0.289^^
							(-1.585)
IncomePC (lg10)	0.706***	0.693***	1.024***	1.021***	1.028***	0.930***	0.593**
	(7.32)	(7.375)	(9.67)	(8.51)	(8.59)	(7.21)	(2.69)
Regional_ assets (Lg10)		0.183*	0.146*	0.148*	0.098	0.102	-0.098
		(2.31)	(2.095)	(2.05)	(1.3)	(1.34)	(-0.825)
RetailPC (Lg10)			-0.639***	-0.64***	-0.541***	-0.440**	-0.350^
			(-4.94)	(-4.72)	(-3.84)	(-2.95)	(-1.673)
Natural_resources (Lg10)				-0.006	0.015	0.016	0.049
				(-0.07)	(0.17)	(0.16)	(0.34)
StudentsPC				-0.011	-0.048	-0.055	0.006
				(-0.135)	(-0.58)	(-0.67)	(0.045)
Small_ businessPC (entrepreneurs)				0.016	0.053	0.034	-0.274^
				(-0.18)	(0.58)	(0.35)	(-1.8)
FDI (Lg10)					-0.210^	-0.258*	0.439*
					(-1.835)	(2.215)	(2.47)
PortfInv (Lg10)					-0.020	-0.053	0.248^
					(-0.22)	(-0.6)	(1.83)
OtherInv (Lg10)					-0.047	-0.078	-0.097
					(-0.46)	(-0.76)	(-0.6)
Cell_ phonesPC (Lg10)						0.080	0.068
						(0.8)	(0.41)
Distance (Lg10)						0.006	0.055
						(0.06)	(0.38)
WTemperature						-0.121	
						(-1.347)	
Border_port (dummy)						-0.115	0.013
						(-1.56)	(0.11)
C (unstandardized coefficient)	-3.151***	-3.167***	-1.178^	-1.152^	-1.815*	-1.977**	-1.919
	(-5.8)	(-5.99)	(-1.92)	(-1.77)	(-2.58)	(-2.78)	(-0.374)
R^2	0.523	0.555	0.665	0.665	0.690	0.711	0.282
R^2_{adj}	0.510	0.537	0.647	0.632	0.644	0.648	0.138
F-statistic	41.647***	31.136***	36.752***	20.168***	15.118***	11.263***	1.962*
Obs.	79	79	79	79	79	79	79

Legend: ^ significant at $\alpha=0.1$, ^^ significant at p=0.118.

Model 15 uses the most subjective (and, thus, arguably the least reliable specification of the dependent variable). It also produces outcomes that are more consistent with the tollbooth hypothesis than with the theory of gate keeping. *C* gains (by increasing her chances of remaining in office), *A* loses. The tollbooth hypothesis does not explain *B*'s gain, however, because this approach does not explicitly take into account *B*'s interests. Public choice theorists' prediction of net loss[102] suggests that *B* should lose as well from their perspective. In other words, it is difficult to interpret the outcomes of Model 15 in an unambiguous manner, which provides an additional reason for being rather sceptical in respect of using subjective experts' assessment in econometric testing.[103]

To summarize, the outcomes of the econometric tests show that the risky predictions of the theory of gate keeping are confirmed. *A*'s and *C*'s pecuniary interests have a positive association. The only ambiguity refers to *B*'s interests. Models 8 through 15 show a positive association of *B*'s interests with the interests of *A* and *C*, whereas Models 1 through 7 show a negative association between them. Thus, it is safe to conclude that the weaker form of the risky predictions was confirmed with the help of empirical testing.

5. Conclusions

The discussion in this chapter produced several important outcomes. First, the theory of gate keeping can eventually be falsified by way of empirically testing the risky predictions made with its help. Predictions of the theory of gate keeping tend to be more specific and, consequently, riskier than predictions of public choice theory. This means that the level of confidence in the results of empirical testing is eventually higher in the case of the theory of gate keeping than in the case of public choice theory.

The testing using the Popperian criteria represents one of the strategies for assessing the validity of the theory of gate keeping, however. The presence of the contested concepts, starting with the concept of power, undermines the prospects of replicating the model of the natural sciences in this case. Neoclassical economists' attempts to do so appear to be hardly successful as their successes are often achieved at the price of relaxing their initial assumptions and, thus, making less risky predictions.

Second, this chapter sheds additional light on the mechanisms of domination by virtue of a constellation of interests in the market. This shows that Foucault's insights in respect of regulation based upon and in accordance with the course of things themselves[104] provide for a better understanding of the situation in both the developed (North American) and emerging (Russian) markets. At the same time, the Foucauldian approach fails to clearly identify the beneficiary of the transformation of the market into a technique of domination.

Agents performing the role of gate keepers in the market are the major beneficiaries, as unveiled by the theory of gate keeping. They restrict and control the access of businesses either to the market (in the periods of economic growth) or to subventions, loans and tax exemptions (in the periods of recession). In exchange for admitting a particular business in the field of transactions, they expect that its owner should transfer a part of the monopoly rent that she captures. In the case of Russia, this transfer takes the form of businesses' voluntary contributions to the power holders' endeavours, political, economic and social. The power holder has full discretion with respect to spending these moneys regardless of whether the business makes the transfer in a transparent (through a treasury account) or non-transparent (in cash or in kind) manner. The power holder spends the voluntary contributions on projects that further her individual and group interests. These projects may eventually benefit the population, but they ultimately must maintain and strengthen the gate keeper's position of power.

5 ACCESS TO JUSTICE: THE RULE OF LAWYERS

The study of the judiciary allows us to see an array of both visible and invisible techniques of domination. On the one hand, the judicial system serves to legitimate the state's monopoly of the use of physical force.[1] A court order gives the clout of legitimacy to a prison sentence as the most manifest expression of the use of physical force. The 'visible' side of the domination exercised by the judiciary can be perceived easily. For instance, countries with a high prison population rate (the number of prisoners per 100,000 of the national population) are often criticized as being too oppressive.[2]

On the other hand, the operation of the judiciary also involves invisible techniques of domination. In contrast to the visible techniques, the invisible ones are rarely accounted for in public discussions and are rarely subject to criticism. Critical sociology partially bridges this gap by directing our attention to the symbolic power of naming or labelling.[3] The actor, who gives names and definitions to things and processes, simultaneously gains power over the other actors, who use these definitions. They see the things in a way that benefits the author of the definitions.

The symbolic power of the jurists (they produce *legal* definitions as the only acceptable ones) does not exhaust the list of invisible techniques of domination in the case of the judiciary, however. Access control to justice represents the other major technique of domination, which explains the inclusion of the present chapter in this monograph. Chapter 5 discusses access control to justice as a tool for sustaining and enhancing the power of the jurists. It applies the concept of the power triad to the context of juridical transactions and explains the inequalities embedded in them with its help. The application of this concept requires making some adjustments, however. In the previous chapters, we considered eventual constellations of interests in the market. In this chapter, I will use the broader notion of field first introduced in Chapter 2, Section 4. As a matter of fact, the restricted-access market represents a special case of the field of transactions. If access to justice turns out to be problematic, the judicial system also transforms into a field of transactions.

The ideal of equal justice is a distinctive feature of Western democracies. For instance, the official mission of the Department of Justice of Canada is 'to ensure that Canada is a just and law-abiding society with an accessible, efficient and fair system of justice'.[4] Equal justice requires free access to justice. Access to justice can be defined as

> the ability of groups and individuals to be able to bring an alleged rights violation to the attention of a court and to have that court adjudicate the claim in a fair and impartial fashion on the basis of the evidence and according to the applicable rules of law.[5]

In reality, however, not everyone can successfully bring an alleged rights violation before a court. The outcome of a legal suit depends less on the merits of the case than on how well a party is represented in the court. An unrepresented party – a *pro se* litigant – experiences court dismissals more often than a party represented by a professional lawyer.[6] Despite a growing number of *pro se* litigants – they initiate up to a quarter of all new civil cases in the United States[7] – the existing judicial system has an institutionalized bias against them.

A common-sense explanation emphasizes the supposed complexity of the law that makes it impenetrable for the untrained litigant. 'It is usually contended by [lawyers] that the rules are so difficult and complex that they can be understood only by experts or those who by long training have become experienced in interpreting them'.[8] This line of reasoning does not explain why the legal rules have to be so difficult to understand. Furthermore, it fails to explain unrepresented litigants' lack of success even in the simplest matters, for instance, in disputes about due procedure.

The existing theories highlight the consequences of the institutionalized bias rather than its origins. The economic theory of the unequal access to justice emphasizes the high costs of obtaining legal assistance, which leaves low- and middle-income groups unrepresented and excludes them from the judicial system. Economists suggest that the high costs result from the monopoly over legal advice. Nevertheless, they do not explain why this monopoly emerged and became sustainable. Critical sociologists link the monopoly over legal advice to the specific interests of the jurists. They show how the acceptance of the rule of lawyers (as opposed to the rule of law) becomes a key condition for gaining access to justice. At the same time, their theory of the jurists' domination undermines the interests of the litigants, assuming that they play a passive role only.

Section 1 of this chapter discusses three theories of access control to justice: economic approaches, critical sociology, and the concept of the power triad adapted to the particularities of juridical transactions. Section 2 compares the academic discourse about access to justice with the public discourse in the mass media. It shows 'the lack of public recognition that there is a serious problem' with respect to the access to justice.[9] This outcome is not surprising, taking into consideration the thesis formulated above about the *invisible* character of access control. References to financial barriers and to an informal hierarchy in the judiciary prevail in the – rare – newspaper articles devoted to the issue of access control.

1. Existing Theories of Domination in the System of Justice

1.1 Economic Approaches

Economists consider the judicial system as a particular market. As in any other market, the price for a commodity or service (legal advice) that is traded is determined by supply and demand. Litigants need the advice of experts (lawyers); lawyers charge a fee for offering it. Some people cannot afford food and shelter, others cannot afford legal services. 'There is certainly broad consensus that middle-income people are closed out of the system'.[10] The 'prohibitive' (for low- and middle-income people) cost of legal advice is nothing other than a 'fact of life': it results from a particular combination of supply and demand.

The specific combination of supply and demand on the 'judicial market' results from several factors. First, traditionally, there were more restrictions on ownership and advertising with respect to law firms, which limited competition in this market. For instance, the relaxation of the rules on advertising in the domestic conveyancing market in the United Kingdom in the 1980s increased competition among the law firms.[11] Second, and more substantially, the supply is limited by the existence of a monopoly over legal advice. Only accredited jurists, i.e. lawyers admitted to the Bar, can legitimately provide legal advice to litigants. Other experts, including paralegals and 'jailhouse lawyers',[12] cannot legitimately offer assistance to litigants, regardless of their experience and know-how. As in the case of any other monopoly, this increases legal fees.

The monopoly over legal advice is not a natural one. On the one hand, it does not exist in all legal systems.[13] On the other hand, even in the countries based in Anglo-Saxon law (the United Kingdom and its former colonies, including the US and Canada) with the most professionalized judiciary, lawyers held no monopoly over legal advice for long periods of time. For example, in the US 'unauthorized practice started to be banned after the [first] Great Depression' only.[14]

Unlike *natural* monopolies (public utilities being a prime example), the production of legal services by a single provider, namely the Bar, has no advantages in terms of costs compared with their supply by multiple competitive providers. The existence and stability of the monopoly over legal advice can hardly be explained in terms of transaction costs, or costs related to contract making, either. Specific assets cannot be redeployed without a loss in their value.

Transaction costs depend on the degree of the specificity of assets involved in the transaction,[15] including human asset specificity (one's know-how specific to the transaction) and procedural asset specificity. The latter type of asset specificity refers to the degree of a provider's workflows and processes that are customized in accordance with a court's requirements.[16] Court documents must be prepared, formatted, filed and served according to court rules that are notoriously complex and impenetrable.[17] Professional lawyers may outperform non-accredited suppliers of legal advice and unrepresented litigants in meeting specific requirements and following particular procedures set by the courts.[18] Economic approaches do not explain, however, why these requirements and procedures are so specific that they require highly idiosyncratic knowledge. Could the rules not be simplified and made more accessible for non-specialists?

A common solution to the problem of the high cost of access to justice – the system of legal aid and assistance – takes the monopoly over legal advice for granted, while trying to mitigate some of its effects. Most countries based on Anglo-Saxon law rely on this system as a unique tool for enhancing access to justice. The Legal Advice and Assistance Act of the British Parliament (1949) provided people who are unable to pay for legal advice with free legal aid.[19] The system of legal aid has been subsequently reformed several times, most recently in the 1990s, which led to 'a retreat from universality and an emphasis on targeting services to those most in need'.[20] In the US, after a ruling of the Supreme Court in *Gideon v. Wainwright* (1963), the right to free legal counsel in criminal prosecutions has been acknowledged and enforced.[21]

Civil litigations are excluded, however, from the legal aid system. The right to civil counsel – the so-called 'civil Gideon' – is still only being debated without much chance of being introduced in the foreseeable future.[22] Both in the UK and the US, the government simply helps the least wealthy to pay a portion of their legal bills without questioning the domination of professional lawyers.

This brief discussion of the economic approaches to the problem of access to justice can be summarized in the following manner. Professional lawyers dominate in the judiciary. Their domination has just one dimension: the high fees charged for legal services. Professional lawyers have a monopoly over legal advice that enables them to charge more than in a competitive market. Lawyers' knowledge of a court's procedural requirements (the specificity of their human and procedural assets) is the source of their comparative advantages over non-specialists.

Economic approaches do not address the question of the stability of the monopoly over legal advice. How can we account for the persistence of requirements that are so specific that they restrict access to justice for low- and middle-income people? Purely economic monopolies, with the exception of natural monopolies, tend to be unstable.[23] Does political power play a role in establishing and sustaining the lawyers' monopoly?

Economic approaches also leave the issue of litigants' interests unaddressed. From an economist's point of view, lawyers maximize their income by charging high fees for legal services. Why are some litigants prepared to pay them? In other words, what leads them to bring their issues before a court despite the associated costs? Economists – neoclassical economists, to be more precise – consider preferences as stable and exogenous to their models.[24] The demand for legal mediation and legal services are no exception.

1.2 Critical Sociology

Probably the most important contribution of critical sociologists to our understanding of how the judiciary works lies in their attempt to make supply and demand endogenous. Instead of taking the interests of professional lawyers and litigants for granted (both presumably maximize their utility), critical sociology offers an explanation of their making. It is presumed that the interests of the professional lawyers and litigants evolve in the process of the interactions between them and with representatives of the state.[25]

Critical sociologists use conflict as a starting point in their analysis. In contrast to economists, who consider mutually profitable transactions (both parties win to some degree) as prevailing on the market, critical sociologists see conflicts everywhere. People disagree over everything: from the distribution of household chores to who has control of an organization or a state. A peaceful solution to these disputes can be found in a court. While not being a critical sociologist, John Commons formulates a relevant argument: 'there is always a third party to every transaction, the judge who decides or is expected to decide every dispute upon the principle of the common rule applicable to all similar transactions'.[26]

From this perspective, transaction as an elementary form of interaction is seen as a site of power struggles. The parties to a transaction attempt to impose their wills on the opposite parties. The parties do not differ in kind. The party that is currently more successful in gaining control over the transaction may be relegated to a subaltern position next time and vice versa. Everything depends on the distribution of the resources in a particular situation and the strategies chosen by the parties. If there were more chances, '*B* [the actor in a subaltern position] would do more or less the same things: *A* [the actor vested in power] and *B* are engaged in plays of power'.[27]

Professional lawyers dominate in the system of justice because their particular interests coincide with the need for peaceful conflict resolution. Pierre Bourdieu argues that the 'specific interest of the jurist' consists in promoting 'the universal', i.e. rules and procedures the universal enforcement of which offers everybody security and justice.[28] Lawyers succeed in persuading the others that their individual and group knowledge serves the common interest. To achieve this result, they rely on techniques of symbolic power representing *specific* rules and procedures as having a *universal* character.

The litigants' interest in having their disputes resolved in a peaceful manner is subsequently reshaped by professional lawyers. Using their power of labelling, they appropriate the right to decide which disputes can be brought before a court and which cannot.

> The specific power of legal professionals consists in *revealing* rights – and revealing injustices by the same process – or, on the contrary, in vetoing feelings of injustice based on a sense of fairness alone and, thereby, in discouraging the legal defense of subjective rights.[29]

Only disputes that can be expressed in specific terms proposed by professional lawyers have a legal solution in these circumstances. This means that by bringing a case before a court, the litigant agrees to have it reformulated in the specific terms proposed by professional lawyers and accepts their domination. Without a lawyer, the litigant is as helpless as a foreigner without knowledge of the local language or a translator's help.

One strategy for 'translating' disputes, namely making them suitable for a legal solution, refers to rationalization. Justice is not inherently rational, i.e. based on strictly formal conceptions and procedures. Max Weber opposes the system of rational justice proper to civil (or 'continental') law and common (or 'Anglo-Saxon') law to what he calls Kadi justice. Kadi justice implies informal judgments rendered in terms of concrete ethical or other practical valuations.[30] In contrast to rational justice, Kadi justice tends to be more personified and emotionally charged. The rationalization of legal arguments is intended to reduce the personal or emotional dimensions of a conflict. The jurists argue that the unrepresented litigant is unable to get rid of what is personal or emotional, which justifies their involvement.

As a result of a power play regarding dispute resolution, the judicial system is transformed into a particular field of power, a juridical field. 'The juridical field is the site of a competition for monopoly of the right to determine the law.'[31] Litigants occupy a subaltern position within this field. The group of professional lawyers is also highly stratified in keeping with their ability to change the law or to interpret it according to individual and sub-group preferences. Big law firms outperform small law firms and sole practitioners in this respect. The resulting informal hierarchy within the legal profession clearly undermines the doctrine of professional collegiality and the theoretical equality of all practising members of the Bar.[32]

As it often happens, the weaknesses of critical sociology are the flip side of its strengths. Critical sociologists explicitly assume that both litigants and professional lawyers seek power. The latter simply turn out to be more successful in the circumstances. An exclusive emphasis on power plays overshadows all other reasons for using the system of justice. A litigant brings a suit hoping to 'get' a particular business or an individual. Such a suit is often 'frivolous'.[33] A lawyer steps in to 'get' the litigant. Such a lawyer is perceived as a 'bloodsucker'. The 'bloodsucker' overcharges the litigant and distorts the substance of the initial claim by 'translating' it into legal parlance. The legal field is populated by 'power freaks'. It must be noted that neither economic approaches nor critical sociology pay special attention to the figure of the judge and the judge's role in controlling access to justice.

In critical sociology, the eventual connection between the law and legitimate interests and plans disappears. Rational considerations emerge as a by-product of 'translating' initial claims into legal ('rational') terms instead of being their eventual source. Professionals differentiate themselves from lay people (litigants) 'by fostering a continual process of rationalization.'[34]

Hernando De Soto demonstrates that people, including the least fortunate, have a rational interest in relying on the law in their everyday activities.[35] The law not only helps *solve* conflicts, it serves to *prevent* their emergence by facilitating the coordination of individual plans and projects. To coordinate their actions – on the road or in the marketplace – individuals need to refer to the same norms and rules. The rules of the road do as much to help solve disagreements between the motorists as to prevent collisions. In its role as a coordination device, the law facilitates predictions and, consequently, makes the rational choice possible. A motorist achieves the ultimate goal – safely moving from point A to point B – being able to calculate manoeuvres of the other motorists and to adjust to them. In other words, the process of rationalization should be considered not only as an outcome, but also as a point of departure for accessing the law. Anyone who interacts with other people when trying to achieve rationally chosen goals needs the law and, consequently, access to the justice system.

1.3 Power Triad

A better approach to understanding the problematic character of access to justice is that it should meet apparently incompatible requirements. First, critical sociology highlights the importance of the desire for power as a motive in human behaviour. Economic approaches assume that actors intend to maximize their utility and do so in a rational manner. A more comprehensive framework shall serve to analyse the interplay between two motives, utility maximization and the desire for power. [36]

Second, both the economic approaches and critical sociology consider the issues of access control and domination separately. The economic approaches show how lawyers dominate litigants by successfully upholding the claim to the monopoly over legal advice. Access to justice turns out to be limited because of the high fees charged for legal advice. Critical sociology links this monopoly to the use of a particular technique of power, namely the symbolic power of labelling (the power of naming things and processes using specific categories). Only the litigants, who agree that the jurists have an upper hand in defining their interests, get access to the juridical field. From this point of view, problems with access to justice also represent an outcome of the lawyers' monopoly instead of being its precondition. Thus, a more comprehensive framework should shed light on access control as a technique of power and its role in establishing and sustaining the lawyers' monopoly.

The concept of the power triad serves to meet these requirements, arguably. As stated before, interactions within the justice system involve at least three parties: two opponents and a 'judge, priest, chieftain, paterfamilias, arbitrator'.[37] The involvement of three parties is not, however, sufficient for the emergence of a power triad. The existence of the power triad requires the interactions to be structured in a particular manner, namely, in a chain of domination, and a party in this chain to perform a specific function, namely, gate keeping.[38]

The triad existing within the justice system includes actors of three types: judges (*C*-type actors), professional lawyers (*A*-type actors) and unrepresented litigants (*B*-type actors). Other parties involved in juridical transactions can be classified in one of these categories. For instance, registry officers, who regulate document turnover at a court, and paralegals (non-accredited and non-professional lawyers) are also *B*-type actors.

The judge plays a central role in the justice system. All other parties agree that the judge has the power to decide matters brought before the court. The judge's power has several sources. Some of them take manifest forms and are commonly acknowledged. For instance, the judge's decisions are believed to derive from legal authority: the judge has the ultimate right to apply and to interpret (in common law) the law in keeping with the circumstances of a particular case. In this sense, the judge 'is himself subject to an impersonal order by orienting his actions to it in his own dispositions and commands'.[39]

This ideal-typical description of the judge's behaviour lacks important nuances, however.[40] First, the nature of the judge's power depends on characteristics of the law that underpin court orders. The law may be either 'good' or 'bad'.[41] Good laws facilitate coordination and mutual adjustments. The rule 'drive on the left' or 'drive on the right' illustrates the idea of a good law in the context of road traffic because it creates certainty as to other motorists' manoeuvres. 'Bad' laws create opportunities for extracting rents instead of facilitating coordination. To continue with the example of road traffic, setting a speed limit when road conditions allow safe driving at a higher speed construes a 'bad' law. It has no other rationale than the extraction of fines and, eventually, bribes.

'Good' laws derive from customs and cannot be imposed 'from above'. The situation in former colonies and countries with various, sometimes divergent legal traditions turns out to be problematic in this respect.[42] If law is associated with actions of occupying states or discriminating groups, then most laws are perceived as 'bad' because they are disconnected from everyday practices.[43]

A simple and most straightforward solution for getting 'good' laws involves legalizing customs, i.e. giving them the force of law.[44] When embedded in customs, 'the rules can be justified by reference to beliefs' prevailing in a society.[45] Traditions are often inconsistent and contradictory, which requires the involvement of the state or the courts.[46] By selecting relevant customs, the judge draws boundaries as to what is legal and what lies outside the justice system.[47] As a result, some transactions (and their parties) are included, whereas others are excluded from legal regulation.

In common law, the judge exercises complete discretion in selection of customs. This discretion extends the scope of the judge's power beyond the limits of legal authority. In addition to the existing law, the judge's choices are determined by the judge's personal preferences, the extent of the judge's knowledge and so forth. 'Discretion resides wherever there is power'.[48]

Second, the circumstances of a case brought before a court are never fully known. The parties involved have different, most often conflicting, takes on what happened. The judge is provided only with bits of the relevant information, which prevents the judge from reconstructing the entire picture. Acting with incomplete information, the judge faces a dilemma. In the case of criminal prosecution, the judge can err by deciding that a person is innocent when, in fact, the suspect is guilty. What is more acceptable then, to send an innocent person to jail or to leave a criminal unpunished?[49] The probabilistic nature of the court's orders has implications for the discussion of the judge's discretionary power.

The more limited the information available to the court is, the larger the scope of the judge's discretion. This postulated regularity can be demonstrated with the help of a thought experiment. Let us first assume that the judge acts with complete information, i.e. there are no information asymmetries between the parties involved in a dispute and the transaction costs are nil. In this case, the judge has the unique task of persuading the party who is clearly wrong and denying evident matter of fact. In a world of zero transaction costs, all contracts would be self-enforceable.[50] Actors would prefer not to bring matters before a court whereas the judge would have no discretion. The judge's discretion would be limited by what is evident to everyone. Unfortunately, this perfect (from several points of view) world has several features of a totalitarian society: it requires the total transparency that undermines privacy and safeguards against total surveillance and control.

If the conditions of zero transaction costs are relaxed, the parties to a dispute act in conditions of information asymmetry. One party has only a part of the relevant information at its disposal. The bits of information possessed by the parties do not necessarily add up and represent the entire picture because the parties share it with the court in a selective manner (the one that maximize their chances to win).[51] No one, including the judge, knows the truth. A court order represents a best guess at what really happened, at best.

Court rules further restrict the amount of evidence available to the judge. Legally admissible evidence refers to a subset of the evidence available to the parties. Not all evidence can be admitted by the court. To be admitted, the evidence must be produced in accordance with specific rules (for instance, 'rules of discovery') and formatted in a particular manner (for example, administered as an affidavit). The judge has the ultimate authority for deciding the admissibility of evidence. By doing so, the court also shapes the scope of the judge's discretionary power. The less evidence is admitted, the larger the scope of the judge's discretion, all other factors being equal.

The judge performs the role of a gate keeper in several respects. The judge selects particular customs and dismisses others. As a result, some stakeholders and their claims get a legal status whereas the others do not. The judge decides the admissibility of the evidence brought by the parties to a dispute. As a result, one party may strengthen its position in the proceedings. The judge allows the actors to become parties in a dispute (granting them the status of an intervenor in the regular proceedings or a class/subclass member in the class proceedings). As a result, the balance of power between the parties may change. Gate keeping in various forms extends the scope of the judge's discretion and, consequently, enhances the judge's power.

It must be noted that no specific assumptions as to the judge's motivation have been made so far. One reason is the lack of comprehensive empirical studies of this issue.[52] Regardless of a particular judge's motives – utility maximization[53] or personal affects and predispositions or the desire for power or the disinterested search for truth and justice – the judge performs the function of gate keeping, or access control to the justice system. The gate keeper's role objectively serves to extend the scope of the judge's power beyond the rather narrow limits of legal authority. Furthermore, the gate keeper's power rarely takes manifest forms. A formal decision regarding the merits of a case turn out to be disconnected in space and time from the seemingly 'technical' decisions as to who is allowed to appear before the court and what is permitted to be brought before it.

This extended power appears to be compatible with both prevailing theories of law, formalism and instrumentalism. According to the former, the justice system has complete autonomy with respect to external sources of influence, including political power. According to the latter, the justice system tends to be subordinated to outside sources of power whereas the law is a 'partisan weapon' in the hands of the power elite.[54] '*Formalism* ... asserts the absolute autonomy of the juridical form in relation to the social world ... *instrumentalism* ... conceives of law as a reflection, or a tool in the service of dominant groups.'[55]

From the formalists' point of view, the judge's powers, enhanced by gate keeping, help to protect the autonomy of the justice system. Only its representatives can decide who and what is 'in' and 'out'. From the instrumentalists' point of view, gate keeping refers to nothing other than an additional 'partisan weapon' complementing other weapons. It can be compared with the preliminary screening of candidates running for public offices in some countries. Screening serves to get rid of unwanted candidates at the very beginning, thereby reducing the need for vote fraud at the end. The only difference lies in an additional layer in the instrumentalists' model of legal stratification: the judge presumably acts on behalf of the higher-ups (for example, state representatives or large corporations).

Litigants, or *B*-type actors, need the law and the justice system to better coordinate their everyday actions, which prevents conflicts or solves them when conflicts emerge nevertheless. Some litigants may indeed aim to 'get' a particular individual or organization, i.e. they seek power, in keeping with the assumption of critical sociology. However, the explanation of the power triad in the justice system does not require this assumption without ruling it out. The litigant's willingness to be 'in', to be admitted into the justice system, represents the key moment. Litigants believe that the legal recognition and enforcement of their rights helps them better fulfil their individual and group interests.

Access to justice is not free, nevertheless, because of the gate keeping exercised by the judge, a *C*-type actor. To be admitted to the justice system, litigants must be able to express their claims in a very particular manner and to produce supporting evidence in keeping with very specific rules. The unrepresented litigant with no or limited previous litigation experience has minimal chances of succeeding. In addition to knowing the rules for each step in litigation, the litigant must predict the discretionary decisions of the judge. 'The citizen can disregard the state – he wants to know what the court and the sheriff will do' in the circumstances.[56] No code or manual or book can help in fully understanding the gate keeping, only extensive experience. Yet, without this full understanding, litigants will see their claims dismissed regardless of their eventual merits. Litigants will appear before the court without being heard and properly understood.

The chances of the litigant, a *B*-type actor, to be heard by the judge, a *C*-type actor, can be increased by involving a professional lawyer, an *A*-type actor. The *A*-type actor translates the claims of the *B*-type actor into the language that is comprehensible for the *C*-type actor and gives them the proper format. The judge has a more limited power to restrict the lawyer's access to justice because the latter normally knows the rules and procedures and has extensive experience in appearing before a court. The lawyer can predict how the judge will use the discretionary power in the circumstances of a particular case.

A's role is far from being purely technical, however. An ordinary translator from one language to the other does not normally gain any power over the individual whose words are translated. The translator is an agent (a *B*-type actor), not a principal (an *A*-type actor). Instead of being satisfied with the technical role of an agent, the lawyer *de facto* performs the role of a principal in relationships with the client, the litigant. The lawyer has some power over the litigant, as paradoxical as this may sound.

The lawyer's power to charge high fees for legal advice refers to just one dimension of *A*'s domination over *B*. *A* also makes changes in *B*'s choice sets by suggesting which claims and evidence can be deemed legally admissible and which cannot.[57] If *A* decides *B*'s strategy in the proceedings, then *A* has power over *B*. 'The will chooses between opportunities, and opportunities are held and withheld by other wills which also are choosing between opportunities'.[58] The litigant's opportunities are 'held and withheld' by the lawyer. As a matter of fact, *B* has two options: either to see *B*'s claims dismissed by *C* or to be heard by *C* in keeping with the conditions imposed by *A*.

A has the power to alter the set of opportunities available to *B* by virtue of *A*'s preferential access to the justice system. In other words, *A*'s power over *B* has a structural nature. *B* can access justice only by changing the initial claims and accepting *A*'s conditions, both financial and other. *A* would not have preferential access to justice without *C* performing the role of a gate keeper and without *A*'s acceptance of *C*'s discretionary power.

To become operational, the power triad requires a constellation of the interests of all three actors, *A*, *B* and *C*. *C* erects barriers (institutional, by setting and enforcing rules and procedures; cultural, by referring to some traditions and excluding the others; and symbolic, by requiring credentials from lawyers), and controls access to the justice system. *C* provides *A* with preferential access to the justice system, whereas *A* accepts *C*'s discretionary power. *A* helps *B* to be heard by *C*. In exchange, *B* pays inflated fees and accepts *A*'s power.

The triad structures transactions within the justice system in such a way that they enhance *C*'s and *A*'s power. Control of access to justice represents a key condition for the operation of the triad in this case. A stratified system emerges as a result. *C* is on the top of the judicial hierarchy, *B* is on its bottom and *A* is in an intermediate position. *C* dominates *B* both directly and indirectly, with the assistance of *A*. *A* would not be able to dominate *B* if access to justice was unrestricted.

B is dominated by both *C* and *A*. The power triad produces the drift toward discrimination against unrepresented litigants. *C*'s and *A*'s prejudice against them is institutionalized in nature. An institutionalized prejudice is differentiated from social, racial or personal prejudice because of its embeddedness in formal institutions. The prejudice against unrepresented litigants depends less on the good or bad will of a particular judge or lawyer than on the consistent patterns of interactions within the justice system. In other words, the prejudice has structural origins. Nevertheless, even *B* gains something from entering the justice system. If *B* decides to stay out of it, the prospects for *B*'s coordination with other individuals and organizations would be undermined.

B's conditional access to the justice system (*B* enters under the condition of being represented by *A*) creates a demand for legal counsel. *B* does not choose between being an unrepresented litigant and being represented by a lawyer. *B* chooses between being represented by a lawyer and not entering the justice system. The first choice implies that *B* prefers to be represented because of the associated advantages (for instance, the need for training and experience to make better use of the court rules and procedures). *B* interacts with *A* as a principal with an agent. The second choice means that *B* decides to be represented as a condition for gaining access to justice. Without being represented by *A*, *B* will see all claims dismissed by *C*.[59] *A* gains power over *B*, relegating the litigant to the role of an agent. The lawyer, legal counsel, also becomes a key figure within organizations.

> Those who tacitly abandon the direction of their conflict themselves by accepting entry into the juridical field (giving up, for example, the resort to force, or to an unofficial arbitrator, or the direct effort to find an amicable solution) are reduced to the status of client.[60]

Access control sustains the lawyers' monopoly over legal advice. In other words, this monopoly does not have an economic nature, as economists believe. It cannot be explained exclusively in terms of *C*'s and *A*'s desire for power as suggested by critical sociologists either. The monopoly results from a combination of rational interests in the justice system and the attempts on the part of its representatives to enhance their power.

The operation of the justice system as a power triad has important implications for the character of the power relationships between the parties involved. In the case of legal authority, law is an independent variable, a cause, judicial power – a dependent variable, an effect. The latter restricts and derives from the former. The existence of the power triad extends the scope of the judge's discretionary power and, consequently, makes it less constrained by legal restrictions. Legal authority transforms into power. The rule of law becomes the rule of lawyers (*C* and, to a lesser degree, *A*). Judicial power changes its place in the causal sequence with law. Judicial power is now an independent variable, law is a dependent one. Judicial power shapes law as its representatives see fit. Namely, when a court changes the defection of something, it 'legislates'.[61]

2. Public Discourse on the Access to Justice

The problematic character of access to justice is not easily recognized either in the professional discourse on the justice system (because the jurists have the symbolic power of labelling) or in public discourse. A study of publications in the major printed mass media helps to empirically demonstrate the latter assertion. The study has two objectives: first, to confirm the lack of public acknowledgement that there is a serious problem with access to justice and, second, to show that the mass media pays more attention to the visible techniques of domination in the justice system (for instance, inflated legal fees and the existence of formal hierarchies) than to the invisible ones (namely, access control).

Publications in the major newspapers of three countries based on Anglo-Saxon law, the UK (*The Times*), the US (the *New York Times*) and Canada (the *Globe and Mail*), were included in the sample.[62] The natural language search terms were 'access to justice' (with two index terms added: 'law & legal system' and the country name). The search covered the period from the start of July 1985 to the end of March 2013, i.e. almost twenty-eight years.

In total, 642 publications were included in the sample after eliminating duplicates: 362 articles, commentaries and letters to the editor from *The Times* ('*T*'), 100 from the *New York Times* ('*NYT*') and 180 from the *Globe and Mail* ('*GM*').[63] A series of additional searches served to assess the relative attention paid by the mass media to the issue of access to justice and, consequently, to verify whether public recognition is indeed lacking. First, the number of publications mentioning 'homicide rate' suggests that in North America (the US and Canada) a particular aspect, the problem of homicides, attracts more public attention than the broader problem of accessing justice (Table 5.1). Overall, the mass media in the three Anglo-Saxon countries mention high homicide rates more than twice as often as problematic access to justice in general. Second, the issues of access to some other goods, namely credit and education, also attracts more public attention in North America than access to justice.

Table 5.1: Relative frequency of mentions for selected key terms, July 1985–March 2013

	Access to justice	Homicide rate	Access to credit	Access to education
The *Globe and Mail*	180	320	239	192
The *New York Times*	100	684	391	254
The *Times*	362	341*	154	109
Total	642	1,345	784	555

Legend: * A total of 57 mentions of 'homicide rate' and 284 mentions of 'murder rate' (this expression is more common in British English, apparently).

The British mass media show a somewhat divergent pattern. They devote relatively more attention to access to justice, which can be explained by a series of reforms of the schemes for legal aid carried out during past twenty years by the New Labour governments.[64]

The US case deserves particular attention. According to common belief, Americans are among the most litigious people on earth. In 2002, a total of 99.72 million suits were filed in state and federal courts in the US.[65] The 2000 census estimated the United States population to be 281,421,906, which amounts to 0.35 lawsuits per person, including newborns, per year. At the same time, the American mass media discusses the issues of access to justice less willingly than the mass media in the less populous and less litigious Canada and the UK. This lack of public recognition sharply contrasts with the intensity of the problem in the US. As one observer notes, '"equal justice under law" ... comes nowhere close to describing the legal system in practice' in this country.[66]

The selected publications were content-analysed using both qualitative and quantitative techniques as well as an original methodology for triangulating the outcomes of qualitative and quantitative content analysis.[67] Namely, 10 per cent of the publications (*N*=67) were randomly selected for manual coding (qualitative content analysis). The structure of a code book for manual coding derives from the three theoretical approaches discussed in the first section of this chapter. Three categories, 'Economic approach', 'Juridical field' and 'Power triad', regroup eleven codes (Table 5.2). The code 'Financial barriers' refers to 'Economic approach'. Five codes ('Government', 'Big law firms', 'Small law firms', 'Judges' and 'Unrepresented litigants') refer to the second category, 'Juridical field'. They operationalize various elements of the formal and informal hierarchies that constitute the juridical field. 'Like the Church and the School, Justice organizes according to a strict hierarchy'.[68] Five remaining codes ('Cultural barriers', 'Institutional barriers', 'Symbolic barriers', 'Excluded actors' and 'Gate keeper') operationalize two distinctive features of the power triad, namely boundaries and access control.

Table 5.2: Code book and frequency of codes and categories
in sample (*N*=642, automated coding with the help of a dictionary based on substitution)
and subsample (*N*=67, manual coding)

Category	Code	Code Frequency		Cases (% of cases)		Category frequency (% of total)	
		subsample	sample	subsample	sample	subsample	sample
Economic approach	Financial barriers	168	2449	46 (65.7%)	436 (67.9%)	158 (36.2%)	2449 (31.8%)
Juridical field	Big law firms	21	396	15 (21.4%)	173 (26.9%)	184 (39.7%)	3662 (47.6%)
	Government	60	1319	31 (44.3%)	413 (64.3%)		
	Judges	44	1086	26 (37.1%)	293 (45.6%)		
	Small law firms	53	687	24 (34.3%)	228 (35.5%)		
	Unrepresented litigants	6	174	6 (8.6%)	86 (13.4%)		
Power triad	Cultural barriers	10	75	6 (8.6%)	31 (4.8%)	112 (24.1%)	1589 (20.5%)
	Institutional barriers	8	158	8 (11.4%)	101 (15.7%)		
	Symbolic barriers	23	191	7 (10%)	96 (15%)		
	Excluded actors	39	759	20 (28.6%)	254 (38.2%)		
	Gatekeeper	32	396	16 (22.9%)	173 (26.9%)		
Total		464	7960			464 (100%)	7690 (100%)

It should be noted that the three approaches partly overlap. After all, they help describe various aspects of the same phenomena (a problematic access to justice). For instance, 'Financial barriers' refer to the idea of the monopoly over legal advice ('Economic approaches') and a particular barrier that a gate keeper may erect ('Power triad'). Elements of the formal and informal hierarchies are relevant to the discussions of both 'Juridical field' and 'Power triad' (for example, the judges perform the role of *C*-type actors and occupy a top position in the formal and informal hierarchies).

The code 'Financial barriers' was applied to fragments discussing fees charged by lawyers as an impediment to free access to justice:

Approximately 70 per cent of those who need legal aid help in connection with family matters are women. Men traditionally have the money. They hire private lawyers independently. So this decision primarily affects women and their dependent children.[69]

Lawyers have indeed encouraged an increasingly litigious society. But Mr. Quayle addresses himself mainly to richer Americans, like manufacturers, municipalities and doctors. He offers nothing for the poor and middle class who need lawyers but can't afford their fees.[70]

Solicitors in England and Wales lost their legal battle yesterday to force the Lord Chancellor to withdraw cuts in legal aid which in effect restrict access to justice for millions of people.[71]

State representatives (the Crown, government officials: the Attorney General, the Lord Chancellor, etc.) play leading roles in the juridical and bureaucratic fields. The bureaucratic field, i.e. 'the space of play within which the holders of capital (of different species) struggle *in particular* for power over the state'[72] is of interest to the extent to which it affects transactions within the juridical field. The legal aid programmes administered by the government and the legal reforms initiated by its representatives are prime examples of how the code 'Government' was applied.

In Ontario, every client has the right to choose any lawyer, and the province pays the bill if the client can't. Ontario's Attorney-General, Howard Hampton, wants to change all this. He is determined to establish a family law clinic by this fall where clients are assigned the next available government-paid lawyer.[73]

The government has been required to provide lawyers for people facing jail because of criminal charges since a landmark ruling by the United States Supreme Court in 1963, *Gideon v. Wainwright.*[74]

A review of legal aid will conclude early next year. The Law Society is willing to work with officials to their tight timetable, Mr. Nally says, but the challenge for the Government was to 'do more and to do it quickly'.[75]

Big law firms occupy dominant positions in the juridical field together with the government and the judges. In contrast to small law firms, they work with corporate clients and wealthy individual clients. They have a significant influence over court decisions and the interpretations of law underlying them. The code 'Big law firms' was applied to fragments referring to the role and operation of these actors.

Plaintiffs' lawyers say the arrangements level the playing field when they take on big corporate defendants with seemingly limitless cash for legal fees.[76]

But, after two years of litigation, Mr. Dowd and a big Chicago law firm to which he referred Ms. Corcoran advised her to settle the case for the $1.4 million she had originally been offered. The lawyers had taken the case on contingency, meaning they were entitled to a percentage of anything she received.[77]

Lord Carter of Coles consulted disproportionately with London firms and practices undertaking very high-cost criminal cases so his proposals do not address the issues facing most legal aid solicitors.[78]

The code 'Small law firms' refers to the role and operation of small law firms and sole practitioners. In contrast to big law firms, they serve small businesses and individuals with limited financial resources. Small law firms have a limited say within the juridical field.

> Lawyer Deanna Ludowicz said the deep cuts left her the only person in the town of Grand Forks doing legal aid. But recently, Ms. Ludowicz said she had to stop doing legal aid work because of inadequate payments and demanding clients. She now refers those seeking help to larger centres.[79]
>
> Mr. Dowd earned his law degree at night at Oklahoma City University. He passed the Illinois bar on his second try and set up shop in Des Plaines, where he works as a solo practitioner handling mostly divorce and bankruptcy cases. As of 2002, his biggest injury case ended in a $14,000 settlement.[80]
>
> Criminal defence lawyers will seek to rebuff a notion that they are 'fat cats', and concentrate on the key role they play in helping the public, and the increasingly straitened circumstances they claim affect their profession. 'The fact of the matter is, an hourly rate for a criminal defence lawyer is less than that of a plumber', said Mark Harrower, the vice-president of the Edinburgh Bar Association.[81]

The judges are in the highest layer of the judicial hierarchy, both formal and informal. The code 'Judges' was applied to references to their leading role within the judicial system.

> In the case last month, a judge refused to let a man be tried for gross indecency, ruling that he could no longer obtain a fair trial after the Sexual Assault Crisis Centre of Essex County destroyed its files. It is believed to be the first such ruling in Canada.[82]
>
> In a speech in Albany, the chief judge, Jonathan Lippman, said his proposal, the first such plan by a top court official in New York, reflected a commitment by the state's courts 'to bring us closer to the ideal of equal access to civil justice' that he described as one of the foundations of the legal system.[83]
>
> As similar cases have revealed, British judges think they smell humbug when they are faced with journalists claiming that a promise of anonymity must override a court's demand to reveal a source.[84]

Unrepresented litigants form the lowest strata in the informal judicial hierarchy. The theoretical equality of the parties in juridical transactions sharply contrasts with the unrepresented litigants' lack of any power in reality. 'The system has been designed by and for lawyers, and too little effort has been made to ensure that it is fair or even comprehensible to the average claimant'.[85] The code 'Unrepresented litigants' highlights various aspects of their situation.

> Mr. Steinberg said the issue of access to justice is inextricably tied to the legal aid funding issue, since people who cannot get legal aid lawyers have to represent themselves.[86]
>
> Ms. Corcoran, negotiating without a lawyer, had already received a settlement offer of $1.4 million.[87]
>
> The inability of the public to understand how barristers can take on awkward cases, and the consistent failure to understand the very clear, if broader, morality of the professional service barristers provide is no reason at all for a change in practices. The apparently guilty must be represented because to have them unrepresented or underrepresented is outrageous.[88]

A set of four codes is intended to describe specific types of barriers delimiting the field of juridical transactions and creating conditions for access control.[89] 'Cultural barriers' exist if the law turns out to be disconnected from customs and traditions. A gap between law and customs makes the former impenetrable for unprofessional claimants and complicates their access to justice.

> I believe the relationship between aboriginal and non-aboriginal peoples of Canada could be the dominant issue of the next decade. It is an affair that is soul-size for Canada, and its outcome will tell us what kind of society we choose to be. Globe columnist Jeffrey Simpson recently called attention to the 'dangerously widening divide' between aboriginal and non-aboriginal Canadians. We need to confront anything within the soul of our nation that indicates weariness with doing justice, or reveals a potential for prejudice or even racism.[90]
>
> With the Assembly now responsible for Welsh subordinate legislation, its bilingual nature is a key feature of its distinctive approach to the drafting and presentation of legislation – an approach similar to that followed in Canada, an important common law jurisdiction with similar bilingual requirements.[91]

'Institutional barriers' refer to the sometimes obscure and contradictory court rules and procedures that complicate interactions between the parties to a dispute instead of facilitating them. 'Court procedures and legal discourse can in themselves, unless popularized, constitute a process of social exclusion rather than empowerment.'[92]

> Ms. Joy managed to obtain a memo on courtroom rules of conduct from Judge Rawlins that stated lawyers shall appear in court in 'conservative clothing'. By any standards, this incident is a farce. It confirms what Dickens's Mr. Bumble said: 'The law is a ass, a idiot.' But it is an ass that insists on a dress code. Although Ms. Joy's treatment is relatively trivial, it does speak to the law's tendency to place form over function and style over substance.[93]
>
> Last year, a group of lawyers, in a concerted campaign, filed petitions with state supreme courts, bar associations or ethics commissions in 12 states seeking to cap contingency fees at 10 percent of the first $100,000 of a settlement, and 5 percent of anything more. The petitions were denied in five states, rejected on procedural grounds in two and remain pending in five.[94]
>
> The first phase of its civil justice reform programme takes effect from April, Lord Irvine said. 'These reforms will unify, simplify and speed up court procedures and protocols, to deliver justice directed towards the needs of court users', he added.[95]

The code 'Symbolic barriers' was applied to fragments discussing professional qualifications and other credentials as a formal requirement for providing legal advice. The division between lawyers and paralegals (individuals who have relevant expertise without meeting formal requirements) is a case in point.

> One type of competition Mr. Gervais worries about is a new class of advisers who have made inroads into what was traditionally a lawyer's bread and butter – areas such as estate planning and tax planning. 'There has been a definite erosion of practices to paralegals and tax advisers. We must use technology to get closer to clients by partnering on source information'.[96]

For a while, that traditional carve-up worked well: the Bar enjoyed a monopoly of advocacy rights in the higher courts; and solicitors of conveyancing and probate.[97]

The code 'Excluded actors' refers to the people, mostly unrepresented litigants, who are excluded from the justice system. The excluded individuals see their claims dismissed not because the claims lack merit, but as a result of the existence of various barriers and access control.

> Judge Wagner said aboriginals were left out of the national discourse for far too long and credited key judgments from the Supreme Court of Canada for ending this injustice.[98]
>
> 'I am not talking about a single initiative, pilot project or temporary program', Judge Lippman said, 'but what I believe must be a comprehensive, multifaceted, systemic approach to providing counsel to the indigent in civil cases'.[99]
>
> Without that [legal] help the most disadvantaged members of our communities cannot defend their fundamental rights.[100]

The code 'Gate keeper' is central for understanding how the power triad operates. The gate keeper benefits from the existence of various barriers (erecting some of them) by providing conditional access to the field of juridical transactions. The judges and state representatives exercise access control more often than the other actors.

> I'm just not convinced there are many people out there with valid claims who are being denied access to justice. We've shifted way to the other side, creating a chance for people to bring lawsuits with no risks.[101]
>
> In the second major revision this week, Assemblywoman Margaret M. Markey, a Queens Democrat, told supporters that her bill would now establish 53 as the maximum age for anyone wishing to file suit claiming sexual abuse as a child.[102]
>
> Accordingly where, as in the present case, the judge gave permission to appeal on terms, the prospective appellant could not appeal against those terms since he would, almost always, have been present when permission was given.[103]

After completing the qualitative content analysis, the validity and reliability of the manual coding were assessed by triangulating the results with the outcomes of the quantitative content analysis in two forms: the analysis of words co-occurrence and the use of a dictionary based on substitution. It was impossible to calculate alternative measures of the reliability, namely, the coefficients of inter-coder agreements, because of the involvement of a single coder, namely the author of this monograph.

The use of two specialized computer programmes, QDA Miner v. 4.0.4 and WordStat v. 6.1.5 served to perform the following tasks. First, coding co-occurrences in the manually coded publications was visualized and the distances of all the publications from the publication lying in the centre of a two-dimensional map ('centroid')[104] were calculated. The distances are expressed in values of Jaccard's coefficient. Second, a dictionary based on substitution was created. It has the same structure as the code book. There is a list of words and expressions for each code. For instance, the words 'judge', 'judges' and 'the court' can be used as substitutes for the code 'Judges'. The selected publications were then coded in an automated manner. The distances from the same centroid were calculated after analysing coding co-occurrences. The distances are expressed in values of cosine coefficient. Third, the distances from the same centroid were also calculated after running the word co-occurrence analysis. These distances are expressed in values of cosine coefficients. Fourth, the distances obtained in the three previous cases were cross-correlated. Moderately strong coefficients of correlation are indicative of an acceptable level of reliability and validity.[105] In the present case, the Pearson correlation coefficients r are .752 (between the qualitative coding and the automated coding using the dictionary based on substitution), .282 (between the automated coding and word co-occurrence) and .223 (between the qualitative coding and word co-occurrence; $N=67$ in all three cases). Fifth, the entire sample ($N=642$) was coded in an automated manner using the dictionary based on substitution. Table 5.2 reports the outcomes of both the manual coding of the subsample and the automated coding of the entire sample.

The mass media pay the most attention to the formal and informal hierarchies in the judiciary (47.6 per cent of the fragments coded in the automated manner, 39.7 per cent of the manually coded fragments). The issues of the cost of access are also in the focus of the public discourse (31.8 per cent of fragments coded in the automated manner, 36.2 per cent of the manually coded fragments). Various aspects of the power triad do not attract much public attention (20.5 per cent of fragments coded in the automated manner, 24.1 per cent of the manually coded fragments).

The relative ignorance of the eventual existence of the power triad in the justice system is consistent with the 'invisibility' of gate keeping as a technique of domination. Even the actors directly affected by access control do not necessarily perform relevant operations in a conscious manner. For instance, the judge may erect additional barriers (e.g. by introducing a new procedural 'filter') attempting to better control the entire process. As a result, however, the number of excluded actors may be increased. The only alternative for the would-be excluded is to hire a lawyer. These processes strengthen the power triad instead of disbanding it.

A more detailed analysis of coding co-occurrences suggests that the public discourse revolves around the financial barriers (Figure 5.1).[106] The financial barriers (in short, high legal fees) are mentioned not only more often than other obstacles to free access to justice, they also co-occur with most other codes. This finding comes as no surprise: the monopoly over legal advice takes obvious forms. The fees charged by lawyers can be relatively easily assessed and studied.[107]

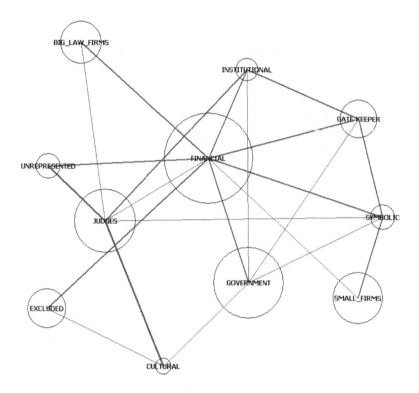

Figure 5.1: Two-dimensional map of coding co-occurrences, multidimensional scaling (*N*=642, automated coding). Stress 0.25, R?=0.69.

The codes included in the category 'Power triad' refer to the invisible technique of domination, namely access control. Not surprisingly, the idea that the problematic character of access to justice is due to the prevalence of access control tends to be overlooked. Common references to the judges in the context of the discussion of the barriers, especially cultural and institutional,[108] suggest that they may perform the role of a gate keeper.

The analysis of the sequences of the qualitative codes shows that in a few cases only there are reasons to believe that a particular sequence is not due to chance alone. Out of 121 eventual sequences (a matrix of eleven codes by eleven codes), only 16 sequences have the probability of occurring by chance alone of 5 per cent or less.[109] Five sequences referring to various aspects of gate keeping have to be discussed in more detail: 'Judges' followed by 'Gate keeper' (p=.009), 'Gate keeper' followed by 'Financial barriers' (p<.001), 'Financial barriers' followed by 'Gate keeper' (p=.001), 'Gate keeper' followed by 'Symbolic barriers' (p<.001),

'Symbolic barriers' followed by 'Gate keeper' (p=.014). Their existence suggests that the judge performs the role of a gate keeper more often than the other actors do. The symbolic and financial barriers help delimit the field of juridical transactions and subsequently control access to it. Here is an example of the code 'Judges' followed by the code 'Gate keeper':

> Apart from Judge Rawlins's perverse and arrogant refusal to give her reasons (which seems a flagrant disregard of basic principles), this incident adds fuel to the critical fire that judges and courts are more concerned about appearance than reality – or, to put it more accurately, that there is some important and deep connection between the two. Indeed, the fact that judges dress in a rather camp style themselves seems to give some credence to this unfortunate idea [...]
>
> But sadly, Judge Rawlins is not on her own. A couple of years ago, in a highly charged trial, a judge asked a spectator to leave the court unless he removed his headgear. When the man said that his kufi (Muslim cap) was an obligatory accessory for a person of his religion, the judge had him removed from the court, insisting that decorum and respect were essential to the judicial process.[110]

This situation refers to the judge's discretionary power to eventually exclude a party whose dress does not conform to the judge's expectations from the court room. This case also illustrates how a party's non-conformity to purely formal, procedural requirements may lead to this party's disqualification regardless of the eventual merits of the party's arguments.

A comparison of the relative frequencies of the codes (automated coding with the help of the dictionary based on substitution) across countries and by the publication format (article, commentary, letter to the editor) did not reveal significant – statistically and substantially – differences with a few exceptions.[111] The public's attention only varies in the case of three codes out of eleven. The North American mass media pay relatively more attention to the excluded actors than the British press does (F=3,620, p=.027). On the contrary, the British mass media discuss the role of the government more actively (F=4,599, p=.010), which can be explained by its active involvement in the above mentioned series of legal reforms. The British press also discusses the role of small law firms more willingly (F=14,328, p<.001).

The publication format plays the role of a differentiating factor with respect to all the codes except three: 'Institutional barriers', 'Judges' and 'Symbolic barriers'. The difference in the coverage of the situation of the excluded authors appears to be particularly noteworthy (Figure 5.2). Most references to the excluded actors can be found in letters to the editors (F=3,506, p=.015). They are written mostly by ordinary people without being commissioned. In the commissioned publications (articles) the mass media devote less attention to this issue. In other words, the journalists tend to under-evaluate the consequences of the operation of the power triad. The technique of access control turns out to be particularly impenetrable for external observers. These consequences are seen more clearly by those who have first-hand experience of the institutional exclusion.

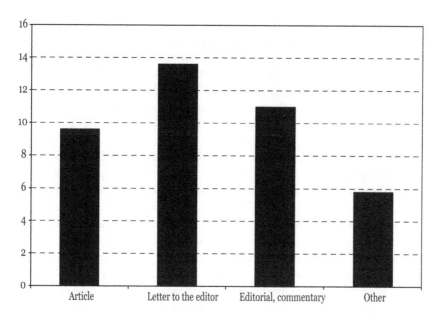

Figure 5.2: Relative frequency of the code 'Excluded actors' by publication format, percentage of total codes (N=642, automated coding)

3. Conclusion

The three analytical approaches to the problem of access to justice depict various aspects of the same phenomena. They all lead to the same conclusion: access to justice is problematic. However, the economic approach serves to discuss the most visible dimension of this problematic access, namely, excessive legal fees. Critical sociology serves to unveil a less visible technique of domination, the symbolic power of labelling. Finally, the concept of the power triad is intended to link the problematic access to the prevalence of access control as one of the most invisible techniques of domination. The concept of the power triad also sheds light on how the formal and informal judicial hierarchies are established and reproduced.

The invisible character of access control accounts for the lack of public recognition of the importance of the problem with respect to access to justice in general and with the existence of access control in particular. The mass media in the three Anglo-Saxon countries under discussion devote less attention to the issue of access to justice than to more specific topics. When discussing problems with respect to access to justice, they often focus on the surface of the problem (emphasizing high legal fees) instead of its essence. Other barriers (institutional, cultural and symbolic) remain on the periphery of the public's attention. The public discourse does not acknowledge the eventual existence of the institutionalized prejudice against unrepresented litigants.

To test the hypothesis of the institutionalized prejudice against unrepresented litigants in a more comprehensive manner, one needs to content-analyse the court rulings, probably using the methodological approaches discussed in this chapter. The researcher should expect several challenges in going down this road. For instance, the status of the parties (unrepresented, represented) is not always unambiguous. A party may be represented by in-house counsel, a small law firm, a large law firm or by several counsel simultaneously. Court records are not always specific enough in this regard.

Some solutions to the problem of access to justice can be briefly outlined without claiming to offer a systematic overview. Deborah Rhode aptly formulates a general principle that a better system should satisfy: 'it should maximize individuals' opportunities to address law-related problems themselves'.[112] This means that a better system should offer more opportunities for unrepresented litigants, which would undermine the current system of the institutionalized prejudice against them.

The simplification of the law, court rules and procedures represent one practical strategy for enhancing access to justice. Another strategy involves unbundling. Unbundling involves the following arrangement: the lawyer performs 'only certain of the required tasks, with the client doing the remainder'.[113] In other words, the litigant determines the overall strategy and division of tasks. The litigant hires the lawyer to perform some of them that require the most specialized knowledge and experience. As a result, the litigant regains power and the status of a principal in the relationship with the lawyer.

The litigant's empowerment will allow lessen the current, almost exclusive, emphasis on legal-aid programmes. The 'do it yourself' principle redirects spending from supporting the monopoly over legal advice to programmes of technical, educational and informational assistance to unrepresented litigants. Being empowered, they could achieve their objectives better and at less cost. The 'do it yourself' system is the exact opposite of the existing system based on access control.

6 AN INVISIBLE DIMENSION OF THE VISIBLE HAND: ENTRY CONTROL IN INTERNAL LABOUR MARKETS

Organizations are conventionally seen as the opposite of the market. Transactions in the market are guided by an invisible hand, whereas organizations are governed by administrative fiat, explicit commands.[1] In this sense, the coordination of individual actions within the organization is achieved with the help of a visible hand. Ronald Coase starts his 1937 article on the nature of the firm by citing Dennis Robertson, who considers organizations as 'islands of conscious power in [the] ocean of unconscious co-operation' and compares them to 'lumps of butter coagulating in a pail of buttermilk'.[2] The theory of gate keeping suggests, however, that the opposition between the market and the organization may not be this clear-cut.

This chapter addresses the question as to whether the organization is governed solely by the visible hand. Is there any room left for the *invisible* hand on the 'island of conscious power'? The discussion in Chapter 2 showed that, in order to explain how the power triad works, one has to take into account both bargaining and rationing transactions. The former prevails in the market; the latter exists within the organization as long as its operation involves setting and enforcing specific game rules. In a sense, my intention at that stage was to bring elements of the employment relationship back to the market, namely a non-clearing market. In this chapter, I will undertake a symmetrical attempt to bring the market back in, i.e. to take into consideration bargaining (market) transactions when making sense of the internal operation of the organization.

If the principal attention was previously concentrated on the market, the 'ocean', now emphasis is placed 'ashore', on the island of conscious power that takes explicit and visible forms. Does the reliance on the visible hand of power make its invisible hand unnecessary and redundant? I will argue, using the theory of gate keeping, that the invisible hand of power complements and eventually replaces the visible hand within the organization. The boss has power over the employee not only by virtue of authority, i.e. the former's power to command and the latter's duty to obey.[3] The boss as a gate keeper also dominates the employee by virtue of a constellation of their interests in the internal labour market.

The argument of this chapter goes beyond a rather straightforward assumption that the boss secures power within the organization either by offering a monetary compensation for the employee's obedience (positive incentives) or by punishing her for disobedience (negative incentives). Both techniques for imposing the boss's will have been well researched. For instance, James Coleman considers the use of positive and negative incentives as a distinctive feature of disjoint authority. The employee transfers the right of control to the boss in exchange 'for some extrinsic compensation' (positive incentives such as salary) or for the boss's promise 'to withhold an action that would make the [employee] worse off' (negative incentives such as the threat of firing).[4] It should be noted that disjoint authority eventually emerges in the relationship between individuals with pecuniary motivations, which allows Coleman to keep a key assumption of neoclassical economics.

Instead, I will discuss the eventual applicability of gate keeping as a particular technique for imposing will within organizations. The boss controls access to the internal labour market by keeping a gate that leads to it from the external labour market. She decides who among the applicants for a job is going to have a permanent position and who is going to be offered only a temporary position.[5] The situation of an individual admitted into the internal labour market depends on external market conditions to a much lesser extent than the situation of a temporary employee. This admission, nevertheless, comes at a price. The would-be permanent employee must accept the boss's control over her actions at the workplace as a condition for accessing the internal labour market. This condition is not necessarily stated in an explicit manner. It turns out to be unavoidable as long as the same job can be performed either by a permanent employee or a temporary one and the boss has discretion with respect to determining the nature of the employment relationship.

This chapter has five sections. Section 1 defines the organization and discusses its particular form, hierarchy, in more detail. I briefly summarize the theory of internal labour markets put forward by Peter B. Doeringer and Michael J. Piore (the 'ILM theory') in Section 2. This theory serves as a key reference point in my subsequent arguments. I will go beyond the original formulation of the ILM theory by proposing my own interpretation of the relationship between the internal and external labour markets in Section 3. I will highlight the role of the boss as a gate keeper who controls access to the internal labour market. Section 4 outlines the particularities of the labour market in academia. Section 5 provides a case study of the labour market in four universities, two in North America and two in Russia.

Only secondary sources of data were available for the case study, which prevents me from making and testing risky predictions. At the same time, the outcomes of the case study suggest that the labour market in academia has an increasingly dual character. As everywhere, the coexistence of the internal and external labour market in academia eventually contributes to the strengthening of the gate keeper's power.

1. The Boss's Visible Hand

It is common in writings about organizations to assume that they emerge virtually from scratch in the ocean of market transactions. Oliver Williamson states that 'in the beginning were markets'[6] and outlines a logical sequence of organizational forms to which market transactions eventually give rise: a peer group, a simple hierarchy, complex hierarchies such as unitary-form and multi-divisional form organizations, and so forth. The question as to which came first, the market or the organization, might be relevant for historical research or for studying the evolution of a particular organization. For the purposes of the present discussion, however, it would be enough to state that both the market and the organization refer to alternative modalities of social action. In contrast to individual action, social action requires coordination and mutual adjustments. Social action 'takes account of the behaviour of others and is thereby oriented in its course'.[7]

A party in the market (bargaining) transaction takes the other party's interests into account and plans, in an implicit manner, by reacting to relative prices of goods and services offered for exchange. Prices convey information about the behaviour of others. The issue of the completeness, reliability and validity of this information deserves a separate discussion. The point is that coordination through the market makes the other information sources irrelevant.

Within the organization, the adjustment of individual actions takes explicit forms and requires conscious efforts. Chester I. Barnard, a founding father of the theory of organizations, writes: 'formal organizations are "associations of cooperative efforts". Formal organization is that kind of cooperation among men that is conscious, deliberate, purposeful'.[8] Commands replace prices as vehicles of relevant information. Commands contain instructions as to how to adjust the individual behaviour of members to particular circumstances. 'Bilateral [and multilateral] adaptation effected through fiat is a distinguishing feature of internal organization'.[9]

Because of its conscious, deliberate and purposeful character, a higher intensity of cooperation can be achieved within organizations than in the market place. A positive side of the organization is the enhanced scope of the possible for its individual members. As members of organizations, they face fewer restrictions. By joining efforts and resources within the organization, they achieve more than by acting individually or by relying on the invisible hand of the market. 'Cooperation justifies itself ... as a means of overcoming the limitations restricting what individuals can do'.[10]

Cooperation within the organization has a downside as well. The visible hand creates a rent, or a surplus of cooperation, but its distribution among the members of the organization turns out to be unequal. The visible hand not as a metaphor but as a practical coordination device is the hand of a particular agent – the owner or the executive (the manager). This agent has a privileged access to the cream and butter (to return to Robertson's comparison) produced by common efforts. She determines the share of the cooperation surplus given to an organization member. Using the terms introduced in Section 1 of Chapter 1, the organization involves exercising both 'power to' and 'power over'.

The exact location of the visible hand depends on the organizational structure. In simple non-hierarchical associations (for instance, self-managed firms), the visible hand acts in a democratic manner. All members of the organization have a say in how it is operated. In the same manner as in a polity, 'the power to control members' options and behaviours must somehow be distributed'.[11] In unitary organizations (Williamson calls them 'U-forms'), or hierarchies,[12] a single agent – the owner or the executive – determines the movements of the visible hand. In complex organizations, for instance, multi-divisional firms ('M-forms', in Williamson's terms), several visible hands coexist.[13] Their areas of operation may overlap partly.

Relationships between the owner and the executive as the owner's representative in day-to-day management deserve some clarifications. The owner's power resides in property rights. 'Property ... means any of the expected activities implied with regard to the thing owned'.[14] The executive has power because it occupies specific organizational positions. Individuals in these positions do not need to have superior abilities or property rights to issue orders.[15] If one has the position of authority, her individual qualities and property play a secondary role.

The question as to whether the owner always has an upper hand in the relationship with the executive or the executive becomes the principal power-holder within the organization[16] is not relevant for the present discussion. For the sake of simplicity, I will call the agent, who determines the movements of the visible hand, the boss. In some organizations the owner is the boss; in the others the executive decides and the visible hand follows. My main task consists in unveiling an often overlooked source of the boss's power, namely her role as a gate keeper. Both the executive (in her relationships with the subordinates) and the owner (in her relationships with the executive) may eventually use this technique for imposing will.

2. Bringing the Market Back In:
The Internal and External Labour Markets

Most organizational theorists since Barnard consider the organization and the market as opposite forms of coordinated action. There is no place for the market within the organization and vice versa.[17] According to certain neoclassical accounts, the organization represents nothing other than 'one form of legal fiction which serves as a nexus of contractual relationships'.[18] Viewed in this perspective, the market exists both outside and inside the organization. The external and internal markets do not differ in nature.

The ILM theory challenges both these assumptions. This theory emerged in the early 1970s as a critical response to a neoclassical take on the labour market. According to the ILM, the labour market has a dual character. The market exists both inside and outside the organization. The internal and external markets differ in nature, however. Neoclassical assumptions remain valid with respect to the external labour market. The internal labour market of the organization does not completely exclude competition and, thus, bargaining transactions. At the same time, the involvement of the visible hand strengthens elements of managerial and rationing transactions within the organization.

> The *internal labour market*, an administrative unit, such as manufacturing plant, within which the pricing and allocation of labour is governed by a set of administrative rules and procedures ... is to be distinguished from the *external labour market* of conventional economic theory where pricing, allocating, and training decisions are governed directly by economic variables.[19]

The ILM predicts that wages in the internal labour market tend to move independently of external wages. The larger the gap between internal and external wages, the more dual the labour market becomes.[20] The internal labour market is still a market, but social forces – customs, norms, power – enter into play and lead to divergent trends in the dynamics of the two labour markets.

Organizations operate in a common external environment, in the external labour market. None of them has full control over its key parameters: the price of a unit of labour (wage rate), the stock of non-specific human assets (the level of general education of labour force), etc. The parameters of the internal labour market tend to be specific to a particular organization, however. Namely, they depend on the location of the visible hand and on the system of checks and balances under which this hand operates. Does the organization have a union? How strong is the union? Does the organization have customs and, speaking more broadly, a culture?[21] How idiosyncratic is the organizational culture? As a result of a plurality of possible organizational arrangements, a single external labour market coexists with multiple internal labour markets.

The essential idea of an ILM is not [that] a particular set of rules is established, but rather that some set (or sets) of rules emerge that shape the employment relationship and have an impact beyond the direct effect of market forces.[22]

The ILM theory reached the peak of its popularity in the late 1970s–80s. Since then, growing concerns have been expressed as to whether the ILM theory remains valid at the time of the subsequent expansion of the markets, including the external labour markets (the 1990s onward). More and more available jobs are temporary in nature, as opposed to permanent. Their parameters tend to be determined in the external labour market. 'Many observers believe that in recent years the market has pushed [social forces – customs, norms, power] aside and that the changes we observe reflect the triumph of market forces'.[23]

There are several counter-arguments in this matter. On one hand, available statistical data tend to produce a mixed picture at best. Job stability – measured by the length of employee's tenure or retention rates (the probability that a job will continue to exist during the next period of observation) – represents a proxy for permanent employment. In contrast to temporary employment, permanent employment has a stable and continuous character. Labour force surveys show that retention rates did not significantly change in North America in the late 1990s compared with the late 1970s. In Canada, 'after controlling for the initial tenure distribution and the age distribution, the conditional one-year retention rate fell from 0.762 in 1978–80 to 0.736 in 1987–9 and recovered to 0.762 in 1999–2001, indicating no period-long decline'.[24]

On the other hand, the internal labour markets eventually exist not only within boundaries of the organization, but also at the regional level (within regional clusters of similar organizations) or in particular industries (they coincide with professions then). If an employee moves from a position in one firm to a similar position in another firm located in the same area, she does not necessarily enter the external labour market. The employee's career may remain unaffected by external economic conditions as long as both employers, previous and present, offer essentially similar conditions. Advocates of the ILM theory argue that the visible hand (various regional associations control its movements) determines careers within regional clusters to a greater extent than external market forces.[25]

Regardless of the relative size and scope of the internal and external markets, the ILM theory is relevant with respect to the argument developed in this book. The ILM theory shows that, without taking power into consideration, economists are unable to offer a satisfactory explanation of employment relationships. Nevertheless, the ILM theory does not consider the eventuality of mutual reinforcement of power and the market. Power shapes the internal market configuration, whereas market forces prevail outside the organizational boundaries.

In order to explore any eventual synergic effects of power and the labour market, I will shift the focus of inquiry from the external and internal labour markets *taken separately* to *connecting links* between them.

The internal and external labour markets are connected through particular positions in the organizations, namely ports of entry and exit. 'Movement between [the two labour markets] occurs at certain job classifications which constitute *ports of entry and exit* to and from the internal labour market'.[26] The employee is initially offered an entry-level position that represents a port of entry. She leaves the organization through a more senior position that can be compared with a port of exit. External market forces influence employment conditions at the ports of entry and exit to a greater extent than employment conditions at intermediate positions within the organization. To get good job applicants, the organization has to make a competitive offer. In the same vein as in recruitment, the employee has incentives for leaving her position in the organization after being offered competitive conditions. In contrast, internal careers – the progression through the ranks – tend to be shaped by the internal labour market.

The boss wants to create an internal labour market because of her interest in minimizing her labour costs. 'The structure of the enterprise internal market is influenced by management's interest in internal allocation as a means of promoting efficiency by reducing training and turnover costs'.[27] The applicant has an interest in applying for the entry-level position because of her expectation of finding protection against the instability of the external labour market and to build a predictable career. 'The structure most efficient in [the] terms [of reducing training and turnover costs], however, is compromised by the work force's interest in the internal market as a means of enhancing job security and advancement'.[28] Entry is not free and unrestricted, however. The number of applicants willing to accept the competitive conditions usually exceeds the number of positions offered. Who keeps the gate, namely who controls movements through the ports of entry and exit?

3. The Boss as a Gate Keeper

The term 'gate keeping' might sound strange to an economist's ear, but it certainly rings a bell for organization theorists. This concept has several meanings in organization studies. First, gate keeping refers to a particular communication technique used in the organization. Second, gate keeping might be related to the process of hiring and promotion, i.e. an employee's progression through the ranks. I will discuss these two forms of gate keeping in the organization briefly before unveiling a new dimension of its second form, which will represent an additional application of the theory of gate keeping, as developed in this book.

Communication and information exchanges represent an important aspect of the organization's operation. Following Barnard, organization theorists consider communication as a raison d'être of the organization because no social action is possible without communication. 'Communication technique shapes the form and the internal economy of [an] organization'.[29]

Williamson offers a hypothetical example illustrating this point. As stated previously, the organization can take the form of peer groups, or simple non-hierarchical associations. Bilateral information exchanges tend to be costly, however. High information costs (this refers to a particular type of transaction costs) characterize an all-channel network in which all members communicate with one another. Transforming the all-channel network into a wheel network serves to reduce information costs. Now, a single agent, who occupies a position in the centre, communicates with all the others. The wheel network is an intermediary form on the way toward the emergence of a hierarchy: 'having more complete information gives [the agent occupying the central position] a strategic advantage over everyone else'.[30]

The information gate keeper holds a position at the intersection of external and internal information flows. She 'funnels information into an organization from the outside world'.[31] In a manner similar to the agent, who eventually converts her position in the centre of the wheel network into a comparative advantage, the information gate keeper 'use[s] external information as a source of power within [her] organization'.[32] This can be achieved, for instance, with the help of sharing external information in exchange for certain services or enhanced reputation. In other words, the information gate keeper acts strategically and aims to convert a strategic component of her power into a structural one (a higher position in a formal or informal hierarchy).[33] The strategy of information gate keeping represents the first technique for enhancing power through access control.

Gate keeping can also be used as a tool for controlling hiring and internal promotions. In the context of internal promotions, gate keeping has a specific meaning. It involves filtering out the least competent employees at the early stages of their careers and offering the others more positive treatment.[34] Chances for promotion depend not only on one's qualifications, general and idiosyncratic skills and performance on the job, however. Opportunities may be either created or reduced purposely by particular organization members, namely gate keepers. A similar observation applies to hiring: the gate keeper influences one's opportunities for being hired, all other factors (work experience, gender, education, etc.) being equal.

The gate keeper as a career shaper has the power 'to provide or deny access to jobs, internal promotions or developmental opportunities'.[35] Superior connections, better information and positions of status enable the career shaper to influence the outcomes of hiring or promotion. This individual does not necessarily make formal decisions – she might simply direct a potential applicant's attention to relevant openings, encourage or discourage applications for a job or promotion, introduce the applicant to organization members in charge of hiring/promotion and so forth. In a manner similar to the information gate keeper, the career shaper uses the strategy of gate keeping for the purpose of further strengthening her power. Thus, gate keeping in hiring and promotion refers to the second technique for enhancing power through access control.

Arguably, the connection between gate keeping and the process of hiring and promotion has some underexplored dimensions. The previously overlooked dimensions can be unveiled by placing the gate keeping in the context of the internal and external labour markets. This approach serves to achieve two objectives. On one hand, the concept of gate keeping serves to further explore the role of power in the functioning of the internal labour market. 'The role of power in shaping work organization is a key element of the ILM perspective'.[36] On the other hand, the organization's operation represents a new context of interactions to which the theory of gate keeping outlined in this book can be applied.

The ILM theory predicts that 'strong points of entry at low job levels and long internal careers' are indicative of the existence of an internal labour market.[37] The ports of entry connect the external and internal labour markets. The agent, who manages to assert her control over the port of entry, occupies a key structural position and is able to enhance her power using the strategy of gate keeping. A conventional take on the control of access to hiring and promotions highlights the benefits of being a middle-person, a third party facilitating a transaction. 'When you take the opportunity to be the tertius, you are an entrepreneur in the literal sense of the word – a person who generates profit from being between others'.[38] An alternative way of considering the control of access to hiring and promotion involves identifying an eventual constellation of interests of three agents: the boss, the permanent employee and the temporary employee.

Three agents form a power triad in the dual labour market:[39] the agent, who restricts access to the internal labour market (C), the agent, who is admitted to the internal labour market (A), and the agent remaining in the external labour market (B). As in the other contexts, the existence of the power triad within the organization requires that two conditions are met, structural and strategic. The dual character of the labour market represents a structural condition. A strategic condition refers to restricting access to the internal labour market.

The power triad might emerge if the labour market has two segments: the internal and external labour markets. Permanent employment prevails in the first segment, whereas temporary, or fixed-term employment characterizes the second segment. It is the coexistence of the internal and external labour markets that creates opportunities for gate keeping, not the internal labour market as such. If the labour market was homogenous, e.g. the individual had a choice between being unemployed and having *some* job, then the interests of the parties involved would not form a constellation. Namely, the unemployed would be a clear loser in this situation.

The dual labour market takes particularly manifest forms in Japan. The J-firm, a country-specific form of the economic organization in Japan, signs long-term incomplete contracts with its employees.[40] The ports of entry into the J-firm are largely restricted to school graduates. The employees start their career in the J-firm early and expect not to change their employer until retirement. A comparative study of two similar firms in Japan and the US shows that the retention rate for employees who entered the organization fifteen years ago in the Japanese case exceeds 80 per cent, which is about 30 per cent higher than in the American case.[41] The fact that both the employer and the employee expect the model of permanent employment to prevail does not altogether exclude the eventuality of temporary employment. The least competent employees tend to be filtered out at the early stages of their careers and thus they return to the external labour market. The internal and external labour markets coexist even in the Japanese case.

A similar situation is observed in the public service and academia (the case of the university will be discussed in more detail in the next two sections) where permanent and temporary employment is also present. In North America, the government employs two types of human resources, permanent and temporary. Employees admitted to the internal labour market of the government as a particular organization enjoy a high level of protection and security. For instance, they can be fired only in exceptional circumstances. More commonly they are simply redeployed within public service organizations.[42] Public employees without permanent contracts return to the external labour market each time after the expiration of their fixed-term contracts. New Public Management – a set of policies for reforming government implemented first in the US and then in several other Western and developing countries in the 1990s – involves placing greater emphasis on the market as a supplier of public goods and government services.[43] In practical terms, this means that more tasks are outsourced to private businesses and the number of temporary workers grows faster than that of permanent public servants.

C, *A* and *B* prefer cooperation to uncoordinated actions. By joining their efforts, the three agents achieve more than by making individual efforts. 'To survive, cooperation must itself create a surplus'.[44] In contrast to the rent captured in the conditions of restricted competition in the market,[45] the cooperation rent does not necessarily involve any loss. It is a bonus attributed to a superior productivity of concerted efforts. There is no guarantee, however, that *C*, *A* and *B* get equal shares of the cooperation rent. As long as each actor's expected utility from joining the organization exceeds her expected utility from acting in an individual manner, she will prefer to enter the internal labour market. In other words, *C*, *A* and *B* prefer cooperation even under conditions of an unequal distribution of the cooperation rent.

The agent can join the organization as either a permanent or temporary employee. In the former case, the agent enters the internal labour market; in the latter, she remains in the external labour market. The agent with a discretionary power to determine the character of a particular individual's employment performs the role of a gate keeper. Gate keeping allows her to further strengthen and enhance her powers.

What functions does the gate keeper, C, perform in the organization? As long as the boss has discretionary powers in this regard, she acts as the gate keeper to the internal labour market. The concept of managerial discretion applies to multiple contexts. It serves to help us understand 'whether, and when, executives have strategic leeway'.[46] The boss's discretion in questions of hiring is of particular interest here. The theory of gate keeping predicts that, if the boss has discretion in selecting candidates for a job and determining the conditions of their employment (namely, permanent versus temporary),[47] then a power triad emerges and the boss becomes a C in the triad.

'Within the limits established by job content and training costs, management can exercise discretion over the kind of workers it is willing to hire'.[48] If C has discretion in hiring, she determines the ratio of permanent positions (occupied by A) to temporary jobs (performed by B). C strengthens her power by increasing the ratio of temporary jobs to permanent positions. The theory of gate keeping predicts that the higher this ratio, the more valuable are permanent positions and, consequently, the stronger C's hold on power is. The relative size of the internal and external labour market represents a key parameter of the power triad in the organization. C may also choose candidates for permanent positions using the acceptance of her power as a selection criterion in addition to (or in lieu of) such formal criteria as professional experience and education.

Barnard identifies three basic functions of the boss: to provide the system of communication, to promote the securing of essential efforts and to formulate and define purpose, i.e. to set organizational goals.[49] It can be argued that gate keeping contributes to the exercise of all three. The conventional interpretation of gate keeping in hiring (the gate keeper as a career shaper) highlights the boss' first function. A's knowledge that, compared with B, she occupies a privileged position makes her work harder, especially at the early stages of A's career. C's access control to promotions in the internal labour market creates additional incentives for A at the subsequent stages of the latter's career.

'A formal system of cooperation requires an objective, a purpose, an aim' distinct from the individual ones.[50] In order to be able to set organizational goals, C needs discretionary powers. If she does not have these powers, then organizational goals are set in consultation with A and, eventually B, i.e. by all members of the organization. Gate keeping allows C to increase the scope of her discretion. If C directs the organization towards profit maximization, then the organization takes the form of the firm. In the firm, C captures the lion's share of the profit generated by concerted efforts of its members. C's decision to maximize the organization's budget, or, as an option, the 'discretionary' budget,[51] is consistent with the transformation of the organization into a bureau. In the bureau, C controls the largest share of the discretionary budget. When C sets non-pecuniary goals, her gains also have a non-pecuniary dimension. For instance, if the organization is a research-intensive university, then C selects priority research areas and so forth.

A's gains from cooperation within the organization as the power triad tend to be more modest. A gets a lesser share of the cooperation rent regardless of its form, namely pecuniary or non-pecuniary. The stable and predictable character of A's compensation (for instance, her salary) matters as much as its size. Under conditions of permanent employment, A's expected utility – the product of her compensation and the probability of securing it – is higher than what she could get in the external labour market.

B is also better off by cooperating than by acting individually. B receives compensation (in a pecuniary or non-pecuniary manner), no matter how insecure it may be. Even if B receives a high wage, her expected utility is lower than A's expected utility because of the insecure character of B's employment. B prefers temporary employment to unemployment, however.

In the power triad within the organization no one loses. All the three agents win, no matter how unequal the distribution of the cooperation rent may be. The power triad is efficient in the sense that it allows C, A and B to satisfy their motives. 'The meaning of "efficiency" as applied to organization is the maintenance of an equilibrium of organization activities through the satisfaction of the motives of individuals sufficient to induce these activities.'[52] C's, A's and B's interests form a constellation within the organization structured as the power triad.

4. Particularities of the Academic Labour Market

The choice of the university as a particular type of the organization for a discussion of the power triad might seem somewhat unusual at first sight. For instance, Doeringer and Piore initially developed their ILM theory studying the situation of skilled and semi-skilled manual workers, 'blue collars'.[53] The choice of the university has several justifications, however.

First, two types of employment, permanent and temporary, exist in academia. Tenured and tenure-track positions refer to permanent employment and, therefore, they constitute an integral element of the internal labour market. The American Association of University Professors defines tenure in the following manner:

> after the expiration of a probationary period, teachers or investigators should have permanent or continuous tenure, and their service should be terminated only for

adequate cause, except in the case of retirement for age, or under extraordinary circumstances because of financial exigencies'.[54]

Temporary employment in academia is represented by fixed-term, or 'contractual' appointments. Their holders operate in the external labour market. Temporary employment progressively replaces permanent positions. In the US, 'full-time faculty are increasingly hired into fixed-term appointments that do not lead to consideration for tenure at the college or university where they are employed'.[55]

Second, the university's internal labour market has a relatively simple structure, which facilitates studies and inter-organization comparisons. Most applicants enter the internal labour market through the port of entry, an assistant professorship (lectureship in the UK). Permanent employees subsequently progress through a simple system of ranks: associate professor (reader in the UK) and full professor. In some countries (for instance, the UK and Russia), there is a fourth rank that occupies an intermediate position between assistant professor and associate professor, senior lecturer.

Third, the study of the university's internal and external labour markets serves to control the impact of asset specificity. Specific assets have a limited redeployability. A specific asset can be used for another transaction with a loss solely of its value.[56] Human assets can be specific as well – to a particular organization. The ILM sees in human assets specificity, or skill specificity, a factor that gives rise to internal labour markets. 'As skills become more specific, it becomes increasingly difficult for the worker to utilize elsewhere the enterprise-specific training he receives'.[57] More neoclassically minded economists agree. For example, Williamson views the organization and its internal labour market as a response to idiosyncrasies of various kinds, including specific human assets.[58]

Fourth, and related to the third point, are human assets specificity results, namely, from the importance of on-the-job training. Some skills can be acquired on site only, as opposed to classrooms. In the case of blue collar workers, on-the-job training plays a particularly important role. On-the-job training loses its importance for white collar workers and managers, however. In professional and managerial occupations 'formal education attainment requirements tend to dwarf skills previously acquired on the job'.[59] This observation applies to academic jobs even to a greater extent, arguably.

The university, as its name suggests, places greater emphasis on universalism than on particularism. 'It is often believed that internal labour market theories have little relevance to universities as human capital is assumed to be general'.[60] If the internal labour market exists in the university, its explanation in terms of asset specificity would not suffice. Alternative theories, including the theory of gate keeping, might help then.

Last, but not least, the importance of depersonalized communication in academia, namely communication through the text,[61] makes informational theories of gate keeping less relevant, at least at the level of normative analysis. If academics believe that who knows what matters more than who knows who, then the gate keeper as a career shaper should be a less important figure at the university than in the other organizations. This assumption also calls for alternative theories of gate keeping, including the concept of the power triad.

The theory of gate keeping predicts that the power triad has some particularities in the case of the university. The administrative head (of the university or faculty) – the boss – has the final say in hiring decisions.[62] She decides the ratio of permanent (tenured and tenure-track) and temporary (non-tenure-track) positions. All other factors (namely, the macroeconomic situation) being held constant, C extends the scope of her discretion by increasing the relative number of temporary positions.

On the one hand, C can hire and fire non-tenure-track faculty members at will. She has no obligation towards them. 'An administrator who dislikes a particular part-time faculty member can choose not to rehire that person, and generally is not required'.[63] B shows a greater dependence on C's good or bad will than A. On the other hand, the scarcer a permanent position is, the more A values it. Under these circumstances, A tends to give more support to C's initiatives and actions because the latter creates additional privileges for the former and enhances her status within the university.

Managerial discretion is a universal phenomenon observed in other organizations as well, but the boss's discretionary powers in the university undermine the basic principles of academic freedom. An eventual constellation of C's and A's interests also undermines the principles of equal and universal exchanges proper to the Republic of Letters. The Republic of Letters represents a web of depersonalized communications between scholars with similar research interests.[64] An eventual coalition of C and A has more features of an oligarchy – it could be called an 'Oligarchy of Letters' – than of a republic. Despite her inferior status, B still prefers participating in the power triad to being excluded from academia altogether. The acceptance of the power triad gives B a unique chance to take part in research and teaching.

C's upper hand in academic relationships enables her to set organizational goals for the university. The traditional orientation with respect to the generation and transmission of knowledge represents one possibility. C also has discretion with respect to prioritizing profit maximization and thus transforming the university into a business enterprise. Thorstein Veblen observed this transformation in the case of American universities at the beginning of the twentieth century: 'in one shape or another this problem of adjustment, reconciliation or compromise between the needs of the higher learning and the demands of business enterprise is for ever present in the deliberations of the university directorate'.[65] *C* may also set religious or political priorities for the university. No matter how diverse these organizational goals might be, they correspond more closely to *C*'s priorities than anyone else's do.

5. Case Study of Four Universities

The labour markets of four universities, two in North America and two in the Russian Federation, were analysed more in-depth. Their selection has both substantial and pragmatic justification. From a substantial point of view, the fact that these universities operate in different institutional and macroeconomic environments increases the generalizability of the findings despite the small size of my sample. In pragmatic terms, the same universities were studied in a previous study I conducted, where I compared their organizational structures, budgets and scientific productivity measured in terms of the number of students and the number of scholarly publications.[66]

The four universities are the Lomonossov Moscow State University (MSU), the National Research University – the Higher School of Economics (HSE), both in Russia, the University of Mississippi (UM) in the US and Memorial University of Newfoundland (MUN) in Canada. The MSU is one of the oldest Russian universities, having been founded in 1755. It embodies the traditional Russian model, which also applies to its internal labour market. In contrast, the HSE has a relatively short history, starting in 1992. Since the first years of its operation, the HSE has focused on replicating Western, initially French and subsequently American, models. The UM is a mid-range American doctoral and research university.[67] The MUN is a mid-range Canadian comprehensive university. The UM has the smallest labour market of the four (846 faculty members in 2006), whereas the MSU has the largest academic labour force (11,021 faculty members in 2010, see Table 6.1).

The analysis of the composition of academic labour force conducted on the basis of official statistics (Table 6.1) shows that the number of contingent (non-track and part-time) positions is growing faster than the internal labour market composed of tenured faculty members and holders of tenure-track academic appointments. Between 2006 and 2011, the share of temporary positions in all full-time academic occupations increased from 26 per cent to 37.3 per cent in the US and from 10 per cent to 14.8 per cent in Canada. At Harvard University, non-tenure track academics constitute about half of the full-time academic labour force, which fuelled criticism of the university administration's policies with respect to hiring and promotion.[68]

Table 6.1: The composition of academic labour force (instructional and research) in the USA, Canada and Russia and at selected universities, 2006 and 2011

	All faculty	Full-time Total	Full-time Tenured %	Full-time Tenure-track, %	Full-time Non-track, %	Part-time Total	Part-time % of all faculty
Doctoral universities, USA, 2011*	480,893	322,838	45.4	17.4	37.3	158,055	32.9
Doctoral universities, USA, 2006**	318,888	224,305	53.2	20.8	26	94,583	29.5
University of Mississippi, 2006***	846	622	71.7		28.3	224	26.5
Stanford University, 2006***	1,014	991	93.6		6.4	23	2.3
UCLA, 2006***	2,168	1,669	82.7		17.3	499	23
Yale University, 2006***	1,599	1,194	66.5		33.5	405	25.3
Harvard University, 2006***	2,974	2,363	54.6		45.4	611	20.5
Princeton University, 2006***	1,013	807	86		14	206	20.3
Columbia University, 2006***	2,036	1,289	88.2		11.8	747	36.7
Cornell University, 2006***	1,966	1,778	80.3		19.7	188	9.6
MIT, 2006***	1,642	1,122	80.4		19.6	520	31.7
Comprehensive universities (Masters' degree universities), USA, 2011*	327,452	148,159	48.1	22.6	29.4	179,293	54.8
Comprehensive universities (Masters' degree universities), USA, 2006**	256,880	132,843	49.2	25.6	25.2	124,037	48.6
Undergraduate universities (Baccalaureate universities), USA, 2011*	121,654	62,678	46.3	22.4	31.4	58,976	48.5
Undergraduate universities (Baccalaureate universities), US, 2006**	85,955	53,698	47.5	25.2	27.3	32,257	37.1
All universities (excluding associate degree colleges), USA, 2011*	929,999	533,675	46.2	19.4	34.4	396,324	42.6

	All faculty	Full-time Total	Full-time Tenured %	Full-time Tenure-track, %	Full-time Non-track, %	Part-time Total	Part-time % of all faculty
All Universities (excluding associate degree colleges), USA, 2006**	661,723	410,846	51.2	22.9	25.9	250,877	37.9
All universities, Canada, 2011****	n.a.	43,455	64.2	21	14.8	n.a.	15.2 (32.2*****)
All universities, Canada, 2006******	n.a.	38,268	70.3	19.7	10	n.a.	13.5 (27.1*****)
MUN, 2011*******	2,272	1,078	66.2	28.8	5	1194	52.6
All universities, Russia, 2003********	409,200	311,300	0	0	100	97,900	23.9
HSE, 2013*********	3,793	3,258	3**********	0	97	535	14.1
MSU, 2010***********	11,021	9,628	0	0	100	1,393	12.6

Sources: * American Association of University Professors (AAUP), 'The Employment Status of Instructional Staff Members in Higher Education, Fall 2011' (2014), pp. 9–11, at http://www.aaup.org/sites/default/files/files/AAUP-InstrStaff2011-April2014.pdf [accessed 12 June 2014]; ** American Association of University Professors (AAUP), '2006 AAUP Contingent Faculty Index', pp. 17–18, at http://www.aaup.org/sites/default/files/files/AAUPContingentFacultyIndex2006.pdf [accessed 12 June 2014]; *** American Association of University Professors (AAUP), '2006 AAUP Contingent Faculty Index', pp. 20–9; **** American Association of University Professors (AAUP), 'The Employment Status of Instructional Staff Members in Higher Education, Fall 2011' (2014), pp. 30, 37; ***** Canadian Association of University Teachers (CAUT), 'CAUT Almanac of Post-Secondary Education in Canada, 2012–2013' (Ottawa, 2013), p. 30, excluding Quebec universities; ***** Canadian Association of University Teachers, 'CAUT Almanac of Post-Secondary Education in Canada, 2012–13', p. 37, including temporary full-time university professors; ****** Canadian Association of University Teachers (CAUT), 'CAUT Almanac of Post-Secondary Education in Canada, 2008–09' (Ottawa, 2009), p. 15; ******* Canadian Association of University Teachers (CAUT), 'CAUT Almanac of Post-Secondary Education in Canada, 2012–13', p. 30 and Memorial University of Newfoundland (MUN), 'President's Report "Great Minds Think Differently"' (2011), p. 57 at http://www.mun.ca/2011report [accessed 12 June 2014]; ******* Federal State Statistics Service, *Obrazovanie v Rossii* [Education in Russia] (Moscow, 2003), Table 5.14; ******** the HSE official website, at http://www.hse.ru/org/persons/ [accessed 12 June 2014] and the author's calculations; ********* HSE ordinary' professors; ********** the MSU official website (http://www.msu.ru/science/2010/sci-study.html) [accessed 12 June 2014].

The labour legislation in Russia requires that the universities sign fixed-term contracts with their employees. All positions are temporary with a notable difference between full-time and part-time employees: the former have more rights and duties than the latter. Under such conditions, the institution of tenure is simply impossible. The HSE offers a poor replacement for this, namely 'ordinary' professorship.[69] In contrast to tenure, an ordinary professor has no legal protection against firing since the stability of her employment depends solely on the university administrator's good (or bad) will. Furthermore, a faculty member cannot apply for tenure: ordinary professors are nominated either by the other ordinary professors or by C, the boss. HSE's ordinary professors represent a tiny fraction, 3 per cent, of all full-time academic occupations. In the case of HSE, the internal labour market most closely approximates the 'oligarchy of letters' mentioned in the previous section.

For this study of the academic labour market, I managed to get access only to secondary and incomplete data. The task of testing truly risky predictions made on the basis of the theory of gate keeping requires the availability of a variety of personal data that are either protected by privacy laws or simply unavailable: employee's gender, age, education, previous work history, current position and history of internal promotions, salary and so forth. It is rare that a researcher has full access to an organization's personnel records.[70]

I used two sources of secondary data: the LinkedIn website and the HSE official website (in my sample, only the HSE requires all of its employees to create professional webpages using a common template and to regularly update them or face the risk of sanctions for non-compliance). LinkedIn is a social networking service oriented toward professional uses, including hiring, as a source of information. Despite the fact that it is the world's largest professional network, LinkedIn is rarely used for the purposes of scholarly research on the labour market.[71] One of the reasons probably refers to researchers' doubts as to the validity of users' personal information that can be retrieved from this website. In order to enhance the scope of information retrievable from LinkedIn, I used a LinkedIn Executive account to construct samples of employees working at the four universities.[72] The sampling frames included 283 individuals in the case of HSE (the accounts of 203 of them were completed at least to some extent and retrievable to constitute the HSE sample), 571 (186) in the case of MUN, 808 (58) in the case of UM and 488 (189) in the case of MSU. The relative (to the total number of employees) size of these samples and the sampling procedure suggest that the standards set for random samples are not met in the circumstances.

The use of the second source of personnel records, the HSE official website, served to assess the validity and reliability of LinkedIn data. Even taking into account the fact that the personal information posted on the HSE website might not be completely valid, both account holders and their superiors have the obligation to correct and update it at least when they renew their contracts.

The sampling frame – 3,793 accounts[73] – coincides with the population in this case. I built a random sample of 209 HSE employees (5.5 per cent of the population). Two samples of HSE employees, one from the LinkedIn site and the other from the HSE site, are similar in size. Thus, in addition to testing some non-risky predictions of the theory of gate keeping, I was able to ask an additional research question, namely how valid is the information on LinkedIn users' employment situation publicly available on this website?

The preliminary data screening revealed that some variables are not normally distributed. Natural logarithm or square root transformation was applied when appropriate. For dummy variables, I ran additional tests to check the assumption of the equality of variance.[74] The length of employment at the current organization was used as a dependent variable[75] under the assumption that employees in the internal labour market have longer tenures than individuals remaining in the external labour market. Scholars of the internal labour markets use the length of tenure as a proxy for being in the internal labour market.[76]

Outcomes of eleven multiple linear regressions based on ordinary least squares (OLS) are reported in Table 6.2. In order to increase the robustness of results, the four LinkedIn samples were initially analysed after being merged (Models 1–5) and then separately (Models 6–9). Models 1–9 use data from the LinkedIn site, whereas Models 10–11 use data from the HSE official website. Personnel records from these two sources are not completely compatible, which explains differences in the selection of independent and control variables across models.

The list of independent variables includes the number of previous employers, the total number of years in academia, the number of LinkedIn connections, dummies for the universities that granted PhD and Masters' degrees[77] and for the port of entry (the entry position at the place of academic's current employment). The number of previous employers and the number of LinkedIn connections serve as a proxy for being in the external labour market. One of LinkedIn's functions consists of facilitating the search for new employment opportunities. The ILM predicts that the length of employment at the current organization will be negatively associated with these independent variables. It also predicts that the academics, who progressed through the ranks at the place of their current employment, will have longer employment records at this organization. The study of a large university in Belgium suggested the presence of a strong port of entry: 75 per cent of entries at this university occur in the lowest professor rank.[78]

The two remaining independent variables, dummies for the universities that granted PhD and Masters degrees, are more specific to the academic internal labour market and its interpretation in the light of the theory of gate keeping. If academia had the features of the Republic of Letters, then there would be no association between the place of an academic's current employment and the university that granted a PhD or Masters degree.

Table 6.2 Results of statistical (Method = Enter) multiple regression to predict the number of years that the academic has worked at her current university, Ln of (Y) from the number of LinkedIn connections (sqrt), the number of years in academia (Ln), the number of previous employers, the number of publications listed on the institutional website (Ln), dummy coefficients for the entry position (1 = lower position than the current one), the university that granted a PhD degree (1 = the place of the current employment), the university that granted a Masters degree, the university, the rank, the administrative position (1 = holds an administrative position), the full-time position (1 = holds a full-time position), HSE's ordinary professorship (1 = holds it), the award of a monetary bonus in addition to a basic salary (1 = has it) and gender (1 = Male), standardized (Beta) coefficients

Model	1	Four universities				MSU	MUN	MU	HSE	HSE_2	HSE_2
	1	2	3	4	5	6	7	8	9	10	11
N of previous employers	-0.324 (-6.85)***	-0.07 (-1.28)	-0.055 (-1.01)	-0.155 (-3.28)**	-0.157 (-3.33)**	-0.531 (-3.15)**	-0.084 (-1.1)	-0.151 (-1.53)	-0.174 (-1.76)^		
Years in academia (Ln)										0.418 (4.18)***	0.483 (4.325)***
N of LinkedIn connections (sqrt)	0.015 (0.325)	0.018 (0.72)	0.037 (0.73)	0.036 (0.83)	-0.041 (-0.94)	-0.039 (-0.34)	-0.059 (-0.76)	-0.014 (0.14)	-0.093 (-1.04)		
Dummy Place of PhD degree		0.01 (0.16)	0.035 (0.48)	0.062 (1.02)	0.054 (0.89)	0.12 (0.83)	0.04 (0.58)	0.089 (0.78)	0.004 (-0.04)	-0.01 (-0.11)	0.066 (0.71)
Dummy Place of Masters' degree		-0.005 (-0.7)	-0.048 (-0.74)	0.045 (0.81)	0.049 (0.88)	0.003 (0.025)	0.04 (0.56)	-0.111 (-0.965)	0.196 (1.75)^	0.17 (1.93)^	0.181 (1.85)^
Dummy Port of entry		0.507 (9.4)***	0.442 (7.87)***	0.213 (3.92)***	0.215 (3.97)***	-0.108 (-0.62)**	0.248 (2.67)**	0.53 (3.12)**	-0.005 (-0.05)		
Dummy HSE			-0.228 (-3.79)***	-0.309 (-5.82)***	-0.304 (-5.75)***						
Dummy MSU			-0.027 (-0.37)	-0.136 (-2.19)*	-0.135 (-2.18)*						
Dummy UM			0.08 (-1.46)	-0.032 (-0.67)	-0.034 (-0.72)						

Model	Four universities					MSU	MUN	MU	HSE	HSE_2	HSE_2
	1	2	3	4	5	6	7	8	9	10	11
Dummy Assistant				-0.277	-0.275	-0.292	-0.331	-0.228	-0.233	-0.044	0.147
				(-5.49)***	(-5.44)***	(-2.13)*	(-3.56)**	(-1.29)	(-2.43)*	(0.465)	(1.34)
Dummy Full				0.316	0.304	0.474	0.338	0.214	0.211	0.045	-0.176
				(7.035)***	(6.67)***	(3.89)***	(4.23)***	(1.81)^	(2.11)*	(0.43)	(-1.38)
Dummy Ordinary											0.218
											(2.27)*
Dummy Full-time											-0.161
											(-1.71)^
Dummy Administrator											0.341
											(3.5)**
Dummy Bonus											0.085
											(0.82)
N of publications (Ln)											0.078
											(0.62)
N of courses (Ln)											-0.119
											(-1.17)
Dummy Male					0.063	-0.029	-0.039	-0.036	0.213	-0.115	-0.065
					(1.5)	(-0.25)	(-0.54)	(-0.35)	(2.34)*	(-1.3)	(0.67)
C (unstandardized coefficient)	2.35	1.727	1.906	2.281	2.22	2.419	2.302	1.962	1.746	0.891	1.161
	(25.03)***	(14.45)***	(14.84)***	(17.4)***	(16.12)***	(5.875)***	(9.25)***	(5.7)***	(8.84)***	(3.88)***	(2.83)*
R^2	0.103	0.287	0.323	0.517	0.521	0.555	0.559	0.727	0.228	0.187	0.295
R^2_{adj}	0.099	0.275	0.304	0.501	0.503	0.466	0.523	0.658	0.168	0.151	0.208
F-statistic	24.309***	24.266***	17.745***	31.697***	29.14***	6.238***	15.24***	10.632***	3.811***	5.075***	3.387***
Obs.	425	306	306	306	306	48	104	40	111	138	109

Legend: * refers to a relationship significant at the 0.05 level; ** at the 0.01 level; *** at the 0.001 level and ^ at the 0.1 level.

Previous studies suggest that the opposite might be true, which is more consistent with the assumption of gate keeping. In the above-mentioned Belgian university, academics with an internally awarded PhD degree receive a 'green light' in hiring. Only 15 per cent of its faculty members had a PhD from another university (6 per cent of which received their degrees from a foreign university).[79] A larger European survey suggested that many other European universities tend to hire their own PhDs as well, with the exception of Germany and the UK.[80] My data shows that MSU hires predominantly its former doctoral students (78.4 per cent of its current employees received their PhD degrees from the MSU) and graduate students (80 per cent graduated from the same university). The other three universities do so to a significantly lesser extent: the percentage of holders of a PhD degree from the same university is 9 per cent at the HSE (7.3 per cent as per data from its official website), 5 per cent at MUN and 6.1 per cent at the MU.

The exploration of eventual links between the place of the academic's current employment and the geographical location of the university that granted a PhD/ Masters degree is also promising. As mentioned in Section 2 above, the ILM has recently evolved toward studying regional clusters. 'A cluster is an agglomeration of similar or complementary firms in a bounded geographic area.'[81] Does the academic internal labour market have a similar regional dimension? Regional clusters seem to play a more important role in Russia than in North America. Neither MUN nor the UM has holders of PhDs from other universities in the same region among their employees. A total of 16.8 per cent of MSU's employees hold a PhD degree from another university in Moscow, 64 per cent (81 per cent as per data from its official website) of HSE's employees received their PhD degrees from other universities in the same region.[82] The two North American universities recruit mostly nationally (90 per cent of UM's employees hold a PhD degree from another American university) and internationally (32 per cent of MUN's employees received their degrees from foreign universities).

In regressions run using the LinkedIn data (Models 1–9), I controlled for the employee's gender, her university and academic rank. The use of the university as a control variable serves to check whether academia uses a single or multiple model of the internal labour market.[83] Does the academic internal labour market have a homogeneous or heterogeneous character? The importance of the academic's progression through the ranks for the operation of the internal labour market calls for controlling the impact of academic rank (dummies for Assistant, Associate and Full professor). The ILM predicts that the longer one stays in the internal labour market, the higher the status in the organizational hierarchy that she achieves. As for the control for gender, gender imbalances characterize even some Western universities.[84]

The list of controls in regressions run using the HSE official data (Models 10–11) included several other variables, namely the employee's scholarly (the number of publications listed on the personal webpage) and teaching activities (the number of courses whose programmes are posted on the personal website), a dummy for receivers of material bonuses in addition to basic salary,[85] dummies for holders of HSE's ordinary professorship, administrative positions (associate department heads, department heads, associate deans and deans) and full-time positions. The HSE academic labour market has a particularly complex structure: this university hires in the external labour market (part-time faculty members represent 14.1 per cent of its labour force), has a small internal labour market (HSE's ordinary professorship as an imperfect substitute for tenure) and a 'hybrid' form of employment with features of both the external and internal labour markets (full-time faculty members).

In keeping with the prediction of the ILM theory, there is a negative association between the length of employment at the current university and the number of previous employers (Model 1). The impact of the number of LinkedIn connections turned out to be insignificant. As a matter of fact, no model suggests that the number of LinkedIn connections might serve as a proxy for the involvement in the external labour market. When the dummy for the port of entry is added to the regression model (Model 2),[86] the contribution of the number of previous employers becomes insignificant. In terms of the elaboration paradigm, the port of entry helps to interpret the original relationship.[87]

Models 3 and 6–9 confirm that the academic labour market tends to be heterogeneous rather than homogeneous. The number of previous employers has a significant negative impact on the dependent variable at the two Russian universities but not at the North American universities. Employees who received their Masters degrees at the university of their current employment, have advantages in the internal labour market solely in the case of HSE. Models 10 and 11 further corroborate this finding. The relative short history of this university might explain why the same does not apply to employees with PhDs granted by the HSE.[88]

The addition of the dummies for two academic ranks, Assistant and Full professors, in Models 4 and 5 made the impact of the number of previous employers significant once again. The external labour market (variable 'N of previous employers') and the internal labour market (the length of employment at the current university) turned out to be connected through the port of entry, as predicted by the ILM theory, and under the conditions of employee's progression through the ranks.[89] On average, assistant professors worked at the current university for shorter periods of time than holders of other academic ranks. On average, full professors worked at the current university for longer periods of time than assistant and associate professors.

The entry of several control variables from a more comprehensive source, the HSE website, allowed me to make several additional observations. Unfortunately, the information on the number of previous employers is unavailable at the HSE site and I used the total number of years spent in academia as an imperfect substitute. Variable 'Years in academia' tells us more about the employee's seniority than about her involvement in the external labour market. Thus, it comes as no surprise that the longer career the HSE employee had, the more years she had spent at the HSE. Models 10–11 show an insignificant impact of the dummies for associate and full professorship on the dependent variable, which might be attributed to the existence of several ports of entry at the HSE. The HSE is the only university out of the four with an insignificant impact of the dummy for the port of entry (Model 9) because its administration tends to hire holders of all academic ranks. HSE's ordinary professors quite expectedly have spent more years at the HSE than non-tenured faculty members. More unexpectedly, full-time employees tend to have shorter track records at the HSE than its part-time employees. The stability of one's employment at the HSE does not seem to depend on the scope of one's involvement in the university's activities.

So far, only findings relevant to various aspects of the ILM theory have been highlighted. Is there any outcome that specifically calls for applying the theory of gate keeping to studies of the academic labour market? Model 11 clearly indicates that the stability of employment at the HSE depends on whether or not the academic holds an administrative position. The value of the standardized (beta) coefficient for the relevant dummy suggests that it is a second most important predictor for the length of employment at the HSE. The closer one is to the boss, the more chances she has of being admitted to the internal labour market, which is fully consistent with the prediction made on the basis of the theory of gate keeping. The transition from the external to the internal labour market results from the exercise of discretionary powers by C. A trades employment stability for the acceptance of C's power.

As for the additional research question on the validity of the information on LinkedIn users' employment situation publicly available at this website, the tentative answer is rather inconclusive. On the one hand, the comparison of data on the average length of employment at the HSE from two sources, LinkedIn and the HSE official website, suggests some consistency (Table 6.3). On the other hand, the combined LinkedIn data for the two Russian universities with respect to the distribution of faculty members across academic ranks diverge from the official nation-level statistics. A total of 39 per cent of LinkedIn users from the MSU and the HSE report having the rank of full professor, whereas full professors represent 10 per cent of faculty working at the Russian universities only.[90] It cannot be excluded that Russian faculty members tend to overstate their academic ranks in their LinkedIn accounts. One cannot rule out either that, at least, the HSE offers more full professorships than the Russian universities on average (as per data from its official website, full professors represent 26.7 per cent of its faculty members, as opposed to 32 per cent as per LinkedIn data for this university). Thus, more careful and large-scale comparisons are needed before any final conclusions can be made.

Table 6.3: The average number of years that the academic worked at her current university, the average number of previous employers and the average number of LinkedIn connections, by academic rank

	HSE_ LinkedIn	HSE_ site	MUN	UM	MSU
N of years, Assistant professor	3.85	1.93	5.89	3.78	6.64
N of previous employers, Assistant professor	0.85	n.a.	0.67	1.44	0.7
N of LinkedIn connections, Assistant professor	161.55	n.a.	136.46	265.37	86.93
N of years, Senior lecturer	n.a.	5.22	n.a.	n.a.	n.a.
N of years, Associate professor	5.91	4.64	11.12	11.29	12.43
N of previous employers, Associate professor	1.14	n.a.	0.75	1.14	0.62
N of LinkedIn connections, Associate professor	161.97	n.a.	185.63	252.25	91.42
N of years, Full professor	8.45	6.07	22.28	16.28	19.67
N of previous employers, Full professor	1.68	n.a.	0.58	1.24	0.63
N of LinkedIn connections, Full professor	180.77	n.a.	113.42	297.32	143.07
N of years, all academic ranks combined[1]	6.32	4.78	13.06	10.43	14.30

Legend: *The corresponding figure for the above discussed university in Belgium is 9.7 years (Haeck and Verboven, 'The Internal Economics of a University', p. 599). To compare: the average in-progress tenure for all occupations in the Canadian economy was 78 months in 1976 and 92 months (7 years 8 months) in 2001 (Heisz, 'The Evolution of Job Stability in Canada', p. 109). In North America, with its institution of academic tenure, university professors tend to have longer in-progress tenures than employees in the other sectors of the economy.

6. Conclusions

The discussion in this chapter focused on two hands of power within the organization, visible and invisible. The existence of the boss's visible hand – her explicit orders and commands – has long been acknowledged and studied. Alfred Chandler, a business historian, refers to the visible hand in the title of one of his most acclaimed books.[91]

The boss's second hand, invisible, often remains unnoticed by both employees and specialists in organization studies. The boss imposes her will on the employees not only by rendering and enforcing her orders, but also by having a discretionary power to decide who will be offered jobs in the organization and under which conditions – permanent or temporary employment. Permanent employees gain access to the internal labour whereas temporary workers remain in the external labour market.

The ILM theory emphasizes the importance of the ports of entry in the operation of the internal labour markets. What remains underexplored, however, is the question as to who might profit from the existence of these ports. The theory of gate keeping offers an answer: the agent, who manages to control the gate, i.e. the port of entry. The boss as a gate keeper strengthens and enhances her powers within the organization. In other words, the boss's toolbox contains not only such well-known techniques as inducements or threats of firing, but also gate keeping.

As long as the university has two types of employment, permanent and temporary, this reasoning also applies to academia. A position of status enables one to have a say in hiring decisions. A final say in hiring decisions further increases the gate keeper's status and extends her powers. Despite the lesser importance of human-specific assets in academia and declared 'universalism', the university has the internal labour market with all opportunities for gate keeping that it creates.

The case study of four North American and Russian universities showed that the academic labour market has a heterogeneous character. Instead of one universal model, there are several sets of rules and procedures that shape the employment relationship in academia. Some arrangements of the academic labour market create particularly ample opportunities for gate keeping. This might be the case of the HSE, where the stability of the academic's employment depends on her proximity to the boss.

7 QUALITY CONTROL AS A WEAPON: GATE KEEPING IN PEER REVIEW

This chapter continues the discussion of academia started in Chapter 6, Sections 4 and 5. The focus of our attention will shift at this stage, however, from the two segments of the academic labour market, external and internal, to more subtle differences between permanent positions in academia. In Chapter 6, tenured and tenure-track positions were treated as similar and constituting integral elements of the internal labour market. Now I will zoom in and consider an uneasy switch from a tenure-track position to tenured employment. This transition normally involves the assessment of an academic's performance, which calls for addressing the issues of quality control in academia.

The concept of gate keeping is not completely absent from the discourse on academia. At the same time, its current uses differ from the conceptualization proposed in this book. Speaking about academia,[1] scholars stress their role as gate keepers to professions. Instructors not only might, but should, as this argument goes, identify students, who will likely fail to meet professional standards, as early as possible in their careers. By advising such students to change, the profession instructors render a service to both the professional community and society as a whole. The operation of social work schools is a case in point. Their mission includes 'screen[ing] out students who appear unable to adhere to social work ethics and values'.[2] If the school of social work fails to do so, the prospective clients of its graduates – senior and disabled people – will suffer.

Scholars do not exclude the eventuality of gate keeping in relationships with colleagues, academics of equal formal status, either. Michèle Lamont acknowledges that restricted access to the most valuable resources in academia – space for scholarly publications, grants and tenure – amount to gate keeping.[3] For instance, editors of scholarly journals[4] and reviewers of manuscripts submitted for publication[5] are sometimes compared with gate keepers. They have the privilege to select authors, who will see their manuscripts published, leaving other authors to virtually perish.

References to gate keeping in the discourse on academia most often have a metaphorical character: they lack analytical and conceptual rigour. This chapter is intended to bridge some gaps that exist in our knowledge of gate keeping in academia. It argues that gate keeping in academia represents a particular case of gate keeping as a technique of power. When combined with gate keeping, the otherwise perfectly legitimate assessment of scientific merit turns into a power struggle. The theory of gate keeping proposed in the present monograph appears applicable not only to the academic labour market, but also to procedures for assessing scientific merit. The specific research question can be formulated in the following manner: does quality control in academia tend to transform into an exercise of power and, if it does, under which conditions?

A look at quality control procedures in academia through the lens of the theory of gate keeping serves to identify the eventual existence of a power triad in relationships between formally equal academics. The power triad existing in the academic labour market includes agents of unequal status, the boss and her employees. The power triad eventually emerging in the process of assessing the scientific merit of a scholar's work includes academics of equal formal status. The latter power triad, similarly to the former or any other power triad, involves a constellation of interests. These interests do not have a pecuniary dimension, however. The university might pursue pecuniary goals, i.e. maximize profits, but such a situation does not represent the rule.[6] The same observation applies to the individual scholar, who is used as a unit of analysis in this chapter. Instead of assuming that she maximizes income, as some neoclassical economists do,[7] I make a less heroic assumption. The academic presumably maximizes her contribution to the body of knowledge in her field. The use of gate keeping helps her to reduce contributions from competitors or to undermine their value. At the same time, the competitors do not disappear altogether; they continue to make their respective contributions.

Similarly to the power triad discussed in Chapter 5, the power triad in the assessment of scientific merit involves a constellation of non-pecuniary interests. In the other chapters of this book, I considered constellations of pecuniary interests. Thus, the significance of the configuration of power relationships outlined in this chapter is twofold. On the one hand, the study of the power triad in the assessment of scientific merit serves to unveil the presence of power relationships even in transactions between seemingly equal parties, namely academic peers. On the other hand, that fact that non-pecuniary interests might also constellate and give rise to a power triad extends the scope of the applicability of the theory of gate keeping beyond the limits of market transactions.

To draw a relevant parallel, the power triads tend to be as diverse as the fields of power studied by Pierre Bourdieu and his followers. Namely, Bourdieu suggested that the juridical field exists in the judicial system,[8] the bureaucratic field in state governance,[9] the economic field in the market[10] and so forth. The concept of the power triad differs from that of the field of power in several aspects, nevertheless. First, in contrast to the field of power, the power triad necessitates the existence of such structural components as boundaries delineating the space of transactions and making access control possible.[11] Second, the field of power does not involve gate keeping as its strategic component. Third, the parties involved in the field of power have conflicting and mutually exclusive interests, as opposed to constellating interests in the case of the power triad.

This chapter has three sections, excluding the introduction and conclusion. Section 1 outlines quality control procedures in academia. It shows that the assessment of scientific merit represents an integral and necessary part of all scholarly endeavours. The eventuality of the transformation of quality control into a technique of power is demonstrated in Section 2. In this section, I discuss gate keeping in the peer review of scholarly publications and gate keeping in the peer review of tenure applications separately. In Section 3, I return to the case of the four universities whose internal labour markets were studied in the previous chapter. This time, the nature of the study is mostly descriptive. It compares procedures for granting tenure at these universities and highlights the ample opportunities for gate keeping that they create.

1. Quality Control in Academia

The assessment of the quality of a good or service is rarely an easy and straightforward task. Even such a simple product as an apple or lettuce might have some hidden vices; for instance, it might contain pesticide residues or be contaminated with Escherichia coli (E. coli). Douglass North showed that measurement costs constitute a key component of transaction costs. Their dynamics shape the path of economic development. 'The technology of measurement and the history of weights and measures is a crucial part of economic history since as measurement costs were reduced the cost of transacting was reduced'.[12] Neoinstitutional economists argue that profit maximization involves minimization of both production and transaction costs. Thus, low transaction costs pave the way to economic growth.

The neoinstitutional approach suggests that measurement costs also have an impact on the choice of organizational form. From this point of view, the organization, namely the firm, emerges in response to high transaction costs in the market. 'The main reason why it is profitable to establish a firm would seem to be that there is a cost of using price mechanism'.[13] Thus, all other factors being equal, the organization exists as long as it serves to save on measurement costs. North made this prediction more specific: 'the choice of organizational form will be influenced by the characteristics of the good or service and by the technology of measurement of the attributes'.[14] I will consider the two predictors for organizational form separately.

First, what are the specific characteristics of knowledge? The body of existing knowledge and particular contributions to its development has the characteristics of a public good. The more basic, fundamental knowledge is, the more characteristics of a public good it has. Advocates of the New Economics of Science, that represent a neoclassical take on academia, use this assumption as a point of departure in their reasoning.

> Codified scientific knowledge possesses the characteristics of a durable public good in that (i) it does not lose validity due to use or the passage of time per se (ii) it can be enjoyed jointly, and (iii) costly measures must be taken to restrict access to those who do not have a 'right' to use it.[15]

In these circumstances, the introduction of property rights on basic knowledge would not make much sense. Property rights impose restrictions on access to knowledge and on possible uses of it.[16] The situation with respect to applied knowledge is different since it combines the features of a public and private good. In the following text, I will focus on the assessment of one's contribution to the body of basic knowledge.

As neoclassical economists well know, self-interested individuals do not have any incentives to contribute to the production of public goods. They prefer to enjoy a 'free ride' instead, i.e. to get public goods produced by someone else. The same applies to the measurement of the quality of a public good since its outcome, an assessment, is a public good itself. Speaking more specifically about quality control in academia, the assessment of contributions to the body of knowledge is problematic as long as self-interested behaviour prevails. All academics have an interest in having contributions to the body of knowledge assessed, but prefer to have this task done by someone else. A possible solution refers to the joint production of public and private goods. One's contribution to the production of a public good enables an individual to simultaneously consume a private good. Todd Sandler defines joint production as 'a technology of supply in which private output may not be separated from the associated collective output'.[17]

Food quality regulation serves as an illustration of the idea of joint production. Food quality regulation produces both private and public goods: higher environmental quality is a public good whereas a lower level of health risk posed by pesticide exposure is a private one.[18] In these circumstances, a self-interested individual favours the regulation of pesticide residues. If an academic's involvement in the assessment of a fellow scientist's contribution to the body of knowledge provides the assessor with some private goods, then the assessor also acts in a situation of joint production. The list of private goods eventually provided to the assessor includes some pecuniary compensation (for instance, the coverage of her travel and accommodation expenses directly or indirectly related to the assessment), her enhanced status in academia, the acknowledgment of her efforts in the evaluation of the assessor's activities, and so forth. The Social Sciences and Humanities Research Council of Canada, SSHRC, explicitly urges the universities, whose representatives participate in the evaluation of project proposals submitted to this granting council, to 'recognize both the contribution to the research enterprise made by committee members and the time commitment involved in peer review'.[19] In practical terms, this means that the participation in SSHRC's committees influences the assessor's chances of obtaining tenure (being accounted for under the category 'service', see Subsection 2.3 below) or a promotion.

Second, what is the technology for measuring the quality of a contribution to the body of knowledge? The assessment of the quality of an academic's contribution cannot be performed by the academic herself. It requires references to externally set criteria and, consequently, the involvement of at least one external assessor. George Simmel saw room for applying his theory of value to the issues of assessing quality in academia. Simmel argues that the nature of value is always relative. 'Things receive their meaning through each other, and have their being determined by their mutual relations'.[20] He believes that the same applies to the production of knowledge. Scientific activities necessarily involve 'the process of reciprocal verification'. He continues: 'cognition is thus a free-floating process whose elements determine their position reciprocally'.[21]

The need for an external validation of one's contribution to the body of knowledge lies at the origin of peer review. Quality control in academia takes the form of peer review.[22] To be accepted as a worthy contribution, one's work must be submitted for evaluation and eventual endorsement by a fellow scholar with a similar expertise, a peer. Peer review operating in a 'bottom-up' manner, i.e. initiated by the academic herself, requires a high level of individualization and personal courage. Thomas Gould claims that 'without the boldness of a single person to submit their works to the judgment of another prior to publication' no system of peer review would have come into existence.[23]

How does the bottom-up process of peer review operate in practice? An academic who wishes to have her work assessed sends it to an established specialist in her field of knowledge. Historically, this was done by sending letters containing short summaries and the principal findings of one's work. 'The "erudite letters" would ask friends and cohorts to examine the logic and, in some cases, suggest that they even attempt to replicate the actions that led to the same conclusions'.[24] The Republic of Letters – a network of corresponding scholars that existed in the late sixteenth and seventeenth centuries – derives its name from this spontaneous system of mutual assessment and peer review.[25]

The ideal of the Republic of Letters has continued to inspire academics even after correspondence by letters became outdated and even somewhat defunct. Michael Polanyi's Republic of Science incorporates the key future of the medieval Republic of Letters, namely the need for external validation in scientific endeavours.

> Scientific opinion is an opinion not held by any single human mind, but one which, split into thousands of fragments, is held by a multitude of individuals, each of whom endorses the others' opinion at second hand, by relying on the consensual chains which link him to all the others through a sequence of overlapping neighbourhoods.[26]

It does not matter exactly how academics communicate and assess one another's claims – by letters, at face-to-face meetings or using the internet. Peer review will continue to exist as long as the need for mutual assessment exists.

Peer review can be compared with triangulation in geodesy. In order to determine the precise location of a point in space, references to at least three points are needed. These three points form a geodesic triangle.[27] One external review does not suffice for a valid assessment of a scholar's work; two or more external references increase our confidence in the reliability and validity of the assessment. Parallels between peer review and triangulation sometimes take explicit forms. For example, in his account of French scientists' efforts to measure the size of the earth and, subsequently, the length of one metre (as a fraction of the length of the Paris meridian), Ken Alder traces several parallels between two sorts of triangulation, in the field work of geodesists and astronomers and in their constant comparisons of the collected data across the teams involved in the survey. He concludes that 'all we know we know by triangulation'.[28] It comes as no surprise that academics now actively use the concept of triangulation outside the scope of geodesy, making it one of the universal research methods.[29]

Peer review has been criticized for a number of flaws. Quality control in academia has an inherent bias against innovative research. Reviewers do their job better when they assess contributions that do not challenge the theories and assumptions that prevail in a particular area of knowledge.[30] A related flaw of peer review is the fact that it reduces the diversity of opinions, thereby making academic discourse more uniform. Peer review undermines John Stuart Mills's arguments on the virtues of the 'marketplace of ideas'. This line of reasoning suggests that 'the expression of multiple and diverging viewpoints is more likely to produce truth than would suppressing some viewpoints', however erroneous the latter might eventually be.[31] The involvement of several reviewers increases the chances of spotting possible errors in an academic's contribution while at the same time reducing the chances of doing justice to its strengths. In the terms of statistical analysis, peer review minimizes the chances of committing Type II errors (the acceptance of an unworthy contribution) at the price of increasing the probability of making Type I errors (the rejection of a worthy contribution).[32] One problem with peer review relevant to our discussion of gate keeping lies elsewhere, however.

2. Keeping the Gate in Academia

The operation of peer review does not exclude the eventual transformation of a quality check into a technique of power.[33] If this happens, the logic of peer review changes. Peer review starts to function in a top-down manner, as opposed to the bottom-up process. An academic submits her work for a peer's evaluation not because the latter has a genuine interest in having a second opinion. Peer review becomes a mandatory requirement for publication or tenure. The peer evaluator imposes and enforces this requirement because it corresponds to her interests.

The theory of gate keeping highlights this aspect, which is often neglected in the literature on peer review. This theory predicts that peer review changes its nature in the presence of two conditions, structural and strategic. The structural condition refers to the existence of boundaries and gates within academia. For instance, the impossibility of publishing everything that has been written by academics due to either technical (e.g. limited space in a journal) or cognitive (attention and information processing capacities as scarce resources)[34] constraints constitutes a boundary. The other boundary separates tenured and tenure-track positions in the academic internal labour market.

Both boundaries have gates:[35] some manuscripts get published and some assistant professors with tenure-track appointments get tenure. An academic's passage through the gates involves peer review of her contribution to the body of knowledge. The fact that the peer review of scholarly publications and the peer review of applications for tenure tend to be related (an academic must publish in order to get tenure, see Subsections 2.2 and 2.3 below) is irrelevant for the purposes of this discussion. If the assessor uses her review as a lever to enhance her relative standing in academia, then she becomes a gate keeper.

The transformation of the reviewer into a gate keeper necessitates the existence of a second, structural condition, namely the assessor's familiarity with the strategy of gate keeping and her willingness to use it in particular circumstances. Why does the assessor eventually have an interest in becoming a gate keeper? One of the incentives for using the strategy of gate keeping refers to joint production. The self-interested academic contributes to the production of a public good – assesses the other academic's contribution – if the former produces some private good for her own consumption in the process. All academics supposedly want to enhance their relative standing within academia and participating in peer review gives them a chance to do so with the help of gate keeping.

2.1 Peer: An Academic of Equal Status or a Superior?

Before outlining the particularities of peer review in academic publishing and in the internal labour market, I will focus on the figure of the peer: who is she, an equal or a superior? The term 'peer' should not be misleading: it designates a specialist in the same area regardless of her formal rank within academia or at the university.[36] If the peer has an equal status, peer review operates in a horizontal manner. Quality control then takes place in the context of networking. In these circumstances, network members as a group might act as a gate keeper. Gate keeping introduces elements of power in transactions between otherwise equal academics.

Networks take various forms: teams, circles, schools of thought, and so forth. For instance, the academic department might be perceived by its members as a team.[37] They cooperate with one another and develop complementary skills. Quality control within a team involves shifting the emphasis from an academic's universal skills and contribution to the general body of knowledge to her network-specific skills and compatibility with the other network members.[38] To pass through the gates – for example, to obtain tenure – an academic must learn how to prioritize the interests of the network over her individual interests and, eventually, the principles of research integrity. In other words, the academic has to subordinate herself to the network as a whole. 'It is not surprising to find that department members assign considerable weight to compatibility and/or collegiality issues in their final tenure decision.'[39]

The priority of being a 'good citizen' (network member) has several consequences that Michel Foucault so persuasively described in his historical study of democracy. Within a network, the criteria for assessing one's contribution have a relative and local character. A network member continuously asks the question: how would the other network members perceive her particular statements, discoveries, or publications.[40] Instead of applying universal criteria for assessing the merit of something (how academics in general would perceive something), the network member tends to validate her assessment by a majority opinion in the network.

The network member is afraid of expressing unpopular opinions and assessments that diverge from the majority point of view. As a result, she becomes a flatterer: flatterers 'speak only because and to the extent that what [they] say represents the prevailing opinion.'[41] The flatterer feels safe: her 'well-roundness' serves as assurance against negative assessments of her contribution to the body of knowledge from the part of the fellow network members. The network member refuses the right to express her true opinion about the contribution of the other network members in exchange for not hearing their true opinions about her own contribution.

Because of the tendency of democratically organized systems, including networks of academic peers, to promote flattery, Foucault saw a solution in more hierarchically organized relationships, namely enlightened absolutism. 'Truthtelling can have its place in relationship to the leader, Prince, king, monarch, quite simply ... because they have a soul, and this soul can be persuaded and educated.'[42] Quality control in hierarchical relationships has its own flaws, however.

If the peer has a superior status, then the peer review process is embedded in hierarchical structures. In the case of the vertically structured process of peer review, gate keeping refers to the strategies at the boss's disposal in her relationships with the subordinate, direct or indirect, as discussed in Section 3 of Chapter 6. In the final account, gate keeping serves to strengthen the superior's power by complementing her visible hand with an invisible one.

Quality control in hierarchies, including academic hierarchies, is performed by a superior. Thus, the boss not only sets goals, but communicates them to the subordinate and motivates her to achieve them[43] and not only adjudicates conflicts between the subordinates acting as a judge in respect of internal disputes,[44] but also assesses the subordinate's contribution. The model of a scholarly journal in which the editor keeps the gate, i.e. makes all key decisions, is a case in point. The editor (eventually with the help of her knowledgeable associates) reads submitted manuscripts, suggests any necessary corrections and decides if a submission deserves publication or should be rejected. The editor might be a good specialist in her area of expertise. Furthermore, the eventual involvement of her associates and the staff members extends the scope of the area in which the editor has an informed opinion. Gould sees the ascension of the journal editor to a position of total power as a possible solution to peer review problems.[45] The chances of having an enlightened editor vested in total power might be higher than the chances of having a submission read by equally enlightened reviewers with no other source of power than gate keeping. In the Soviet Union, most scholarly journals in the social sciences followed the editorial model of quality control. This system continues to exist in the post-Soviet countries, including Russia.

By definition, the editor has a superior status in the academic hierarchy. Nevertheless, she further strengthens her power and extends its scope by using the strategy of gate keeping. To secure her passage through the gates, the prospective author must show her respect toward the editor by all possible means and nurture good relationships with the latter. If, in the case of peer review performed by academics of equal status, the most desirable qualities are 'well-roundedness' and 'likableness', in the case of peer review carried out by a superior one needs to be submissive or at least appear to be so. In other words, regardless of the modality of peer review, the academic has to pay a price for securing a positive assessment of her contribution to the body of knowledge even when this contribution has merits.[46]

The hierarchical model of quality control applies not only in academic publishing, but also in the academic internal labour market, the management of academic curriculum and other academic activities. Furthermore, there is a growing tendency to substitute the hierarchical model of peer review for the 'egalitarian' model of peer review.[47] The tenure and promotion committees lose the final say in the peer review of tenure applications. The university administration sets, enforces and controls tenure and promotion policies.[48] This substitution happens despite the available evidence that faculty control over appointment, promotion and tenure decisions tends to be associated with the increased performance of the academic organization.[49] If the implied association does indeed exist, then does the substitution have more to do with the issues of power within academia than with considerations of performance?

2.2 Peer Review in Academic Publishing

Despite the similarity of the substance of the peer review in academic publishing and the peer review of tenure applications, these modalities of quality control in academia have several particularities. The former modality has a longer history (the institution of tenure is a relatively recent invention – in the US, tenure was introduced in the first half of the twentieth century) that includes various combinations of the hierarchical and 'egalitarian' models of peer review.

Gould identifies several stages in the history of the peer review in academic publishing. Initially the church performed quality checks assessing the soundness of an academic's arguments from the point of view of religious doctrines. The church conducted reviews in a hierarchical manner: after the appearance of a new work, a church official read it and rendered his judgment. 'Works were judged appropriate either prior to publication or afterward by church officials, usually those within the region of the author'.[50] The invention of printing led to a significant increase in the number of published works. The church progressively lost its capacity to produce an informed opinion about all published works, which called for an assessment by specialists, peers. The 'egalitarian' model of peer review started to prevail. Growing individualization created incentives to initiate peer review 'from below', in a bottom-up manner. The author's identity was known to the reviewers, whereas the author did not know the reviewers' names (a half-blind peer review). The next major change occurred in the 1950s when the double-blind peer review became the standard.[51] The use of the internet as a vehicle for disseminating scholarly works made an open peer review possible. 'Open peer review is review by the scholarly community at large, instead of a few anonymous referees along with an editor or board'.[52] Some combinations of an open review and a more traditional closed peer review are equally possible. Namely, the editor posts a blindly reviewed manuscript and comments made by the anonymous assessors on the internet and invites any interested and capable reader to submit commentary before rendering her final decision on publication.[53]

If one considers these stages in the evolution of the peer review in academic publishing through the lens of power relationships, a few observations can be made. The church officials' review derived from their position of power. It is the exercise of the church officials' power that enabled them to assess and control scholarly publications. A half-blind and double-blind review by specialists changes the configuration of the power relationships. Now, participation in quality control becomes a source of power. If the reviewer uses the strategy of gate keeping, then she enhances her status and power as a result of her involvement in the peer review process. The progressive changes in the organization of peer review, namely the transition from a half-blind to a double-blind peer review, was intended to reduce the reviewers' opportunities for gate keeping. These opportunities have not disappeared, however. They will exist as long as there is a power triad in the peer review process.

As elsewhere, the power triad in peer review does not necessary take manifest, visible forms, which undermines efforts to minimize the opportunities for gate keeping. The power triad includes three academics in this case: a reviewer and an editor play the role of the gate keeper, C, the author of a manuscript accepted for publication occupies the position of A, and its reader finds herself in the position of B. The interests of C, A and B form a constellation: no one, including B, loses in absolute terms. B values the fact that the available readings passed the quality check. However restricted B's readings may be, she prefers reading peer reviewed material to dealing with self-published (or published through 'vanity' presses) material only. A adds a new item to her list of publications, establishing herself as a well-published scholar.[54] In addition to enhancing A's reputation in academia, a long list of publications also increases her chances in the academic internal labour market, as discussed in the next subsection. The author of a rejected manuscript performs the role of A'. She keeps trying to get her work published. The rejection of her submission to a particular journal does not automatically lead to her disqualification and exclusion from academia.

For the sake of clarity, let us consider two gate keepers, the reviewer (C_1) and the editor (C_2), separately. As long as C_1 has discretionary power to suggest that C_2 rejects an otherwise worthy manuscript, C_1 acts as a gate keeper. By doing so, C_1 benefits in several ways. She might defend or enhance the relative standing of a network in which she participates. As a result, she strengthens her own position within the network. C_1 also gets an opportunity to give A and A' a 'lesson'. The teacher–pupil relationship necessarily involves the exercise of power, at least in a highly symbolic manner.[55] C_1 'teaches' A by suggesting revisions that correspond to C_1's take on the issue and by eventually inviting A to cite C_1's publications (C_1's reputation in academia – conventionally measured by the number of references to her works – gets a boost as a result).

The position of the editor arguably provides even more opportunities for gate keeping. C_2 can influence the outcomes of the peer review process by selecting reviewers that will likely produce a desirable outcome, whether this is acceptance or rejection. 'It is well known among editors that a deliberate bad choice of referees can always ensure that a paper is either accepted or rejected, as preferred.'[56] C_2 knows the biases of the potential reviewers or predicts them on the basis of her knowledge of their membership in particular networks. If C_2 has a 'hidden agenda' of promoting a particular network or theory, she can use gate keeping to achieve the desirable outcome without being noticed and exposed to criticism.

C_2 acts behind the scenes: her crucial role remains invisible for A, B and even C_1.

> Although editors select reviewers, interpret reviews, and make the decision about the future of the manuscript (acceptance, revisions, rejection), they ordinarily engage in discourses that make it appear as if they had little to do with the decision about the fate of the manuscript.[57]

The fact that gate keeping in C_2's case takes less visible forms than in C_1's case is of particular relevance to the argument developed in this book.

A rather radical proposal for putting an end to the scholarly journal as a primary vehicle for disseminating knowledge illustrates the difficulties with unveiling the true role played by C_2 in determining the outcome of a submission. Gould, the author of the proposal, puts forward, as an alternative, the option of posting manuscripts in online archives and depositories run by professional bibliographers. 'What would be produced would not be a journal, per se. It would be merely a large collection of gathered data, possibly indexed, but not necessarily, given that a researcher's search engine would probe the contents.'[58] Manuscripts deposited in the online collections and archives will still be peer reviewed using, for example, the model of an open peer review, as discussed above. Unlike the editor, however, the depositary manager will play a rather technical role of indexing,[59] formatting and eventually style editing the submission. Gould intends to leave no room for gate keeping in the system so designed. He notes that, with the arrival of search engines such as Google Scholar or the Web of Science, the 'researcher seeks only articles, not by journal, but by best fit by subject or author to the topic at hand.'[60]

2.3 Peer Review of Tenure Applications

A power triad emerges in the peer review of tenure applications as well. Academics with tenure-track appointments apply for tenure, i.e. for permanent admission to the internal labour markets. Holders of tenure-track appointments are tentatively admitted to the academic internal labour market. The final decision as to their admission is usually taken after a probationary period lasting four to seven years. At the end of the probationary period, a number of peers of both equal and superior status consider the academic's application for tenure by assessing her performance as a teacher, researcher and member of the academic community. These assessors manage the gate to the internal labour market and have an opportunity to transform this role into a lever to enhance their status and power.

In the content of the peer review of tenure applications, the position of B is occupied by a student studying and a colleague working at this particular university but not involved in the process of evaluation. They both gain from interacting with a scholar whose qualifications are certified. Interactions with a scholar whose credentials remain obscure tend to be risky and uncertain. An academic who obtains tenure occupies the position of A in the power triad. A obtains a secure position and a privileged status within academia. Now she can be expelled from the internal labour market only 'for cause', i.e. as a result of a serious breach of law or academic ethics. A profits from the existence of the power triad to a greater extent than B. C, the gate keeper, benefits the most. An unsuccessful applicant plays the role of A', who did have her chance, after all. The denial to grant tenure to A' nevertheless does not involve her expulsion from academia. A' simply returns to the external labour market and might try her luck elsewhere.[61]

As in the case of the power triad in academic publishing, several academics, Cs, keep the gate to the internal labour market. This group of gate keepers includes members of the promotion and tenure committees or all members of the academic unit (C_1), external assessors (C_2) and the university administration, the 'boss' (C_3).[62] All parties of the power triad but C_3 have similar formal statuses in academia; there is no formal subordination of A and B (if B is a colleague) to C_1 and C_2. In other words, transactions between A, B, C_1 and C_2 refer to the 'egalitarian' model of peer review, whereas transactions between A, B and C_3 represent its hierarchical version.

With the help of gate keeping, C_1 makes sure that no colleague overshadows her contribution to the body of knowledge. C_1's colleagues tend to be well-rounded and unchallenging in the good and bad senses of this word. C_2 has an opportunity to eventually weaken a rival network by giving one of its members a negative assessment. Or, alternatively, C_2 strengthens her own network by supporting a similarly minded applicant. C_3 further enhances her power by complementing her visible hand as the university administrator with the invisible hand of the gate keeper.

C_3 usually selects C_2, acting in a manner similar to the editor in academic publishing. The privilege to select C_2 increases C_3's opportunities for keeping the gate and, thus, contributes to strengthening her superior status at the university. 'The appointment of external readers is far from being innocent; it eventually lays the ground for discriminatory practices'.[63] University administrators use external academic reviews as a management tool. Namely, 'university presidents and their staff mobilize these reviews to legitimate decisions made at the university level'.[64] The more attention C_1 pays to external reviews, the more powerful the management tool C_3 obtains in addition to the other techniques of power at the latter's disposal. A survey shows that C_1 at the comprehensive (Masters degree) and undergraduate (baccalaureate) universities consider external reviews particularly seriously.[65] C_1 at the doctoral (research) universities prefer to rely on their own expertise.

The other factor that increases the opportunities for gate keeping refers to the vagueness of criteria used by the assessors. Academics involved in the peer review of tenure applications commonly consider three dimensions of the applicant's performance: teaching, research and service.[66] The nature of the criteria used for assessing each of these dimensions is contested, however. For instance, can students' evaluations of the applicant's teaching performance be deemed a valid source of information given conditions of grade inflation?[67] Can the number of the applicant's publications and even the impact factor of the journals in which they appeared inform the assessor about the quality of the former's research? Some scholars argue that the true impact of one's work can be evaluated only after publication, which calls for a careful post-publication review as a part of tenure consideration.[68] From this point of view, the prepublication review discussed in the previous subsection is never sufficient. Service, the third area of assessment for tenure, turns out to be equally challenging. If well-roundedness and flattery are used as proxies for being a good citizen of the academic unit or the university community, then critically-minded academics and whistle-blowers will not pass through the gates.[69]

Attempts to deal with the lack of agreement as to how to evaluate the applicant's performance in the three areas of assessment by merging these areas into a single one have not been successful so far. There was a proposal to broaden the definition of research performance by introducing a more encompassing concept of scholarship. The assessment of one's scholarship involves paying attention to such components as discovery (generation of new knowledge), integration (efforts to put isolated facts in perspective), application (implementation of knowledge in practice) and teaching.[70] The number of publications as a criterion for evaluating the applicant's record of research has to be complemented then by several other measures. A work meets the standards of excellence in scholarship 'to the extent that it exhibits clear goals, adequate preparation, appropriate methods, significant results, effective presentation, and reflective critique'.[71] The drift into gate keeping will persist, however, as long as the criteria used in the assessment remain incompletely specified and operationalized. It is the assessors' discretion in the selection and application of evaluation criteria that makes the use of the strategy of gate keeping possible, not the degree of comprehensiveness of these criteria.

3. Case of the Four Universities

A case study of four universities, two North American (the University of Mississippi (UM) in the US and Memorial University of Newfoundland (MUN) in Canada) and two Russian (the Lomonossov Moscow State University (MSU) and the National Research University – the Higher School of Economics (HSE), was intended to highlight those aspects of tenure consideration that facilitate gate keeping. Only secondary data – organization charts, tenure policies and procedures available at the four universities' official websites – informed this case study.

The Russian universities do not grant tenure to their employees because of the legal requirement to sign only fixed-term contracts. The HSE offers a poor substitute for tenure, HSE's ordinary professorship (an academic cannot apply for ordinary professorship, it can only be awarded). The MSU reappoints its full-time employees every three or five years. The assessment of a full-time employee's teaching and research performance precedes all her reappointments.

The UM also acts in an institutional environment that undermines the core principles of tenure: 'Mississippi law does not empower the Board of Trustees to contract the services of faculty for indefinite periods'.[72] This legal obstacle does not prevent the UM, however, from adopting policies of continuing employment. The UM and the MUN set a five-year probationary period before allowing their faculty members with tenure-track appointments to apply for tenure. 'A faculty member with the rank of assistant professor shall be considered for tenure in the sixth year of service'.[73]

None of the four universities spelled out the criteria of performance required for obtaining tenure (for getting reappointed in the Russian case) in a clear, unambiguous and detailed manner. For instance, the MUN expects applicants for tenure at that university to demonstrate 'documented effectiveness and scholarly competence as a teacher ... [have] a demonstrated record, since the date of appointment, of research, scholarship, or creative and professional activities appropriate to the rank ... [and have] a demonstrated record of academic service'.[74] The Russian by-law regulating academics' reappointment falls short of spelling out requirements even in the most general terms. It simply states that the applicant must have the credentials stated in the relevant job advertisement.[75] As per the discussion in this chapter, Subsection 2.3, the vagueness of criteria for assessing an academic's performance represents a necessary condition for gate keeping.

The group of gate keepers, Cs, has a different make-up at the four universities (Table 7.1). Academics of equal status, C_1, participate in the assessment at all the universities included in the sample. C_1 includes members of the promotion and tenure committees at the MUN, all tenured members of the academic unit at the UM and all members of the academic unit at the MSU and the HSE. The UM and the MUN solicit the opinion of external reviewers, C_2. At the MUN they are selected by the university administration, C_3. C_1 – tenured members of the applicant's home department and its administrative head – have a similar privilege at the UM.

Table 7.1: Organization of the tenure process, four universities, 2014

	HSE*	HSE's ordinary professorship**	MSU***	MUN******	UM********
1	Academic unit meeting, the administrative head	College of HSE ordinary professors (98)	Academic unit meeting	External referees (3-5)	Outside evaluators
2	*Human Recourses Commission*	**Academic council of the university** (150)	**Academic council of a faculty** (44*****)	Promotion and tenure committee (5)	Departmental evaluation (3+ and the chair)
3	**Academic council of a faculty** (58****) **or the university,** in the case of full professors (150)	Rector (1)	Dean (1)	Administrative head (1)	*Advisory Committee to the Dean*
4	Rector (1)			*The Dean's consultative committee* (17*******)	Dean (1)
5				Dean (1)	Dean of the Graduate School (1)
6				Vice-President (Academic) (1)	Tenure and Promotion Review Committee (10)
7				President and Vice-Chancellor (1)	Provost/Vice-Chancellor for Academic Affairs (1)
8				**Board of Regents** (30)	**Chancellor** (1)
9					*Board of Trustees* (12)
10					Tenure and Promotion Appeal Committee (10)
No of Peers involved	60+	249	45+	42-4 (+17)	18+

Legend: Consultative bodies (their recommendations are not binding) are indicated in *italics*; decision makers with the final say are shown in **bold**

Sources: * Ministry of Education of the Russian Federation, 'Polozhenie o poryadke zameshcheniya dolzhnostei naugno-pedagogicheskikh rabotnikov v vyshem uchebnom zavedenii Rossiiskoi Federatsii' enacted on 26 November 2006 [Principles of the appointment to research and teaching positions at the universities in the Russian Federation], clauses 6, 10, 17; ** HSE Rector, 'Polozhenie ob ordinarnykh professorakh NIU VShE' [Regulations regarding HSE ordinary professorship], clauses 2.2–2.3; *** Ministry of Education of the Russian Federation, 'Polozhenie c poryadke zameshcheniya' and HSE Rector, 'Reglament organizatsii i provedeniya konkursnogo otbora pretendentov na dolzhnosti professorsko-prepodavatel'skogo sostava v NIU VShE' [Regulations regarding the selection of applicants for teaching positions at the HSE], clauses 2.10–2.14; **** F-SE Faculty of Economics; ***** MSU Faculty of Economics; ****** Collective agreement between MUN and MUN Faculty Association, 26 February 2010 – 31 August 2013, clauses 8.03, 11.16, 12.06, 12.07; ******* MUN Faculty of Arts; ******** The UM Tenure Policies and Procedures effective 9 September 2013, at https:// secure4.olemiss.edu/umpolicyopen/GetPdfActive?pol=10647010&ver=active&file=10647010_active_20130909.pdf [accessed 6 August 2014].

The academic council of a faculty or university has the final say in reappointment decisions in Russia. In North America, 'as a rule, institutional by-laws make it clear that votes by faculty committees are strictly advisory; they can be, and now and then are, overturned by administrators and governing boards'.[76] The UM illustrates this pattern: its chancellor makes a final decision as to the award of tenure. At the MUN, the board of regents has the ultimate authority to decide this matter. At no university does the 'egalitarian' or hierarchical model exist in its pure form, however. Instead, we observe various combinations of their elements.

A supervisory body – the board of regents, the board of trustees, or the governing board – deserves separate discussion. The supervisory board 'supervises and/or controls the executive management of a higher education institution'.[77] The growing popularity of supervisory bodies at the universities, both public and private, can be attributed to reforms inspired by New Public Management.[78] New Public Management involves using templates of private business in the system of higher education.[79] 'These [supervisory] bodies are gradually becoming more similar to their counterparts in the corporate world with regards to formal authority, composition and functions'.[80] The existence of a supervisory board in the organization structure potentially limits C_3's opportunities for gate keeping and, thus, her discretionary power.[81] From this point of view, a fourth type of gate keeper, C_4, might come into existence. Nevertheless, the capacity of the members of the supervisory board, who usually serve on a part-time basis and lack sufficient academic credentials, to effectively control C_3 remains questionable.

The appeal procedure imposes another limit on C's capacity for gate keeping. It is also possible that the appellate instance also acts as a gate keeper, but the more gate keepers are involved, the more divergent interests they might have. In these circumstances, A has a chance to 'squeeze in' using the eventual inconsistencies in the gate keepers' positions to her advantage. Best practices require that even students shall have recourse to appellate instances when they are denied access to a programme or a degree as a result of gate keeping performed by faculty members.[82] 'To protect the student's rights to challenge academic decisions, programs must have an academic appeals process in place that allows for review and re-evaluation of those decisions'.[83]

The appeal procedure can take a purely rudimental form, as in the case of MUN. At this university, a would-be A' (an applicant informed of a negative recommendation prepared by members of her promotion and tenure committee) has the right to state her concerns and counter-arguments at a meeting with the committee. A' also can include in the assessment file rebuttal or written comments about the accuracy or meaning of any document in her file, including documents inserted at the request of the committee or the administrative head.[84]

The UM has a more developed procedure for appealing decisions regarding tenure. The tenure and promotion review committee considers applicants' files before they reach the office of the chancellor. Its members pay attention solely to procedural issues. 'The committee shall not undertake to make its own judgment on the merits of an application, but it shall make an assessment on whether the tenure process has been applied properly.'[85] If the provost/vice-chancellor for academic affairs makes a negative recommendation concerning an applicant, the latter can file an appeal with the tenure and promotions appeal committee. This committee is composed of tenured full professors representing all UM's colleges and schools. The committee considers the applicant's written submissions and conducts an oral hearing with the eventual participation of witnesses. The appeal procedure at the UM is designed using juridical templates.

In addition to being very short – applications for teaching and research positions are considered in three to four stages – the assessment procedure at the Russian universities does not give the applicant the right of appeal. The Russian universities are not even bound by a requirement to inform the academic that a negative decision will be made with respect to her application. If the applicant is duly informed before the promotion and tenure committee or a university administrator (dean or provost) makes a negative recommendation, then she has an opportunity to express her concerns. A recent court decision – upheld by an appellate court – confirmed that the Russian universities do not have any legal obligation to inform an academic that her contract is not going to be renewed before a final decision is made.[86]

It turns out that despite its apparently egalitarian character – C_1 has the final say, not C_3 – the procedure for evaluating applications for teaching and research positions at the Russian universities provides less protection against the eventual drift into gate keeping. On the one hand, the academic councils, which have the final say in this country, usually include several dozen members (up to 150 at the HSE). At the meetings, they consider a large number of applications, from dozens to hundreds. The councils simply lack the time to give due consideration to each application, which increases their dependence on the university administration, C_3, whose representatives prepare the assessment files and do all other paperwork. On the other hand, the applicants do not have the right of appeal. Last, but not least, because the institution of tenure does not exist in Russia, academics must go through the ordeal of reappointment every three to five years. What initially looked like an 'egalitarian' system actually creates more opportunities for C_3's gate keeping than the formally more hierarchical procedure of the peer review of tenure applications at the two North American universities. In the final account, no model of peer review considered in this subsection excludes the drift into gate keeping, especially in the case of the university administration, C_3.

4. Conclusions

As in the other contexts, a power triad emerges in peer review in academia if two sets of conditions, structural and strategic, exist. Structural conditions refer to boundaries delineating the space of transactions and restricted access to this space. The boundaries have a technical (limited space in a journal, difficulties with indexing a large volume of qualitative data), cognitive (scarcity of attention and information procession capacities), or legal (legal environment in general and labour laws in particular) nature. A strategic condition refers to the agents' familiarity with gate keeping and their willingness to use it as a means for imposing their will on the other agents. Agents should, namely, be prepared to overlook or disregard the existence of a conflict of interest when they evaluate the quality of one's contribution to the body of knowledge. The assessor's failure to manage a conflict between her interests as a member of a particular network (team, circle and school of thought) and her interests as a citizen of the Republic of Science is indicative of the strategic component of gate keeping in peer review.

Why might an academic who has been asked to take part in an assessment be willing to keep the gate? An incentive to do so derives from the character of the assessment as a public good. All academics benefit from having the contribution made by one of them to the body of knowledge duly evaluated. Under the assumption of self-interested behaviour, however, no academic has an interest in spending her time and efforts on quality control in science unless she receives some private good in compensation for her involvement. The compensation does not necessarily have a pecuniary character: the assessor might want to enhance her status in academia, to promote a particular theory or a network. The use of the strategy of gate keeping provides the assessor with an opportunity to achieve these objectives. As a result, procedures for quality control turn into a weapon in the assessor's hands.

The transformation of quality control into a technique for enhancing power also involves a change in relationships between academics. Transactions between parties of unequal status replace transactions between parties of equal status. The concept of oligarchy, then, captures the essence of academia better than the concept of republic: an 'oligarchy of letters' emerges in the place of the Republic of Letters.[87]

> Rather than the term embedded within our civil rights – a trial by one's peers – and suggestive of a panel of those of equal station and education, the academic peer hearkens back to a more royal term, referencing the landed gentry who might be most often found in the British House of Lords.[88]

The emphasis on peer review as a vehicle of rising inequality might seem exaggerated to some. My task was to unveil this tendency without claiming that it always takes extreme forms. While we used to think of peer review in the same terms as we think of democracy, namely that 'it is the worst form of valuation – except for all the others,'[89] then nothing precludes offering a critique of it. Such a critique will guide the search for solutions for arguably improving the existing system of peer review. The discussion proposed in this chapter suggests that we need to limit the opportunities for gate keeping, both structural (by more actively using the open review model or a combination of a closed peer review and open commentary) and strategic (by selecting reviewers on a random basis from a list of all academics with the necessary credentials and expertise in a relevant area).[90]

To conclude, I will indicate a possible direction for further research. As long as reviewers have opportunities for keeping the gate (to publication, to the internal labour market), the academic whose contribution is being assessed can opt for securing an individual guarantee against eventual biases in the evaluation of her contribution. The academic simply maintains good relationships with any possible assessors. In the hierarchical system of peer review, one is better off maintaining good relationships with superiors. In the 'egalitarian' system of peer review, one should be on good terms with academics of equal status who will likely be involved in the assessment. The task of building and maintaining networks takes time and resources. It might be instructive to compare the average number of peers with whom the academic needs to have good relationships in both cases. A tentative conclusion informed by the data on the four universities (last row in Table 7.1) suggests that the 'egalitarian' model of peer review might impose higher costs on the academic than the hierarchical model, all other conditions being equal.

WORKS CITED

Aghion, P., M. Dewatripont, C. Hoxby, A. Mas-Colell and A. Sapir, 'The Governance and Performance of Universities: Evidence from Europe and the US', *Economic Policy*, 25 (2010), pp. 7–59.

Aidis, R., S. Estrin and T. M. Mickiewicz, 'Size Matters: Entrepreneurial Entry and Government', *Small Business Economics*, 39 (2012), pp. 119–39.

Ailon, G., 'What *B* Would Otherwise Do: A Critique of Conceptualizations of "Power" in Organizational Theory', *Organization*, 16 (2006), pp. 771–800.

Alder, K., *The Measure of All Things: The Seven-Year Odyssey and Hidden Error That Transformed the World* (New York: The Free Press, 2002).

American Association of University Professors (AAUP), '1940 Statement of Principles on Academic Freedom and Tenure', at http://www.aaup.org/report/1940-statement-principles-academic-freedom-and-tenure [accessed 12 June 2014].

—, '2006 AAUP Contingent Faculty Index', at http://www.aaup.org/sites/default/files/files/AAUPContingentFacultyIndex2006.pdf [accessed 12 June 2014].

—, 'The Employment Status of Instructional Staff Members in Higher Education, Fall 2011', 2014, at http://www.aaup.org/sites/default/files/files/AAUP-InstrStaff2011-April2014.pdf [accessed 13 June 2014].

Anderson, M. J., 'Legal Education Reform, Diversity, and Access to Justice', *Rutgers Law Review*, 61 (2009), pp. 1011–36.

Aoki, M., *Economie japonaise: information, motivations et marchandage*, trans. H. Bernard (1989; Paris: Economica, 1991).

Arendt, H., *On Violence* (New York: Harcourt, Brace & World, 1969).

Babbie, E. and G. Benaquisto, *Fundamentals of Social Research*, 1st Canadian edn (Scarborough: Nelson, 2002).

Barnard, C. I., *The Functions of the Executive*, 30th anniversary edn (1938; Cambridge, MA: Harvard University Press, 1968).

Basu, K., 'One Kind of Power', *Oxford Economic Papers*, 38 (1986), pp. 259–82.

Baumgartner, S. P., 'Does Access to Justice Improve Countries' Compliance with Human Rights Norms? – An Empirical Study', *Cornell International Law Journal*, 41 (2011), pp. 441–91.

Beetham, D., *The Legitimation of Power* (Atlantic Highlands, NJ: Humanities Press International: 1991).

Bernard, H. R., *Social Research Methods*, 2nd edn (Thousand Oaks, CA: Sage, 2013).

Bordalo, P., N. Gennaioli and A. Shleifer, 'Salience and Consumer Choice', *Journal of Political Economy*, 121 (2013), pp. 803–43.

Bosley, S. L. C., J. Arnold and L. Cohen, 'How Other People Shape our Careers: A Typology Drawn from Career Narratives', *Human Relations*, 62 (2009), pp. 1487–520.

Bourdieu, P., 'The Force of Law: Toward a Sociology of the Juridical Field' (1986), *Hastings Law Journal*, 38 (1987), pp. 805–53.

—, 'Rethinking the State: Genesis and Structure of the Bureaucratic Field', *Sociological Theory*, 12 (1994), pp. 1–18.

—, *The Social Structures of the Economy*, trans. C. Turner (2000; Cambridge: Polity, 2005).

— and J-C. Passeron, *La reproduction: Éléments pour une théorie du système d'enseignement* (Paris: Éditions de Minuit, 1970).

Bowles, S. and H. Gintis, 'Contested Exchange: New Microfoundations for the Political Economy of Capitalism', *Politics & Society*, 18 (1990), pp. 165–222.

—, 'Power in Competitive Exchange', in S. Bowles, M. Franzini, and U. Pagano (eds), *The Politics and Economics of Power* (London: Routledge, 1999), pp. 13–30.

—, 'Power', in S. N. Durlauf and L. E. Blume (eds), *The New Palgrave: Dictionary of Economics*, 2nd edn, 8 vols (Houndmills: Macmillan, 2008), vol. 6, pp. 565–70.

Boyer, E. L., *Scholarship Reconsidered: Priorities of the Professoriate* (New York: The Carnegie Foundation for the Advancement of Teaching, 1990).

Broadman, H. G., 'Reducing Structural Dominance and Entry Barriers in Russian Industry', *Review of Industrial Organization*, 17 (2000), pp. 155–76.

Brown, W. O. Jr, 'Faculty Participation in University Governance and the Effects on University Performance', *Journal of Economic Behavior and Organization*, 44 (2001), pp. 129–43.

Bruno, R. L., M. Bytchkova and S. Estrin, 'Institutional Determinants of New Firm Entry in Russia: A Cross-Regional Analysis', *Review of Economics and Statistics*, 95 (2013), pp. 1740–9.

Brym, R., L. Roberts and J. Lie, 'Networks, Groups, Bureaucracies, and Societies', in R. Brym (ed.), *New Society*, 7th edn (Toronto: Nelson Education), ch. 21, at http://www.society-inquestion7e.nelson.com/instructor [accessed 11 March 2014].

Buchanan, J. M., 'Rent-Seeking and Profit Seeking', in J. M. Buchanan, R. D. Tollison and G. Tullock (eds), *Toward a Theory of the Rent-Seeking Society* (College Station, TX: Texas A & M University Press, 1980), pp. 3–15.

Burt, R., 'The Social Structure of Competition', in N. Nohria and R. Eccles (eds), *Networks and Organizations: Structure, Form, and Action* (Boston, MA: Harvard Business School Press, 1992), pp. 56–90.

Burton, D. M., 'Revisiting Internal Labour Markets', in P. Osterman (ed.), *Economy in Society: Essays in Honor of Michael J. Piore* (Cambridge, MA: The MIT Press, 2013), pp. 11–42.

Cabral, L. M. B., 'Barriers to Entry', in S. N. Durlauf and L. E. Blume (eds), *The New Palgrave: Dictionary of Economics*, 2nd edn, 8 vols (Houndmills: Macmillan, 2008), vol. 1, pp. 382–4.

Callon, M., 'From Science as an Economic Activity to Socioeconomics of Scientific Research: The Dynamics of Emerged and Consolidated Techno-economic Networks', in P. Mirowski and E.-M. Sent (eds), *Science Bought and Sold: Essays in the Economics of Science* (Chicago, IL: The University of Chicago Press, 2002), pp. 277–317.

Canadian Association of University Teachers (CAUT), 'CAUT Almanac of Post-Secondary Education in Canada, 2008–2009' (Ottawa, 2009).

—, 'CAUT Almanac of Post-Secondary Education in Canada, 2012–2013' (Ottawa, 2013).

Carnegie, G. D. and J. Tuck, 'Understanding the ABC of University Governance', *Australian Journal of Public Administration*, 69 (2010), pp. 431–41.

Castiglione, C., Y. Gorbunova, D. Infante and J. Smirnova, 'FDI Determinants in an Idiosyncratic Country: A Reappraisal over the Russian Regions during Transition Years', *Communist and Post-Communist Studies*, 45 (2012), pp. 1–10.

Chandler, A., *The Visible Hand: The Managerial Revolution in American Business* (Cambridge, MA: Harvard University Press, 1977).

Chase, S., 'Tories Plan "Buy Canada" Military Budget', *Globe and Mail*, 24 September 2012.

Coase, R. H., 'The Nature of the Firm', *Economica*, new series, 4 (1937), pp. 386–405.

Cole, B. S. and R. G. Lewis, 'Court Cases and Judicial Opinions Related to Gatekeeping in Colleges, Universities, and Professional Schools', in P. Gibbs and E. H. Blakely (eds), *Gatekeeping in BSW Programs* (New York: Columbia University Press, 2000), pp. 212–35.

Coleman, J. S., *Foundations of Social Theory* (Cambridge, MA, and London: The Belknap Press of Harvard University Press, 1990).

Collins, R., *The Sociology of Philosophies: A Global Theory of Intellectual Change* (Cambridge, MA: The Belknap Press of Harvard University Press, 1998).

Commons, J. R., 'Institutional Economics', *American Economic Review*, 21 (1931), pp. 648–57.

—, *Legal Foundations of Capitalism* (1924; Madison, WI: The University of Wisconsin Press, 1959).

Congleton, R. D., 'On the Political Economy of the Financial Crisis and Bailout of 2008–2009', *Public Choice*, 140 (2009), pp. 287–317.

—, 'On the Political Economy and Limits of Crisis Insurance: The Case of the 2008–11 Bailouts', *Public Choice*, 150 (2012), pp. 399–423.

Cooter, R. D., 'Coase Theorem', in J. Eatwell, M. Milgate and P. Newman (eds), *The New Palgrave: A Dictionary of Economics*, 1st edn, 4 vols (London: Macmillan, 1987), vol. 1, pp. 457–60.

Cox, A., 'Business Relationship Alignment: On the Commensurability of Value Capture and Mutuality in Buyer and Supplier Exchange', *Supply Chain Management: An International Journal*, 9 (2004), pp. 410–20.

Christensen, T., 'University Governance Reforms: Potential Problems of More Autonomy?', *Higher Education*, 62 (2011), pp. 503–17.

Crossland, C. and D. C. Hambrick, 'Differences in Managerial Discretion Across Countries: How Nation-Level Institutions Affect the Degree to which CEOs Matter', *Strategic Management Journal*, 32 (2011), pp. 797–819.

Cunningham, B. M., 'Faculty: Thy Administrator's Keeper? Some Evidence', *Economics of Education Review*, 28 (2009), pp. 444–53.

Dasgupta, P. and P. A. David, 'Toward a New Economics of Science' (1994), in P. Mirowski and E.-M. Sent (eds), *Science Bought and Sold: Essays in the Economics of Science* (Chicago, IL: The University of Chicago Press, 2002), pp. 219–48.

Dean, M., 'Three Conceptions of the Relationship between Power and Liberty', in S. R. Clegg and M. Haugaard (eds), *The Sage Handbook of Power* (Los Angeles, CA: Sage, 2009), pp. 177–93.

De Boer, H., J. Huisman and C. Meister-Scheytt,'Supervision in "Modern" University Governance: Boards under Scrutiny', *Studies in Higher Education*, 35 (2010), pp. 317–33.

Deleuze, G., 'Les intellectuels et le pouvoir: Entretien entre Michel Foucault et Gilles Deleuze', *L'Arc*, 49 (1972), pp. 3–10.

De Soto, H., *The Other Path: The Economic Answer to Terrorism* (1989; New York: Basic Books, 2005).

Department of Justice of Canada. Mandate and Strategic Outcomes, at http://www.justice. gc.ca/eng/abt-apd/mandat/index.html [accessed 17 June 2013].

Djankov, S., R. La Porta, F. Lopez-de-Silanes and A. Shleifer, 'The Regulation of Entry', *Quarterly Journal of Economics*, 117 (2002), pp. 1–37.

Doeringer, P. B. and M. J. Piore, *Internal Labour Markets and Manpower Analysis* (Cambridge, MA: Harvard University and Massachusetts Institute of Technology, 1970).

Dorsch, M., 'Bailout for Sale? The Vote to Save Wall Street', *Public Choice*, 155 (2013), pp. 211–28.

Dowding, K. M., *Rational Choice and Political Power* (Aldershot: Edward Elgar, 1991).

—, *Power* (Minneapolis, MN: University of Minnesota Press, 1996).

Dugger, W. M., 'Power: An Institutional Framework of Analysis', *Journal of Economic Issues*, 14 (1980), pp. 897–907.

—, 'The New Institutionalism: New but Not Institutionalist', *Journal of Economic Issues*, 24 (1990), pp. 423–31.

Eckstein, H., *Division and Cohesion in Democracy: A Study of Norway* (Princeton, NJ: Princeton University Press, 1966).

Eggertsson, T., *Economic Behavior and Institutions* (Cambridge: Cambridge University Press, 1990).

Elg, U., P. N. Ghauri and V. Tarnovskaya, 'The Role of Networks and Matching in Market Entry to Emerging Retail Markets', *International Marketing Review*, 25 (2008), pp. 674–99.

Eliaz, K. and R. Spiegler, 'Consideration Sets and Competitive Marketing', *Review of Economic Studies*, 78 (2011), pp. 235–62.

Etzioni, A., *A Comparative Analysis of Complex Organizations* (1961; New York: The Free Press, 1975).

—, 'The Need for Quality Filters in Information Systems', *Science*, new series, 171 (1971), p. 133.

—, *The Moral Dimension: Toward a New Economics* (New York: The Free Press, 1988).

Fabry, N. and S. Zeghni, 'Foreign Direct Investment in Russia: How the Investment Climate Matters', *Communist and Post-Communist Studies*, 35 (2002), pp. 289–303.

Federal State Statistics Service of the Russian Federation, *Obrazovanie v Rossii* [Education in Russia] (Moscow, 2003).

—, Struktura and osnovnye pokazateli deyatel'nosti khozyaistvuyushchikh sub'ektov za 2012 god [Structure and key parameters of operation of economic subjects in 2012], at http://www.gks.ru/free_doc/doc_2013/bul_dr/xoz-12.rar [accessed 18 April 2014].

—, *Finansy Rossii, 2012 god* [Russian Finances, 2012] (Moscow, 2012), at http://www.gks.ru/free_doc/doc_2012/fin12.rar [accessed 19 April 2014].

—, *Sostav rabotnikov, zameshchavshikh gosudarstvennye (munitsypal'nye) dolzhnosti i dolzhnosti gosudarstvennoi grazhdanskoi (munitsipal'noi) sluzhby po polu, vozrastu, stazhy raboty, obrazovaniyu* [Socio-demographic characteristics of state (municipal) employees working at state (municipal) bodies] (Moscow, 2013), at http://www.gks.ru/free_doc/doc_2013/bul_dr/goskadr_13.rar [accessed 19 April 2014].

—, *Regiony Rossii: Sotsial'no-ekonomicheskie pokazateli, 2013 god* [Regions of Russia: Socio-Economic Data, 2013] (Moscow, 2013), at http://www.gks.ru/free_doc/doc_2013/region/soc-pok.rar [accessed 18 April 2014].

—, *Regiony Rossii: Osnovnye kharakteristiki sub'ektov RF, 2013 god* [Regions of Russia: Basic Characteristics of the subjects of the Russian Federation] (Moscow, 2013), at http://www.gks.ru/free_doc/doc_2013/region/subject.rar [accessed 18 April 2014].

—, National Accounts: GDP annual growth rates, at http://www.gks.ru/free_doc/new_site/vvp/tab3.xls [accessed 17 April 2014].

Ferris, S. J. and M. McKee, 'Matching Candidates with Academic Teams: A Case for Academic Tenure', *International Journal of Law and Economics*, 25 (2005), pp. 290–310.

Fligstein, N. and L. Dauter, 'The Sociology of Markets', *Annual Review of Sociology*, 33 (2007), pp. 105–28.

Foucault, M., *Surveiller et punir: Naissance de la prison* (Paris: Gallimard, 1975).

—, *Security, Territory, Population: Lectures at the Collège de France, 1977–1978*, trans. G. Burchell (Basingstoke and New York: Palgrave Macmillan, 2007).

—, *The Government of Self and Others: Lectures at the Collège de France, 1982–1983*, trans. G. Burchell (New York: Picador/Palgrave Macmillan, 2011).

—, *The Courage of Truth (The Government of Self and Others II): Lectures at the Collège de France, 1983–1984*, trans. G. Burchell (New York: Palgrave Macmillan, 2011).

Fredricksen, L. 'The Fraser Institute Annual Survey of Mining Companies', *Applied Earth Science (Trans. Inst. Min. Metall. B)*, 111 (2002), pp. B171–B176.

Galbraith, J. K., *The New Industrial State* (London: H. Hamilton, 1967).

—, *Anatomy of Power* (Boston, MA: Houghton Mifflin, 1983).

George, J. P., 'Access to Justice, Costs and Legal Aid', *American Journal of Comparative Law*, 54 (2006), pp. 293–315.

Gibbs, P. and H. J. Macy, 'Introduction: The Arena of Gatekeeping', in P. Gibbs and E. H. Blakely (eds), *Gatekeeping in BSW Programs* (New York: Columbia University Press, 2000), pp. 3–21.

Gintis, H., *Game Theory Evolving: A Problem-Centered Introduction to Modeling Strategic Interactions* (Princeton, NJ: Princeton University Press, 2000).

Glöckner, A. and T. Betsch, 'The Empirical Content of Theories in Judgment and Decision Making: Shortcomings and Remedies', *Judgment and Decision Making*, 6 (2011), pp. 711–21.

Göhler, G., '"Power to" and "Power over"', in S. R. Clegg and M. Haugaard (eds), *The Sage Handbook of Power* (Los Angeles, CA: Sage, 2009), pp. 27–39.

Goldsmith, W., 'Harvard has Lowest Percentage of Tenure-Track Profs in Ivies', *Harvard Crimson*, 13 December 2006.

Gould, T. H., *Do We Still Need Peer Review? An Argument for Change* (Lanham, MA: Scarecrow Press, 2013).

Guo, Y. and A. Hu, 'The Administrative Monopoly in China's Economic Transition', *Communist and Post-Communist Studies*, 37 (2004), pp. 165–280.

Haeck, C. and F. Verboven, 'The Internal Economics of a University: Evidence from Personnel Data', *Journal of Labour Economics*, 30 (2012), pp. 591–626.

Hamilton, S. F., D. L. Sunding and D. Zilberman, 'Public Goods and the Value of Product Quality Regulations: The Case of Food Safety', *Journal of Public Economics*, 87 (2003), pp. 799–817.

Hannaford-Agor, P. and N. Mott, 'Research on Self-Represented Litigation: Preliminary Results and Methodological Considerations', *Justice System Journal*, 24 (2003), pp. 163–81.

Harnad, S. J., 'The Invisible Hand of Peer Review' (2000), in D. Shatz, *Peer Review: A Critical Inquiry* (Lanham, MA: Rowman & Littlefield Publishers, 2004), pp. 235–42.

Harsanyi, J., 'The Dimension and Measurement of Social Power' (1962), in K. W. Rothschild (ed.), *Power in Economics: Selected Readings* (Harmondsworth: Penguin, 1971), pp. 77–96.

Heisz, A., 'The Evolution of Job Stability in Canada: Trends and Comparisons to US Results', *Canadian Journal of Economics*, 38 (2005), pp. 105–27.

Herbener, J. M., 'The Rise and Fall of the Japanese Miracle', *Mises Daily* (20 September 1990), at http://mises.org/story/298 [accessed 10 October 2012].

Hodgson, G. M., 'On the Institutional Foundations of Law: The Insufficiency of Custom and Private Ordering', *Journal of Economic Issues*, 43 (2009), pp. 143–66.

Hofstede, G., *Cultures and Organizations: Software of the Mind* (London: McGraw-Hill Book Company, 1991).

—, 'What did GLOBE really Measure? Researchers' Minds versus Respondents' Minds', *Journal of International Business Studies*, 37 (2006), pp. 882–96.

Holt, P. F. R. and D. T. Greenwood, 'Negative Trickle-Down and the Financial Crisis of 2008', *Journal of Economic Issues*, 46 (2012), pp. 363–70.

Howard, R. D., G. W. McLaughlin, W. E. Knight and Associates, *The Handbook of Institutional Research* (San Francisco, CA: Jossey-Bass, 2012).

Hutchings, P., M. T. Huber and A. Ciccone, *The Scholarship of Teaching and Learning Reconsidered* (San Francisco, CA: Jossey-Bass: A Wiley Imprint and Stanford, CA: The Carnegie Foundation for the Advancement of Teaching, 2011).

International Centre for Prison Studies. World Prison Brief, at http://www.prisonstudies.org/info/worldbrief/wpb_stats.php?area=all&category=wb_poprate [accessed 17 June 2013].

Ishida, H., Kuo-Hsien-Su and S. Spilerman, 'Models of Career Advancement in Organizations', *European Sociological Review*, 18 (2002), pp. 179–98.

Jensen, M. and W. Meckling, 'Theory of the Firm: Managerial Behavior, Agency Costs and Ownership Structure', *Journal of Financial Economics*, 3 (1976), pp. 305–60.

Jick, T. D., 'Mixing Qualitative and Quantitative Methods: Triangulation in Action', *Administrative Science Quarterly*, 24 (1979), pp. 602–11.

Kagel, J. H. and A. E. Roth (eds), *The Handbook of Experimental Economics* (Princeton, NJ: Princeton University Press, 1995).

Kaldor, N., 'Speculation and Economic Stability', *Review of Economic Studies*, 7 (1939), pp. 1–27.

Kamensky, J. M., 'The Obama Performance Approach: A Midterm Snapshot', *Public Performance and Management Review*, 35 (2011), pp. 133–48.

Karhunen, P. and S. Ledyaeva, 'Corruption Distance, Anti-corruption Laws and International Ownership Strategies in Russia', *Journal of International Management*, 18 (2012), pp. 196–208.

Kelly, T., 'Law, Culture and Access to Justice under the Palestinian National Authority', *Development and Change*, 36 (2005), pp. 865–86.

Keynes, J. M., *The General Theory of Employment Interest and Money* (1936; London: Macmillan, 1964).

Killian, J. and N. Eklund, *Handbook of Administrative Reform: An International Perspective* (Boca Raton, FL: CRC Press, 2008).

Klein, P. A., 'Power and Economic Performance: The Institutionalist View', *Journal of Economic Issues*, 21 (1987), pp. 1341–77.

Knight, F. H., *Risk, Uncertainty, and Profit* (1921; New York: Augustus M. Kelley, 1964).

Kreps, D., 'Corporate Culture and Economic Theory', in J. Alt and K. Shepsle (eds), *Perspectives on Positive Political Economy* (Cambridge: Cambridge University Press, 1990), pp. 90–143.

Kretek, P. M., Ž. Dragšić and B. M. Kehm, 'Transformation of University Governance: On the Role of University Board Members', *Higher Education*, 65 (2013), pp. 39–58.

Kritzer, H. M., 'To Lawyer or Not to Lawyer: *Is* that the Question?', *Journal of Empirical Legal Studies*, 5 (2008), pp. 875–906.

Krugman, P., *The Return of Depression Economics and the Crisis of 2008* (New York: W. W. Norton, 2009).

—, 'How Did Economists Get it So Wrong?', *New York Times*, 2 September 2009, p. 36, at http://www.nytimes.com/2009/09/06/magazine/06Economic-t.html?_r=3&pagewanted=all [accessed 16 April 2014].

Lamont, M., *How Professors Think: Inside the Curious World of Academic Judgment* (Cambridge, MA: Harvard University Press, 2009).

Lawson, T., *Economics and Reality* (London and New York: Routledge, 1997).

Lewis, L. S., *When Power Corrupts: Academic Governing Boards in the Shadow of Adelphi Case* (New Brunswick, NJ: Transaction Publishers, 2000).

Ledyaev, V. G., *Power: A Conceptual Analysis* (Commack, NY: Nova Science Publishers, 1997).

Ledyaeva, S., P. Karhunen and R. Kosonen, 'The Global Economic Crisis and Foreign Investment in Russia from the EU: Empirical Evidence from Firm-Level Data', *Eurasian Geography and Economics*, 53 (2012), pp. 772–89.

Libman, A., 'Democracy, Size of Bureaucracy, and Economic Growth: Evidence from Russian Regions', *Empirical Economics*, 43 (2012), pp. 1321–52.

—, 'Natural Resources and Sub-National Economic Performance: Does Sub-National Democracy Matter?', *Energy Economics*, 37 (2013), pp. 82–99.

— and L. P. Feld, 'Strategic Tax Collection and Fiscal Decentralization: The Case of Russia', *German Economic Review*, 14 (2013), pp. 449–82.

Lovett, F., *A General Theory of Domination and Justice* (Oxford: Oxford University Press, 2010).

Lukes, S., 'Power and Agency', *British Journal of Sociology*, 53 (2002), pp. 491–6.

—, *Power: A Radical View* (1974; Houndmills: Palgrave Macmillan, 2005).

Ma, A. and B. Norwich, 'Triangulation and Theoretical Understanding', *International Journal of Social Research Methodology*, 10 (2007), pp. 173–84.

Macdonald, S. and C. Williams, 'Beyond the Boundary: An Information Perspective on the Role of the Gatekeeper in the Organization', *Journal of Product Innovation Management*, 10 (1993), pp. 417–27.

—, 'The Survival of the Gatekeeper', *Research Policy*, 23 (1994), pp. 123–32.

McPherson, M. S. and M. O. Shapiro, 'Tenure Issues in Higher Education', *Journal of Economic Perspectives*, 13 (1999), pp. 85–98.

Makarenko, V. P., *Politicheskaya kontseptologiya: obzor povestki dnya* [Political concepts: an overview of the research agenda] (Moscow: Praxis, 2005).

Malia, M., *Russia under Western Eyes: From the Bronze Horseman to the Lenin Mausoleum* (Cambridge, MA: The Belknap Press of Harvard University Press, 1999).

Mann, M., *The Sources of Social Power*, 4 vols (Cambridge: Cambridge University Press, 1986–2013).

Marshall, A., *Principles of Economics*, 8th edn (1890; London: Macmillan, 1920).

Marx, K., *Capital*, trans. B. Fowkes, 3 vols (1867; New York: Vintage Books, 1977), vol. 1.

Matza, D., *Delinquency and Drift* (1964; New Brunswick, NJ: Transaction Publishers, 1990).

Mau, V. and K. Yanovskiy, 'Political and Legal Factors of Economic Growth in Russian Regions', *Post-Communist Economies*, 14 (2002), pp. 321–39.

Medema, S., 'The Trial of Homo Economicus: What Law and Economics Tells us about the Development of Economic Imperialism', *New Economics and its History: History of Political, Economy Annual Supplement*, 29 (1997), pp. 122–42.

Memorial University of Newfoundland (MUN), 'Collective Agreement between MUN and MUN Faculty Association', 26 February 2010–31 August 2013, at http://www.mun.ca/munfa/CA201013.htm [accessed 29 June 2014].

—, 'President's Report "Great Minds Think Differently"' (2011), at http://www.mun.ca/2011report/ [accessed 13 June 2014].

Ménard, C., 'Transaction Cost Economics: From the Coase Theorem to Empirical Studies', in A. Oleinik (ed.), *The Institutional Economics of Russia's Transformation* (Aldershot: Ashgate, 2005), pp. 45–64.

—, 'Theory of Organizations: The Diversity of Arrangements in a Developed Market Economy', in A. Oleinik (ed.), *The Institutional Economics of Russia's Transformation* (Aldershot: Ashgate, 2005), pp. 88–111.

Merton, R. K., 'Bureaucratic Structure and Personality', *Social Forces*, 18 (1940), pp. 560–8.

Milgrom, P., D. C. North and B. Weingast, 'The Role of Institutions in the Revival of Trade: The Law Merchant, Private Judges, and the Champaign Fairs', *Economics and Politics*, 2 (1990), pp. 1–23.

Mills, C. W., *The Power Elite* (New York: Oxford University Press, 1957).

Ministry of Education of the Russian Federation, 'Polozhenie o poryadke zameshcheniya dolzhnostei naugno-pedagogicheskikh rabotnikov v vyshem uchebnom zavedenii Rossiiskoi Federatsii' enacted on 26 November 2006 [Principles of the appointment to research and teaching positions at the universities in the Russian Federation].

Ministry of Finance of the Russian Federation, Struktura postuplenii v konsolidirovannyi byudzhet RF [Structure of revenues of the consolidated budget of the Russian Federation], at http://info.minfin.ru/kons_doh.php [accessed 18 April 2014].

Mitra, A. and Lynch, J. G. Jr, 'Toward a Reconciliation of Market Power and Information Theories of Advertising Effects on Price Elasticity', *Journal of Consumer Research*, 21 (1995), pp. 644–59.

Mixon, F. G. Jr and R. W. McKenzie, 'Managerial Tenure under Private and Government Ownership: The Case of Higher Education', *Economics of Education Review*, 18 (1999), pp. 51–8.

Moorhead, R. and P. Pleasence, 'Access to Justice after Universalism: Introduction', *Journal of Law and Society*, 30 (2003), pp. 1–10.

Morriss, P., *Power: A Philosophical Analysis* (New York: St Martin's Press, 1987).

Mueller, D. C., *Public Choice III* (Cambridge: Cambridge University Press, 2003).

Musselin, C., 'How Peer Review Empowers the Academic Profession and University Managers: Changes in Relationships between the State, Universities and the Professoriate', *Research Policy*, 42 (2013), pp. 1165–73.

— and F. Pigeyre, 'Les effets des mécanismes du recrutement collégial sur la discrimination: le cas des recrutements universitaires', *Sociologie du travail*, 50 (2008), pp. 48–70.

Newman, W. L., *Social Research Methods: Qualitative and Quantitative Approaches*, 6th edn (Boston, MA: Allyn & Bacon, 2006).

Ngo, T.-W., 'Rent-Seeking and Economic Governance in the Structural Nexus of Corruption in China', *Crime, Law and Social Change*, 49 (2008), pp. 27–44.

Niskanen, W. A., 'Bureaucrats and Politicians', *Journal of Law and Economics*, 18 (1975), pp. 617–43.

North, D. C., *Structure and Change in Economic History* (New York: W. W. Norton, 1981).

—, 'Three Approaches to the Study of Institutions', in D. C. Colander (ed.), *Neoclassical Political Economy: The Analysis of Rent-Seeking and DUP Activities* (Cambridge, MA: Ballinger, 1984), pp. 33–40.

Nye, J. S., *The Future of Power* (New York: Public Affairs, 2011).

Oleinik, A., 'Mixing Quantitative and Qualitative Content Analysis: Triangulation at Work', *Quality & Quantity*, 45 (2010), pp. 859–73.

—, *Market as a Weapon: The Socio-Economic Machinery of Dominance in Russia* (New Brunswick, NJ: Transaction Publishers, 2011).

—, *Knowledge and Networking: On Communication in the Social Sciences* (New Brunswick, NJ: Transaction Publishers, 2014).

—, 'Sbor, agregirovanie i obrabotka kachestvennykh dannykh' [Collection, aggregation and processing of qualitative data], *SOTsIS – Sotsiologicheskie Issledovaniya*, 5 (2014), pp. 121–31.

Olson, M., *Power and Prosperity: Outgrowing Communist and Capitalist Dictatorships* (New York: Basic Books, 2000).

Osborne, J. W., 'Best Practices in Data Transformation: The Overlooked Effect of Minimal Values', in J. W. Osborne (ed.), *Best Practices in Quantitative Methods* (Thousand Oaks, CA: Sage, 2008), pp. 197–204.

Osterman, P. and D. M. Burton, 'Ports and Ladders: The Nature and Relevance of Internal Labour Markets in a Changing World', in S. Ackroyd, R. Batt, P. Thompson and P. S. Tolbert (eds), *The Oxford Handbook of Work and Organization* (Oxford: Oxford University Press, 2005), pp. 425–45.

Palermo, G., 'Economic Power and the Firm in New Institutional Economics: Two Conflicting Problems', *Journal of Economic Issues*, 34 (2000), pp. 573–601.

Paterson, A., L. Farmer, F. Stephen and J. Love, 'Competition and the Market for Legal Services', *Journal of Law and Society*, 15 (1988), pp. 361–73.

Pen, J. 'Bilateral Monopoly, Bargaining and the Concept of Economic Power' (1959), in K. W. Rothschild (ed.), *Power in Economics: Selected Readings* (Harmondsworth: Penguin, 1971), pp. 97–115.

Peterbugskaya Politika Foundation, 13-i reiting politicheskoi vyzhivaemosti gubernatorov [13th ranking of governors' political survival] (2013), at http://www.fpp.spb.ru/rate13.php [accessed 18 April 2014].

Peterson, W. C., 'Market Power: The Missing Element in Keynesian Economics', *Journal of Economic Issues*, 23 (1989), pp. 379–91.

Pindyck, R. S. and D. L. Rubinfeld, *Microeconomics*, 5th edn (Upper Saddle River, NJ: Prentice Hall, 2001).

Polanyi, K., *The Great Transformation: The Political and Economic Origins of Our Time* (1944; Boston, MA: Beacon Press, 1957).

Polanyi, M., 'The Republic of Science: Its Political and Economic Theory' (1969), in P. Mirowski and E.-M. Sent (eds), *Science Bought and Sold: Essays in the Economics of Science* (Chicago, IL: The University of Chicago Press, 2002), pp. 465–85.

Popper, K., *Conjectures and Refutations* (London: Routledge and Kegan Paul, 1963).

—, *The Logic of Scientific Discovery*, 3rd edn (London: Hutchinson, 1968).

—, *The Two Fundamental Problems of the Theory of Knowledge*, trans. A. Pickel and J. Kinory (1978; Abington: Routledge, 2009).

Putterman, L., 'The Firm as Association versus the Firm as Commodity: Efficiency, Rights and Ownership', *Economics and Philosophy*, 4 (1988), pp. 243–66.

Reisinger, W. M., 'Congruency Theory as a Perspective on Russian Politics', in H. Eckstein, F. J. Fleron, E. P. Hoffmann and W. M. Reisinger (with R. Ahl, R. Bova and P. Roeder), *Can Democracy Take Root in Post-Soviet Russia? Exploration in State–Society Relations* (Lanham, MA: Rowman & Littlefield, 1998), pp. 151–62.

Reporters without Borders, *World Press Freedom Index 2014* (2014), at https://rsf.org/index2014/en-index2014.php [accessed 17 April 2014].

Rhode, D. L., *Access to Justice* (New York: Oxford University Press, 2004).

Robertson, D. H., *Control of Industry: Cambridge Economic Handbooks IV* (London: Nisbet, 1923).

Roth, W.-M., 'Editorial Power/Authorial Suffering', *Research in Science Education*, 32 (2002), pp. 215–40.

Rothschild, K. W., 'New Worlds – New Approaches: A Note on Future Research Strategies', *Kyklos*, 58 (2005), pp. 439–47.

Russian Federal Treasury, Otchet ob ispolnenii byudzhetov sub'ektov RF i mestnykh byudzhetov [Report on the Execution of the Budgets of the Subjects of the Russian Federation and the Local Budgets], at http://www.roskazna.ru/byudzhetov-subektov-rf-i-mestnykh-byudzhetov/doc/Otch_2012.rar [accessed 18 April 2014].

—, Otchet ob ispolnenii konsolidirovannogo byudzheta sub'ekta RF i byudzheta territorial'nogo gosudarstvennogo vnebyudzhetnogo fonda za 2012 god [Report on the Execution of the Consolidated Budget of the Subject of the Russian Federation and the Budget of the Regional State Social Security Fund], at http://www.roskazna.ru/byudzhetov-subektov-rf-i-mestnykh-byudzhetov/doc/Otch_2012.rar [accessed 18 April 2014].

Sack, R. D., *Human Territoriality: Its Theory and History* (Cambridge: Cambridge University Press, 1986).

Sala-I-Martin, X. X., 'I Just Ran Two Million Regressions', *American Economic Review*, 87 (1997), pp. 178–83.

Sandler, T., *Collective Action: Theory and Applications* (Ann Arbor, MI: The University of Michigan Press, 1992).

Schelling, T. S., *The Strategy of Conflict* (Cambridge, MA: Harvard University Press, 1960).

Schutz, E., 'Markets and Power', *Journal of Economic Issues*, 29 (1995), pp. 1147–70.

Scott, J., *Power* (Cambridge: Polity Press, 2001).

Shatz, D., *Peer Review: A Critical Inquiry* (Lanham, MA: Rowman & Littlefield Publishers, 2004).

Simmel, G., *The Philosophy of Money*, trans. T. Bottomore and D. Frisby (1970; London: Routledge & Kegan Paul, 1978).

Simon, H. A., 'A Formal Theory of the Employment Relationship', *Econometrica*, 19 (1951), pp. 293–305.

—, 'Rationality as Process and as Product of Thought', *American Economic Review*, 68 (1978), pp. 1–16.

Skopol, T. and K. Finegold, 'State Capacity and Economic Intervention in the Early New Deal' (1982), in J. Scott (ed.), *Power: Critical Concepts*, 3 vols (London: Routledge, 1994), vol. 3, pp. 370–92.

Smith, A., *Inquiry into the Nature and Causes of the Wealth of Nations* (1776; New York: Modern Library, 1937).

Social Sciences and Humanities Research Council, Memorandum of Understanding 'Roles and Responsibilities in the Management of Federal Grants and Awards' (2007), at http://www.nserc-crsng.gc.ca/nserc-crsng/policies-politiques/mouroles-protocolroles/index_eng.asp [accessed 27 June 2014].

Solari, S., 'The "Practical Reason" of Reformers: Proudhon vs. Institutionalism', *Journal of Economic Issues*, 46 (2012), pp. 227–40.

Sommerlad, H., 'Some Reflections on the Relationship between Citizenship, Access to Justice, and the Reform of Legal Aid', *Journal of Law and Society*, 31 (2004), pp. 345–68.

Spears, D. 'Intertemporal Bounded Rationality as Consideration Sets with Contraction Consistency', *B.E. Journal of Theoretical Economics*, 11:1 (2011), Article 12.

Spencer, M. and J. Spencer, 'Coping with *Conway* v. *Rimmer* [1968] AC 910: How Civil Servants Control Access to Justice', *Journal of Law and Society*, 37 (2010), pp. 387–411.

Stigler, G. J., 'The Theory of Economic Regulation', *Bell Journal of Economics and Management Science*, 2 (1971), pp. 3–21.

Stiglitz, J. E., 'Principal and Agent', in J. Eatwell, M. Milgate and P. Newman (eds), *The New Palgrave: A Dictionary of Economics*, 4 vols, 1st edn (London: Macmillan), vol. 3, pp. 966–71.

Swedberg, R., *Principles of Economic Sociology* (Princeton, NJ: Princeton University Press, 2003).

Taber, J., 'Ottawa Hails Buy American Deal', *Globe and Mail*, 5 February 2010.

Taylor, K. and K. Svechnikova, *What Does it Cost to Access Justice in Canada? How Much is "Too Much"? And How Do We Know?* (Edmonton: The Canadian Forum on Civil Justice, 2010).

Tilly, C., 'Contentious Repertoires in Great Britain, 1758–1834', in M. Traugott (ed.), *Repertoires and Cycles of Collective Action* (Durham, NC: Duke University Press, 1995), pp. 15–42.

Traugott, M., 'Barricades as Repertoire: Continuities and Discontinuities in the History of French Contention', *Social Science History*, 17 (1993), pp. 309–23.

Tullock, G., 'The Backward Society: Static Inefficiency, Rent Seeking, and the Rule of Law', in J. M. Buchanan and R. D. Tollison (eds), *The Theory of Public Choice II* (Ann Arbor, MI: The University of Michigan Press, 1984), pp. 224–37.

—, *Public Goods, Redistribution and Rent Seeking* (Cheltenham: Edward Elgar, 2005).

Turk, A. T., 'Law as a Weapon in Social Conflict', *Social Problems*, 23 (1976), pp. 276–91.

University of Mississippi, 'Tenure Policies and Procedures' (2013), at https://secure4.olemiss.edu/umpolicyopen/GetPdfActive?pol=10647010&ver=active&file=10647010_active_20050330.pdf [accessed 29 June 2014].

US Department of Defense, 'News Briefing' of 12 February 2002, at http://www.defense.gov/Transcripts/Transcript.aspx?TranscriptID=2636 [accessed 15 April 2014].

Veblen, T., *The Theory of the Leisure Class: An Economic Study of Institutions* (1899; Don Mills, ON: Dover Publications, 1994).

—, *Imperial Germany and Industrial Revolution* (1915; New York: The Viking Press, 1939).

—, *The Higher Learning in America: A Memorandum on the Conduct of Universities by Business Men* (1918; New York: Sagamore Press, 1957).

Venard, B. 'Organizational Isomorphism and Corruption: An Empirical Research in Russia', *Journal of Business Ethics*, 89 (2008), pp. 59–76.

Waller, W., 'John Kenneth Galbraith: Cultural Theorist of Consumption and Power', *Journal of Economic Issues*, 42 (2008), pp. 13–24.

Walmsley, R., *World Prison Population List*, 10th edn (London: International Centre for Prison Studies, 2013), at http://www.prisonstudies.org/sites/prisonstudies.org/files/resources/downloads/wppl_10.pdf [accessed 17 April 2014].

Warner R. M., *Applied Statistics: From Bivariate through Multivariate Techniques* (Thousand Oaks, CA: Sage, 2008).

Wartenberg, T. E., *The Forms of Power: From Domination to Transformation* (Philadelphia, PA: Temple University Press, 1990).

Weber, M., *Economy and Society: An Outline of Interpretative Sociology*, ed. R. Guenther and C. Wittich, 2 vols (1922; New York: Bedminster Press, 1968).

Wedig, G. J., 'The Value of Consumer Choice and the Decline in HMO Enrollments', *Economic Inquiry*, 51 (2013), pp. 1066–86.

Weintraub, R. E., 'Neoclassical Economics', *The Concise Encyclopedia of Economics* (2002), at http://www.econlib.org/library/Enc1/NeoclassicalEconomics.html [accessed 10 March 2014].

Welch, C. and I. Wilkinson, 'Network Perspectives on Interfirm Conflict: Reassessing a Critical Case in International Business', *Journal of Business Research*, 58 (2005), pp. 205–213.

Wettersten, J. 'Philosophical Anthropology Can Help Social Scientists Learn from Empirical Tests', *Journal for the Theory of Social Behaviour*, 37 (2007), pp. 295–318.

Williamson, O. E., *Markets and Hierarchies, Analysis and Antitrust implications: A Study in the Economics of Internal Organization* (New York: The Free Press, 1975).

—, *The Economic Institutions of Capitalism: Firms, Markets, Relational Contracting* (New York: The Free Press, 1985).

—, 'Comparative Economic Organization: The Analysis of Discrete Structural Alternatives', *Administrative Science Quarterly*, 36 (1991), pp. 269–96.

Wilson, A., *Virtual Politics: Faking Democracy in the Post-Soviet World* (New Haven, CT and London: Yale University Press, 2005).

World Bank, World Development Indicators, at http://data.worldbank.org/data-catalog/world-development-indicators [accessed 17 April 2014].

—, Doing Business Project, at http://www.doingbusiness.org/ [accessed 17 April 2014].

Wrong, D. H., *Power: Its Forms, Bases and Uses* (New York: Harper Colophon Books, 1980).

Yefimov, V., *Economie institutionnelle des transformations agraires en Russie* (Paris: L'Harmattan, 2003).

Zaheer, A. and N. Venkatraman, 'Determinants of Electronic Integration in the Insurance Industry: An Empirical Test', *Management Science*, 40 (1994), pp. 549–66.

Zorza, R., 'Access to Justice: The Emerging Consensus and Some Questions and Implications', *Judicature*, 94 (2011), pp. 156–67.

NOTES

1 Visible and Invisible Hands of Power: Theoretical Preliminaries

1. Steven Lukes, namely, starts his analysis of power by asking what would have happened in a relationship if there were no application of power by one of the parties involved (S. Lukes, *Power: A Radical View* (1974; Houndmills: Palgrave Macmillan, 2005), pp. 43–4; see Chapter 2, Section 4, endnote 2). Peter Morriss offers the following definition of counterfactual thinking: 'The counterfactual asserts that we are to pretend things are different from the way we know they are ("if Verdi and Berlioz were compatriots"), and then asserts a conclusion ("they would be Italian") that follows if, and only if, we pretend things are different in some specific way, where the counterfactual itself is completely silent about whether this is the right way of pretending things are different' (P. Morriss, *Power: A Philosophical Analysis* (New York: St Martin's Press, 1987), p. 73).
2. T. E. Wartenberg, *The Forms of Power: From Domination to Transformation* (Philadelphia, PA: Temple University Press, 1990), p. 12; V. G. Ledyaev, *Power: A Conceptual Analysis* (Commack, NY: Nova Science Publishers, 1997), p. x; V. P. Makarenko, *Politicheskaya kontseptologiya: obzor povestki dnya* [Political concepts: an overview of the research agenda] (Moscow: Praxis, 2005), C. 73; F. Lovett, *A General Theory of Domination and Justice* (Oxford: Oxford University Press, 2010), p. 65; J. S. Nye, *The Future of Power* (New York: Public Affairs, 2011), p. 5.
3. M. Weber, *Economy and Society: An Outline of Interpretative Sociology*, ed. R. Guenther and C. Wittich, 2 vols (1922; New York: Bedminster Press, 1968), vol. 1, p. 53.
4. 'She' is used throughout this book instead of the rather awkward constructions 'he/she' or 's/he'.
5. Several taxonomies will be discussed later in this book, namely Lukes's three dimensions of power (in Chapter 2, Section 4), Amitai Etzioni's three types of power within organizations (in this chapter, Section 3), and Nye's three types of power in politics (in this chapter, Section 2). Among the other approaches are Weber's typology of legitimate power (Weber, *Economy and Society*, vol. 1, p. 215), Thomas Mann's classification of sources of power (M. Mann, *The Sources of Social Power: A History of Power from the Beginning to A. D. 1760*, 4 vols (Cambridge: Cambridge University Press, 1986), vol. 1, p. 2) and my two-dimensional taxonomy of power built with the help of two variables, the technique for imposing will and the type of social action (A. Oleinik, *Market as a Weapon: The Socio-Economic Machinery of Dominance in Russia* (New Brunswick, NJ: Transaction Publishers, 2011), ch. 2.

6.   R. Collins, *The Sociology of Philosophies: A Global Theory of Intellectual Change* (Cambridge, MA: The Belknap Press of Harvard University Press, 1998), p. 535. According to this author, the two sufficient components are research technology and mathematical modelling.

7.   G. Hofstede, *Cultures and Organizations: Software of the Mind* (London: McGraw-Hill Book Company, 1991), p. 28.

8.   The data were collected by surveying 'matched groups of employees in seven occupational categories, two managerial and five non-managerial', working at the branches of an international company, IBM, in various countries (G. Hofstede, 'What did GLOBE really Measure? Researchers' Minds versus Respondents' Minds', *Journal of International Business Studies*, 37 (2006), pp. 882–96, on p. 884).

9.   H. Eckstein, *Division and Cohesion in Democracy: A Study of Norway* (Princeton, NJ: Princeton University Press, 1966), pp. 240–1.

10. 'It takes enormous work to measure the concepts of congruence theory' (W. M. Reisinger, 'Congruency Theory as a Perspective on Russian Politics', in H. Eckstein, F. J. Fleron, E. P. Hoffmann and W. M. Reisinger (with R. Ahl, R. Bova and P. Roeder), *Can Democracy Take Root in Post-Soviet Russia? Exploration in State–Society Relations* (Lanham, MA: Rowman & Littlefield, 1998), pp. 151–62, on p. 152.

11. A. Smith, *Inquiry into the Nature and Causes of the Wealth of Nations* (1776; New York: Modern Library, 1937), book 4, ch. 2, p. 423.

12. M. Olson, *Power and Prosperity: Outgrowing Communist and Capitalist Dictatorships* (New York: Basic Books, 2000), p. 13.

13. M. Foucault *Security, Territory, Population: Lectures at the Collège de France, 1977–1978*, trans. G. Burchell (Basingstoke and New York: Palgrave Macmillan, 2007), p. 200.

14. Ledyaev, *Power*, p. 98; see also Wartenberg, *The Forms of Power*, p. 18; K. M. Dowding, *Rational Choice and Political Power* (Aldershot: Edward Elgar, 1991), ch. 4; K. M. Dowding, *Power* (Minneapolis: MN: University of Minnesota Press, 1996), ch. 1.

15. D. H. Wrong, *Power: Its Forms, Bases and Uses* (New York: Harper Colophon Books, 1980), p. 248.

16. Power is not *the* solution, however, as other solutions also exist. For instance, individuals may coordinate their actions on the basis of trust maintaining their equality. The comparison of power with trust and the other coordination devices goes beyond the specific scope of this book (see, for instance, Oleinik, *Market as a Weapon*, pp. 45–9).

17. Mann, *The Sources of Social Power*.

18. H. Arendt, *On Violence* (New York: Harcourt, Brace & World, 1969), p. 44.

19. Dowding, *Power*, p. 8.

20. Arendt, *On Violence*; see also Lukes, *Power*, p. 33; G. Göhler, '"Power to" and "Power over"', in S. R. Clegg and M. Haugaard (eds), *The Sage Handbook of Power* (Los Angeles, CA: Sage, 2009), pp. 27–39, on p. 34.

21. Wartenberg, *The Forms of Power*, p. 184.

22. Lukes, *Power*, p. 112.

23. Lovett, *General Theory of Domination and Justice*, pp. 82, 119.

24. G. Simmel, *The Philosophy of Money*, trans. T. Bottomore and D. Frisby (1970; London: Routledge & Kegan Paul, 1978), p. 209.

25. Wrong, *Power*, p. 236.

26. Simmel, *The Philosophy of Money*, p. 235.

27. Oleinik, *Market as a Weapon*, ch. 3.

28. S. Bowles and H. Gintis, 'Power', in S. N. Durlauf and L. E. Blume (eds), *The New Palgrave: Dictionary of Economics*, 8 vols, 2nd edn (Houndmills: Macmillan, 2008), vol. 6, p. 569. They also offer a broader theory of power in the market that will be discussed at length in Section 2 of Chapter 2.

29. An overview of an institutionalist take on power will be offered in Chapter 3, Section 3.

30. J. R. Commons, 'Institutional Economics', *American Economic Review*, 21 (1931), pp. 648–57, on p. 651; emphasis in the original.

31. Dowding, *Power*, p. x.

32. T. S. Schelling, *The Strategy of Conflict* (Cambridge, MA: Harvard University Press, 1960), ch. 5; Dowding, *Rational Choice and Political Power*, p. 63; Dowding, *Power*, p. 56.

33. J. Harsanyi, 'The Dimension and Measurement of Social Power' (1962), in K. W. Rothschild (ed.), *Power in Economics: Selected Readings* (Harmondsworth: Penguin, 1971), pp. 77–96, on p. 89. Game theorists formalize bargaining in the conditions of bilateral monopoly with the help of the Rubinstein bargaining model; see H. Gintis, *Game Theory Evolving: A Problem-Centered Introduction to Modeling Strategic Interactions* (Princeton, NJ: Princeton University Press, 2000), pp. 97–8.

34. Mann, *The Sources of Social Power*, p. 8.

35. K. Marx, *Capital*, trans. B. Fowkes, 3 vols (1867; New York: Vintage Books, 1977), vol. 1, p. 230.

36. Marx, *Capital*, p. 448.

37. Dowding, *Power*, p. 82.

38. Marx, *Capital*, p. 739. Contemporary Marxists and heterodox economists also agree that the capitalist has power only as long as her behaviour conforms to rules and principles embedded in the market structures. William Dugger, for instance, emphasizes the importance of primary and secondary socialization in a specific institutional environment. 'The power of corporate executives is not individual but institutional, in both its source and in its direction ... The ends of power are institutionally determined because the motives, goals, and ideals of the powerful have been learned in their role-by-role climb to the top' (W. M. Dugger, 'Power: An Institutional Framework of Analysis', *Journal of Economic Issues*, 14 (1980), pp. 897–907, on p. 904).

39. M. Foucault, *Surveiller et punir: Naissance de la prison* (Paris: Gallimard, 1975).

40. Foucault, *Security, Territory, Population*, p. 45. The notions of exit and entry control and their particularities are discussed in more detail in Chapter 2, Section 4.

41. Foucault, *Security, Territory, Population*, p. 47.

42. Foucault, *Security, Territory, Population*, p. 353.

43. Lovett, *General Theory of Domination and Justice*, p. 72; see also Lukes, *Power*, pp. 92–5. Debates as to whether the deterministic interpretation of Foucault's thought correctly captures his ideas still continue. Foucault made some statements that seem to support it, however. In an interview with Gilles Deleuze he once acknowledged that no one has power because of its diffused character (G. Deleuze, 'Les intellectuels et le pouvoir: Entretien entre Michel Foucault et Gilles Deleuze', *L'Arc*, 49 (1972), pp. 3–10).

44. S. Lukes, 'Power and Agency', *British Journal of Sociology*, 53 (2002), pp. 491–6, on p. 492; emphasis in the original.

45. 'The power elite is composed of men whose positions enable them to transcend the ordinary environments of ordinary men and women; they are in positions to make decisions having major consequences' (C. W. Mills, *The Power Elite* (New York: Oxford University Press, 1957), pp. 3–4).

46. Boris Berezovsky, a now deceased Russian mathematician and tycoon, reportedly dreamed of developing a system that would function in his interests without human input. His input would have consisted in designing a system of incentives for making other people work for him without shirking. He died before finding an opportunity to actually realize this project.

47. Weber, *Economy and Society*, vol. 1, pp. 32–4.

48. K. Polanyi, *The Great Transformation: The Political and Economic Origins of our Time* (1944; Boston, MA: Beacon Press, 1957).

49. Lukes, *Power*, p. 25.

50. 'To identify a given process as an "exercise of power", rather than as a case of structural determination, is to assume that it is *in the exerciser's or exercisers' power* to act differently' (Lukes, *Power*, p. 57).

51. Nye, *The Future of Power*, p. 54.

52. M. Foucault, *The Government of Self and Others: Lectures at the Collège de France, 1982–1983*, trans. G. Burchell (New York: Picador/Palgrave Macmillan, 2011), p. 42.

53. C. Tilly, 'Contentious Repertoires in Great Britain, 1758–1834', in M. Traugott (ed.), *Repertoires and Cycles of Collective Action* (Durham, NC: Duke University Press, 1995), pp. 15–42, on p. 26; see also M. Traugott, 'Barricades as Repertoire: Continuities and Discontinuities in the History of French Contention', *Social Science History*, 17 (1993), pp. 309–23, on p. 310.

54. A. Etzioni, *A Comparative Analysis of Complex Organizations* (1961; New York: The Free Press, 1975), p. 5. John Kenneth Galbraith offers a similar classification of power. It contains three types: condign, compensatory and conditioned (J. K. Galbraith, *Anatomy of Power* (Boston, MA: Houghton Mifflin, 1983), pp. 4–6). Galbraith's condign power has features in common with Etzioni's coercive power. Compensatory power involves the remuneration for *B*'s compliance. Conditioned power is exercised by changing *B*'s beliefs.

55. More detailed classifications can be found, namely in Ledyaev, *Power*, ch. 12; Wartenberg, *The Forms of Power*, ch. 5 and Oleinik, *Market as a Weapon*, ch. 2.

56. Wrong, *Power*, p. 24.

57. Wrong, *Power*, p. 32.

58. Ledyaev, *Power*, p. 190.

59. Wrong, *Power*, p. 35; Ledyaev, *Power*, p. 193.

60. Weber, *Economy and Society*, vol. 1, p. 215.

61. D. Beetham, *The Legitimation of Power* (Atlantic Highlands, NJ: Humanities Press International: 1991), p. 16.

62. Foucault, *Surveiller et punir*, pp. 13–20.

63. Lukes, *Power*, p. 1.

2 Domination by Virtue of a Constellation of Interests: Benefits of Gate Keeping

1. M. Weber, *Economy and Society: An Outline of Interpretative Sociology*, ed. R. Guenther and C. Wittich, 2 vols (1922; New York: Bedminster Press, 1968), vol. 1, p. 946.

2. J. Scott, *Power* (Cambridge: Polity Press, 2001), p. 17.

3. See Chapter 1, Section 3.

4. Scott, *Power*, p. 71.

5. T.-W. Ngo, 'Rent-Seeking and Economic Governance in the Structural Nexus of Corruption in China', *Crime, Law and Social Change*, 49 (2008), pp. 27–44; Y. Guo and A. Hu, 'The Administrative Monopoly in China's Economic Transition', *Communist and Post-Communist Studies*, 37 (2004), pp. 165–280.

6. See Chapter 4.

7. S. Bowles and H. Gintis, 'Power', in S. N. Durlauf and L. E. Blume (eds), *The New Palgrave: Dictionary of Economics*, 2nd edn, 8 vols (Houndmills: Macmillan, 2008), vol. 6, pp. 565–70, on p. 567; emphasis in the original.

8. S. Bowles and H. Gintis, 'Power in Competitive Exchange', in S. Bowles, M. Franzini and U. Pagano (eds), *The Politics and Economics of Power* (London: Routledge, 1999), pp. 13–30, on p. 23.

9. See Chapter 1, Section 2.

10. S. Bowles and H. Gintis, 'Contested Exchange: New Microfoundations for the Political Economy of Capitalism', *Politics & Society*, 18 (1990), pp. 165–222, on p. 184.

11. A. Oleinik, *Market as a Weapon: The Socio-Economic Machinery of Dominance in Russia* (New Brunswick, NJ: Transaction Publishers, 2011), ch. 2; see also Chapter 1 of this book.

12. R. E. Weintraub, 'Neoclassical Economics', *The Concise Encyclopedia of Economics* (2002), at http://www.econlib.org/library/Enc1/NeoclassicalEconomics.html [accessed 10 March 2014].

13. Bowles and Gintis, 'Contested Exchange', p. 172.

14. See Chapter 1, Section 1.

15. A. Cox, 'Business Relationship Alignment: On the Commensurability of Value Capture and Mutuality in Buyer and Supplier Exchange', *Supply Chain Management: An International Journal*, 9 (2004), pp. 410–20, on p. 415.

16. R. D. Cooter, 'Coase Theorem', in J. Eatwell, M. Milgate and P. Newman (eds), *The New Palgrave: A Dictionary of Economics*, 4 vols, 1st edn (London: Macmillan, 1987), vol. 1, pp. 457–60; S. Medema, 'The Trial of Homo Economicus: What Law and Economics Tells us about the Development of Economic Imperialism', *New Economics and its History: History of Political, Economy Annual Supplement*, 29 (1997), pp. 122–42.

17. R. H. Coase, 'The Nature of the Firm', *Economica*, new series, 4 (1937), pp. 386–405.

18. C. Ménard, 'Theory of Organizations: The Diversity of Arrangements in a Developed Market Economy', in A. Oleinik (ed.), *The Institutional Economics of Russia's Transformation* (Aldershot: Ashgate, 2005), pp. 88–111, on p. 94.

19. H. A. Simon, 'A Formal Theory of the Employment Relationship', *Econometrica*, 19 (1951), pp. 293–305; J. E. Stiglitz, 'Principal and Agent', in J. Eatwell, M. Milgate and P. Newman (eds), *The New Palgrave: A Dictionary of Economics*, 4 vols, 1st edn (London: Macmillan, 1987), vol. 3, pp. 966–71.

20. Ménard, 'Theory of Organizations', p. 94.

21. Bowles and Gintis, 'Power in Competitive Exchange', p. 24.

22. D. Kreps, 'Corporate Culture and Economic Theory', in J. Alt and K. Shepsle (eds), *Perspectives on Positive Political Economy* (Cambridge: Cambridge University Press, 1990), pp. 90–143.

23. Bowles and Gintis, 'Contested Exchange', p. 177; see also Bowles and Gintis, 'Power in Competitive Exchange', p. 18.

24. $EU_B > \bar{U}$ see [1].

25. Bowles and Gintis, 'Power in Competitive Exchange', p. 18.

26. Bowles and Gintis, 'Contested Exchange', p. 179; emphasis in the original.

27. Bowles and Gintis, 'Power in Competitive Exchange', p. 22.

28. Bowles and Gintis, 'Power', p. 566; emphasis in the original.
29. Bowles and Gintis, 'Contested Exchange', p. 183.
30. Bowles and Gintis, 'Power', p. 569.
31. Bowles and Gintis, 'Power in Competitive Exchange', p. 23.
32. Bowles and Gintis, 'Contested Exchange', p. 188.
33. H. Gintis, *Game Theory Evolving: A Problem-Centered Introduction to Modeling Strategic Interactions* (Princeton, NJ: Princeton University Press, 2000), p. 138.
34. D. C. North, *Structure and Change in Economic History* (New York: W. W. Norton, 1981); see also Chapter 7, Section 1.
35. Bowles and Gintis, 'Contested Exchange', p. 193.
36. I am setting aside here the approaches that are either too descriptive, or too remotely connected to the study of transactions in the market. For instance, one study in business management concludes that conflicts between firms in the international market rarely take a dyadic form. 'Other actors outside the interfirm dyad may be important in explaining conflict, conflict may emanate from or be exacerbated by relationships connected to the dyad, conflict resolution may depend on other relationships outside the dyad, conflict outcomes should be considered in network as well as dyadic terms' (C. Welch and I. Wilkinson, 'Network Perspectives on Interfirm Conflict: Reassessing a Critical Case in International Business', *Journal of Business Research*, 58 (2005), pp. 205–13, on p. 212). The authors do not offer a theory of multilateral business transactions, however. Sociologists offer several insights as to how the transition from the dyad to the triad and the other multilateral structures makes transactions between their parties more and more sophisticated (R. Brym, L. Roberts and J. Lie, 'Networks, Groups, Bureaucracies, and Societies', in R. Brym (ed.), *New Society*, 7th edn (Toronto: Nelson Education), pp. 21/8–14). Unfortunately, a structuralist approach does not allow us to emphasize the particularities of transactions in the market, which are the subject of this chapter.
37. K. Basu, 'One Kind of Power', *Oxford Economic Papers*, 38 (1986), pp. 259–82, on p. 259.
38. Basu, 'One Kind of Power', p. 268. I changed the notations to make them consistent with those previously used, namely in equation [1].
39. Oleinik, *Market as a Weapon*, pp. 183–4.
40. A public choice approach to theorizing power at the macro level will be considered in Chapter 3, Sections 1 and 2. As a result of its influence in economic sciences, a public choice theory view of power in the market deserves special and in-depth discussion.
41. In a manner similar to the definition of power, the definition of the state has a contested character. The state can be defined either in a broad, encompassing manner or narrowly. The first approach appears relevant in holistic societies with little differentiation between their functional subsystems. Germany in the first half of the twentieth century represented such a holistic society: 'It is neither the territorial area, nor the population, nor the body of citizens or subjects, nor the aggregate wealth or traffic, nor the public administration, nor the government, nor the crown, nor the sovereign; yet in some sense it is all these matters, or rather all these organs of the state' (T. Veblen, *Imperial Germany and Industrial Revolution* (1915; New York: The Viking Press, 1939), p. 161). A narrow definition of the state applies to societies with clearly differentiated functional subsystems: politics, the economy, and so forth. Here, 'the state is not "the people", nor "the public", it is the working rules of the discretionary officials of the past and present who have had and now have the legal power to put their will into effect within the limits set by other officials, past and present, and through the instrumentality of other officials or employees, present and future' (J. R. Commons, *Legal Foundations of Capitalism* (1924; Madison, WI: The University of Wisconsin Press, 1959), p. 149).

42. K. W. Rothschild, 'New Worlds – New Approaches: A Note on Future Research Strategies', *Kyklos*, 58 (2005), pp. 439–47, on p. 443.

43. Rothschild, 'New Worlds – New Approaches', p. 445.

44. J. R. Commons, *Legal Foundations of Capitalism* (1924; Madison, WI: The University of Wisconsin Press, 1959), p. 66.

45. Commons, *Legal Foundations of Capitalism*, p. 262.

46. Commons, *Legal Foundations of Capitalism*, p. 67.

47. Commons, *Legal Foundations of Capitalism*, p. 88.

48. L. M. B. Cabral, 'Barriers to Entry', in S. N. Durlauf and L. E. Blume (eds), *The New Palgrave: Dictionary of Economics*, 8 vols, 2nd edn (Houndmills: Macmillan, 2008), vol. 1, p. 383.

49. S. Lukes, *Power: A Radical View* (1974; Houndmills: Palgrave Macmillan, 2005), pp. 43–4.

50. Oleinik, *Market as a Weapon*, pp. 159–60.

51. The scholarly literature offers several definitions of 'field'. Neil Fligstein and Luke Dautier call the field a set of economic agents who 'engage in strategic behaviour vis-à-vis one another and look to one another for clues as to what constitutes successful behavior' (N. Fligstein and L. Dauter, 'The Sociology of Markets', *Annual Review of Sociology*, 33 (2007), pp. 105–28, on p. 111). Pierre Bourdieu defines a field through conflicts over the access to the different species of capital: physical force, economic, informational and symbolic (P. Bourdieu, 'Rethinking the State: Genesis and Structure of the Bureaucratic Field', *Sociological Theory*, 12 (1994), pp. 1–18, on p. 4). I place primary emphasis on boundaries as a constitutive element of the field. The field refers to a set of transactions delimited in space. Consequently, it has some elements in common with the concept of territoriality developed in political geography. 'Territoriality establishes control over area as means of controlling access to things and relationships' (R. D. Sack, *Human Territoriality: Its Theory and History* (Cambridge: Cambridge University Press, 1986), p. 20).

52. Oleinik, *Market as a Weapon*, p. 158.

53. O. E. Williamson, *The Economic Institutions of Capitalism: Firms, Markets, Relational Contracting* (New York: The Free Press, 1985), p. 30.

54. Oleinik, *Market as a Weapon*, pp. 155–7.

55. *C* in Rothschild's triad, the state, has power. Rothschild explains the state's power in terms of its role in establishing and enforcing rules of the game. The state can also perform the role of gate keeper, as we will see in Chapters 3 and 4.

56. John Pen describes the indirect exercise of power in the following words: 'The exercise of power by *C* over *B* is built up of two elements: the influence (and possibly power) exerted by *C* over *A*, and that exercised by *A* over *B*' (J. Pen, 'Bilateral Monopoly, Bargaining and the Concept of Economic Power' (1959), in K. W. Rothschild (ed.), *Power in Economics: Selected Readings* (Harmondsworth: Penguin, 1971), pp. 97–115, on p. 110; I changed Pen's system of notations to make it consistent with that previously used).

57. Sack, *Human Territoriality*, p. 16.

58. Such as first-, second- and third-degree price discrimination, intertemporal price discrimination, peak-load pricing, two-part tariffs or bundling; see R. S. Pindyck and D. L. Rubinfeld, *Microeconomics*, 5th edn (Upper Saddle River: Prentice Hall, 2001), pp. 370–92.

59. M. Foucault, *Security, Territory, Population: Lectures at the Collège de France, 1977–1978*, trans. G. Burchell (Basingstoke and New York: Palgrave Macmillan, 2007), p. 344.

60. A. Etzioni, *The Moral Dimension: Toward a New Economics* (New York: The Free Press, 1988), p. 227; see also Chapter 3, Section 2.

61. See Chapter 1, Section 1.

62. Weber, *Economy and Society*, vol.1, p. 54; emphasis added.
63. Ménard, 'Theory of Organizations', p. 94; emphasis added.
64. Lukes, *Power*, pp. 19–28.
65. Lukes, *Power*, p. 27.
66. Gintis, *Game Theory Evolving*, p. 251.
67. Pindyck and Rubinfeld, *Microeconomics*, p. 62.
68. Several terms may be used in the place of the words 'choice sets'. Marketing literature uses the 'consideration set' (K. Eliaz and R. Spiegler, 'Consideration Sets and Competitive Marketing', *Review of Economic Studies*, 78 (2011), pp. 235–62, on p. 239). Economic literature uses the term 'opportunity sets' (F. Lovett, *A General Theory of Domination and Justice* (Oxford: Oxford University Press, 2010), p. 41). I prefer the expression 'choice set' also found in economic literature (D. Spears, 'Intertemporal Bounded Rationality as Consideration Sets with Contraction Consistency', *B.E. Journal of Theoretical Economics*, 11 (2011), Article 12, p. 3) because of its neutrality and connection with the problem of choice, one of the fundamental issues in the economic sciences.
69. Eliaz and Spiegler, 'Consideration Sets and Competitive Marketing', p. 239.
70. 'Attention rather than information [is] the scarce resource' (H. A. Simon, 'Rationality as Process and as Product of Thought', *American Economic Review*, 68 (1978), pp. 1–16, on p. 13).
71. T. Lawson, *Economics and Reality* (London and New York: Routledge, 1997), p. 187.
72. Spears, 'Intertemporal Bounded Rationality as Consideration Sets with Contraction Consistency', p. 7.
73. G. Simmel, *The Philosophy of Money*, trans. T. Bottomore and D. Frisby (1907; London: Routledge & Kegan Paul, 1978), p. 213. Gerard Wedig applies a similar idea in his empirical research on the value of options given to the buyer of health insurance. The list of hospitals providing medical services to the owner of a particular insurance plan tends to be restricted. The customer's gains in terms of volume-based price discounts offered by the eligible hospitals do not offset the utility losses caused by the restrictions on the range of her choices, however (G. J. Wedig, 'The Value of Consumer Choice and the Decline in HMO Enrollments', *Economic Inquiry*, 51 (2013), pp. 1066–86).
74. G. Palermo, 'Economic Power and the Firm in New Institutional Economics: Two Conflicting Problems', *Journal of Economic Issues*, 34 (2000), pp. 573–601, on p. 582. Analytical philosophers studying power make similar observations. For instance, Keith Dowding asserts that 'the ability to structure others' choice situations is a major power resource' (K. Dowding, *Power* (Minneapolis, MN: University of Minnesota Press, 1996), p. 66). Frank Lovett echoes this idea: 'the method of raising or lowering costs and benefits [in the other agent or group's choice set] might be thought of as a direct exercise of social power'(Lovett, *A General Theory of Domination and Justice*, p. 76). In the same vein, Thomas Wartenberg claims that 'an agent's constraint of either the action-alternatives that another agent faces or of that agent's assessment of those alternatives is what constitutes the power that the former has over the latter' (T. E. Wartenberg, *The Forms of Power: From Domination to Transformation* (Philadelphia, PA: Temple University Press, 1990), p. 86).
75. M. Dean, 'Three Conceptions of the Relationship between Power and Liberty', in S. R. Clegg and M. Haugaard (eds), *The Sage Handbook of Power* (Los Angeles, CA: Sage, 2009), pp. 177–93, on p. 186.
76. J. K. Galbraith, *The New Industrial State* (London: H. Hamilton, 1967), chs 18, 19.

77. A. Mitra and J. G. Lynch Jr, 'Toward a Reconciliation of Market Power and Informa-tion Theories of Advertising Effects on Price Elasticity', *Journal of Consumer Research*, 21 (1995), pp. 644–59.

78. P. Bordalo, N. Gennaioli and A. Shleifer, 'Salience and Consumer Choice', *Journal of Political Economy*, 121 (2013), pp. 803–43, on p. 805.

79. Oleinik, *Market as a Weapon*, ch. 6.

80. This fact allows clearly differentiated the present case for the case of coercion (see Chapter 1, Section 3). If *A* was coerced, then her expected utility would be negative all the time. *A* would try to minimize her losses.

81. It should rather be called 'rent-seeking function'.

82. The supermarket's management performs the role of a gate keeper in retail trade: because not all potential sellers willing to sell their products in the supermarket are allowed to do so, the buyer's choices are determined by the gate keeper's decisions as to which sellers are actually admitted and under what conditions (see Oleinik, *Market as a Weapon*, pp. 166–70).

83. For the sake of simplicity none of the systems of equations, [1], [2] or [3], accounts for the input of capital (the variable K in the standard production function). The variable E here is analogous to the variable L, the input of labour, in the standard production function.

84. According to Thomas Schelling, any place can become a focal point, it has only to be recognized as such by the parties involved, namely *A* and *B*. 'Any key that is mutually recognized as the key becomes *the* key – may depend on imagination more than on logic, it may depend on analogy, precedent, accidental arrangement, symmetry, aes-thetic or geometric configuration, casuistic reasoning, and who the parties are and what they know about each other' (T. S. Schelling, *The Strategy of Conflict* (Cambridge, MA: Harvard University Press, 1960), p. 57; emphasis added).

85. This situation has structural similarities with that studied by Bowles and Gintis: 'the employee excluded from access to *her current employer's asset* may not find access to *any asset*' (see this chapter, Section 2).

86. MMBtu refers to 1 Million British thermal unit, a common measure.

87. Pindyck and Rubinfeld, *Microeconomics*, pp. 385–7.

88. J. R. Commons, 'Institutional Economics', *American Economic Review*, 21 (1931), pp. 648–57, on p. 652.

89. Foucault, *Security, Territory, Population*, pp. 43–4.

3 The 2008 Financial Crisis through the Lens of Power Relationships

1. The 1946 recession occurred in very specific circumstances during the transition from the World War II economic mobilization to post-War development.

2. The US Bureau of Economic Analysis provides a more optimistic estimate for the drop in the US GDP in 2009: -2.8 per cent.

3. World Bank. World Development Indicators, at http://data.worldbank.org/data-catalog/world-development-indicators [accessed 25 November 2013].

4. J. M. Keynes, *The General Theory of Employment Interest and Money* (1936; London: Macmillan, 1964), p. 152.

5. The central place of the housing market in the economic system can be demonstrated by other means as well. Pierre Bourdieu argues that the government is interested in stimulat-ing this market in order to enhance its social base: 'What is being tacitly asserted through the creation of a house is the will to create a permanent group, united by stable social rela-

tions, a lineage' (P. Bourdieu, *The Social Structures of the Economy*, trans. C. Turner (2000; Cambridge: Polity, 2005), p. 20; see also Chapter 5, Section 1, endnote 16).

6. Recovery policies had been started at the very end of President Bush's second term, but their scope and size were expanded at the beginning of President Obama's first term. Namely, the Troubled Asset Relief Program, TARP, was passed late during the Bush administration, whereas the Recovery and Reinvestment Act was signed into law by President Obama. The term 'bailout funds' refers to the former, the term 'stimulus funds' – to the latter. For instance, money received by the automakers and the banks came from TARP. The difference between the Recovery and Reinvestment Act and the TARP may be important from a political point of view, but it has a limited bearing on the substance of the argument about using the distribution of bailout and stimulus funds as a lever of influence developed in this chapter. The Republicans and Democrats divide does not explain the variance in the distribution of the stimulus funds, as reported below. The author is indebted to Professor Christopher Brown, the *Journal of Economic Issues* Editor, for highlighting this aspect.

7. R. D. Congleton, 'On the Political Economy of the Financial Crisis and Bailout of 2008–2009', *Public Choice*, 140 (2009), pp. 287–317, on p. 312.

8. T. Skopol and K. Finegold, 'State Capacity and Economic Intervention in the Early New Deal' (1982), in J. Scott (ed.), *Power: Critical Concepts*, 3 vols (London: Routledge, 1994), vol. 3, pp. 370–92.

9. D.C. Mueller, *Public Choice III* (Cambridge: Cambridge University Press, 2003), p. 360.

10. R. H. Coase, 'The Nature of the Firm', *Economica*, new series 4 (1937), pp. 386–405.

11. O. E. Williamson, *The Economic Institutions of Capitalism: Firms, Markets, Relational Contracting* (New York: The Free Press, 1985).

12. W. M. Dugger, 'The New Institutionalism: New but not Institutionalist', *Journal of Economic Issues*, 24 (1990), pp. 423–31, on p. 424.

13. Congleton, 'On the Political Economy of the Financial Crisis and Bailout of 2008–2009'; R. D. Congleton, 'On the Political Economy and Limits of Crisis Insurance: The Case of the 2008–11 Bailouts', *Public Choice*, 150 (2012), pp. 399–423.

14. See Chapter 1, Section 1.

15. See Chapter 1, Section 1.

16. Mueller, *Public Choice III*, p. 360.

17. F. H. Knight, *Risk, Uncertainty, and Profit* (1921; New York: Augustus M. Kelley, 1964).

18. Mueller, *Public Choice III*, p. 362.

19. Mueller, *Public Choice III*, p. 362.

20. W. A. Niskanen, 'Bureaucrats and Politicians', *Journal of Law and Economics*, 18 (1975), pp. 617–43, on p. 618.

21. G. Tullock, *Public Goods, Redistribution and Rent Seeking* (Cheltenham: Edward Elgar, 2005), p. 224; see also J. M. Buchanan, 'Rent-Seeking and Profit Seeking', in J. M. Buchanan, R. D. Tollison and G. Tullock (eds), *Toward a Theory of the Rent-Seeking Society* (College Station, TX: Texas A & M University Press, 1980), pp. 3–15.

22. I avoid using the term 'dyad' here because of its connection with the study of power relationships, see Chapter 1, Section 1 and Chapter 2, Section 1.

23. Tullock, *Public Goods, Redistribution and Rent Seeking*, p. 96.

24. G. Tullock, 'The Backward Society: Static Inefficiency, Rent Seeking, and the Rule of Law', in J. M. Buchanan and R. D. Tollison (eds), *The Theory of Public Choice II* (Ann Arbor, MI: The University of Michigan Press, 1984), pp. 224–37, on p. 228.

25. Mueller, *Public Choice III*, p. 346.

26. S. Djankov, R. La Porta, F. Lopez-de-Silanes and A. Shleifer, 'The Regulation of Entry', *Quarterly Journal of Economics*, 117 (2002), pp. 1–37, on p. 3.

27. G. J. Stigler, 'The Theory of Economic Regulation', *Bell Journal of Economics and Management Science*, 2 (1971), pp. 3–21.

28. Djankov, La Porta, Lopez-de-Silanes and Shleifer, 'The Regulation of Entry', p. 3.

29. Mueller, *Public Choice III*, p. 362.

30. Congleton, 'On the Political Economy and Limits of Crisis Insurance: The Case of the 2008–11 Bailouts', p. 410; see also Congleton, 'On the Political Economy of the Financial Crisis and Bailout of 2008–2009', p. 306.

31. World Bank, World Development Indicators.

32. The content analysis was carried out using the specialized computer programme QDA Miner v. 4.0.4 with the module for quantitative content analysis WordStat v. 6.1.4. Namely, a dictionary based on substitution was created in order to locate all references to crisis in the presidential addresses (in two versions: English and Russian).

33. The State of the Union address delivered by President Obama on 24 February 2009.

34. The presidential address delivered by President Yeltsin on 31 March 1999.

35. Congleton, 'On the Political Economy and Limits of Crisis Insurance: The Case of the 2008–11 Bailouts', p. 418.

36. Congleton, 'On the Political Economy and Limits of Crisis Insurance: The Case of the 2008–11 Bailouts', p. 407.

37. Congleton, 'On the Political Economy of the Financial Crisis and Bailout of 2008–2009', p. 310. A historical example of regulatory capture can be seen in the operation of the US National Recovery Administration established in the early 1930s under the National Industrial Recovery Act. As a matter of fact, this government body was staffed and run by corporate representatives. 'Business executives and their organizations held all the good cards' (Skopol and Finegold, 'State Capacity and Economic Intervention in the Early New Deal', p. 378).

38. Congleton, 'On the Political Economy and Limits of Crisis Insurance: The Case of the 2008–11 Bailouts', p. 412.

39. M. Dorsch, 'Bailout for Sale? The Vote to Save Wall Street', *Public Choice*, 155 (2013), pp. 211–28, on p. 212; emphasis added.

40. Congleton, 'On the Political Economy and Limits of Crisis Insurance: The Case of the 2008–11 Bailouts', p. 402.

41. Calculated on 22 November 2013, using the *Web of Knowledge* database and the following search operators: Topic = (power) AND Publication Name = (*Journal of Economic Issues*).

42. W. M. Dugger, 'Power: An Institutional Framework of Analysis', *Journal of Economic Issues*, 14 (1980), pp. 897–907, on p. 897; G. Palermo, 'Economic Power and the Firm in New Institutional Economics: Two Conflicting Problems', *Journal of Economic Issues*, 34 (2000), pp. 573–601, on p. 582; E. Schutz, 'Markets and Power', *Journal of Economic Issues*, 29 (1995), pp. 1147–70, on pp. 1148.

43. T. E. Wartenberg, *The Forms of Power: From Domination to Transformation* (Philadelphia, PA: Temple University Press, 1990), p. 117; see also Chapter 1, Section 1.

44. P. A. Klein, 'Power and Economic Performance: The Institutionalist View', *Journal of Economic Issues*, 21 (1987), pp. 1341–77, on p. 1342.

45. See Chapter 2, Section 4 and especially endnote 15 in that chapter.

46. J. R. Commons, 'Institutional Economics', *American Economic Review*, 21 (1931), pp. 648–57, on p. 653; see also the conclusion to Chapter 2.

47. J. K. Galbraith, *The New Industrial State* (London: H. Hamilton, 1967).
48. W. Waller, 'John Kenneth Galbraith: Cultural Theorist of Consumption and Power', *Journal of Economic Issues*, 42 (2008), pp. 13–24; see also Chapter 2, Section 5.
49. S. Bowles and H. Gintis, 'Contested Exchange: New Microfoundations for the Political Economy of Capitalism', *Politics & Society*, 18 (1990), pp. 165–222; S. Bowles and H. Gintis, 'Power', in S. N. Durlauf and L. E. Blume (eds), *The New Palgrave: Dictionary of Economics*, 2nd edn, 8 vols (Houndmills: Macmillan, 2008), vol. 6, pp. 565–70.
50. See Chapter 2, Section 2 for more details.
51. G. Palermo, 'Economic Power and the Firm in New Institutional Economics: Two Conflicting Problems', *Journal of Economic Issues*, 34 (2000), pp. 573–601.
52. See Chapter 2, Section 4.
53. T. Veblen, *The Theory of the Leisure Class: An Economic Study of Institutions* (1899; Don Mills, ON: Dover Publications, 1994), pp. 43–62.
54. P. F. R. Holt and D. T. Greenwood, 'Negative Trickle-Down and the Financial Crisis of 2008', *Journal of Economic Issues*, 46 (2012), pp. 363–70.
55. It must also be noted that Keynes 'had little awareness of, nor any serious interest in, the matter of economic power' (W. C. Peterson, 'Market Power: The Missing Element in Keynesian Economics', *Journal of Economic Issues*, 23 (1989), pp. 379–91, on p. 383).
56. A. Oleinik, *Market as a Weapon: The Socio-Economic Machinery of Dominance in Russia* (New Brunswick, NJ: Transaction Publishers, 2011), pp. 143–76.
57. Oleinik, *Market as a Weapon*, pp. 177–97; see also Chapter 2, Section 5.
58. J. M. Kamensky, 'The Obama Performance Approach: A Midterm Snapshot', *Public Performance and Management Review*, 35 (2011), pp. 133–48, on p. 143.
59. The search was performed using the key sentences 'access to bailout funds', with the help of *LexisNexis Academic*, on 7 October 2009 and 10 October 2012.
60. Similar policies in Japan in the late 1990s induced the process of concentration in the banking industry because regional banks did not get access to the bailout funds, which only amplified structural biases favouring the 'selected few' (J. M. Herbener, 'The Rise and Fall of the Japanese Miracle', *Mises Daily* (20 September 1990), at http://mises.org [accessed 10 October 2012]).
61. The corresponding data were retrieved from recovery.gov and from www.bea.gov, the Bureau of Economic Analysis website. The data cover the period from 17 February 2009 to 30 June 2012. The state was used as a unit of analysis (N=51, including Washington, DC). After visual inspection of the data ('eye-balling'), a log transformation (LG10) was applied to get some of them closer to the normal distribution.
62. It varies from zero (the Democrats do not control any top elected public office in this state) to five (they control the five top elected public offices: that of the governor, those of the state's representatives in the US Senate and House of Representatives, and hold a majority in the upper and lower houses of the state's legislature).
63. The 'Forward' method, with the probability of F set at the 0.05 significance level was used when running Ordinary Least Squares regressions. The overall regression, including one of the four candidate predictors, was statistically significant, R=.922, R^2=.85, adjusted R^2=.847, $F(1, 49)$=277.361, p<.001. Approximately 85 per cent of the variance in the total value of awards could be predicted from the number of electors.
64. The overall regression, including two of the four candidate predictors, was statistically significant, R=.704, R^2=.495, adjusted R^2=.49, $F(2, 188)$=92.149, p<.001. Approximately 50 per cent of the variance in the number of awards could be predicted from this set of two variables. To assess the statistical significance of the contributions of

individual predictors, the F ratio for R^2 increment was examined for each variable in the step when it first entered the analysis. In Step 1, the export–import share was entered; it produced an R^2 increment of .423, $F(1, 189)=138.747$, $p<.001$. In Step 2, the Freedom House composite index was entered; it produced an R^2 increment of .072, $F(1, 188)=26.690$, $p<.001$

65. J. Taber, 'Ottawa Hails Buy American Deal', *Globe and Mail*, 5 February 2010.
66. S. Chase, 'Tories Plan "Buy Canada" Military Budget', *Globe and Mail*, 24 September 2012.

4 Welcome to Russia: Benefits of Obedience

1. The former US Secretary of Defense, Ronald Rumsfeld, defined terrorism as an 'unknown unknown': 'There are known knowns; there are things we know we know. We also know there are known unknowns; that is to say we know there are some things we do not know. But there are also unknown unknowns – the ones we don't know we don't know' (US Department of Defense, 'News Briefing', 12 February 2002, at http://www.defense.gov/Transcripts/Transcript.aspx?TranscriptID=2636 [accessed 15 April 2014]). A financial crisis would be a 'known unknown' in these terms.
2. R. D. Congleton, 'On the Political Economy and Limits of Crisis Insurance: The Case of the 2008–11 Bailouts', *Public Choice*, 150 (2012), p. 418; see also Chapter 3, Section 2.
3. R. Swedberg, *Principles of Economic Sociology* (Princeton, NJ: Princeton University Press, 2003), p. 15; emphasis in the original.
4. J. M. Keynes, *The General Theory of Employment Interest and Money* (1936; London: Macmillan, 1964), p. 156. Nicholas Kaldor applies a similar reasoning to his analysis of speculative activity in the market: 'it may become, in fact, more profitable for the individual speculator to concentrate on forecasting the psychology of other speculators, rather than the trend of the non-speculative elements' (N. Kaldor, 'Speculation and Economic Stability', *Review of Economic Studies*, 7 (1939), pp. 1–27, on p. 2).
5. Keynes, *The General Theory of Employment Interest and Money*, p. 161.
6. Paul Krugman, a Keynesian economist, complains that the 'saltwater economists [Krugman refers here to Keynesian economists], who had comforted themselves with the belief that the great divide in macroeconomics was narrowing, were shocked to realize that freshwater economists [Krugman attaches this label to neoclassical economists] hadn't been listening at all' (P. Krugman, 'How Did Economists Get it so Wrong?', *New York Times*, 2 September 2009, p. 36, at http://www.nytimes.com/2009/09/06/magazine/06Economic-t.html?_r=3&pagewanted=all [accessed 16 April 2014]). Unfortunately, the unwillingness to listen to the opponent's arguments often characterizes economists and other social scientists regardless of their theoretical affiliation.
7. As Alfred Marshall, one of the founding fathers of modern economics, states, 'the laws of human action are not indeed as simple, as definite or as clearly ascertainable as the law of gravitation; but many of them may rank with the laws of those natural sciences which deal with complex subject-matter' (A. Marshall, *Principles of Economics*, 8th edn (1890; London: Macmillan, 1920), book 1, ch. 4, §1).
8. P. Krugman, *The Return of Depression Economics and the Crisis of 2008* (New York: W. W. Norton, 2009), p. 190.
9. K. Popper, *Conjectures and Refutations* (London: Routledge and Kegan Paul, 1963), p. 35.
10. A. Glöckner and T. Betsch, 'The Empirical Content of Theories in Judgment and Decision Making: Shortcomings and Remedies', *Judgment and Decision Making*, 6 (2011), pp. 711–21, on p. 716.

11. K. Popper, *The Logic of Scientific Discovery*, 3rd edn (London: Hutchinson, 1968), p. 86.
12. K. Popper, *The Two Fundamental Problems of the Theory of Knowledge*, trans. A. Pickel and J. Kinory (1978; Abington: Routledge, 2009), p. 417.
13. Popper, *Conjectures and Refutations*, p. 36.
14. Experimental economics represent a vibrant, rapidly developing area of knowledge; see J. H. Kagel and A. E. Roth (eds), *The Handbook of Experimental Economics* (Princeton, NJ: Princeton University Press, 1995).
15. Case studies and qualitative data are actively used by original institutionalists (see, for instance, V. Yefimov, *Economie institutionnelle des transformations agraires en Russie* (Paris: L'Harmattan, 2003)) and some other heterodox economists.
16. X. X. Sala-I-Martin, 'I Just Ran Two Million Regressions', *American Economic Review*, 87 (1997), pp. 178–83, on p. 178.
17. S. Djankov, R. La Porta, F. Lopez-de-Silanes and A. Shleifer, 'The Regulation of Entry', *Quarterly Journal of Economics*, 117 (2002), pp. 1–37. As of 21 April 2014, this paper was cited 543 times in the Web of Science, which suggests a high impact.
18. Djankov, La Porta, Lopez-de-Silanes and Shleifer, 'The Regulation of Entry', p. 3.
19. See also Chapter 3, Section 1.
20. Djankov, La Porta, Lopez-de-Silanes and Shleifer, 'The Regulation of Entry', p. 26.
21. See Chapter 1, Section 1.
22. Glöckner and Betsch, 'The Empirical Content of Theories in Judgment and Decision Making', p. 717.
23. As specified in the equation [3] in Chapter 2, Section 5.
24. Glöckner and Betsch, 'The Empirical Content of Theories in Judgment and Decision Making', p. 711.
25. J. Wettersten, 'Philosophical Anthropology Can Help Social Scientists Learn from Empirical Tests', *Journal for the Theory of Social Behaviour*, 37 (2007), pp. 295–318, on p. 296.
26. See the introduction to Chapter 1.
27. See Chapter 1, Section 3.
28. A. Oleinik, *Market as a Weapon: The Socio-Economic Machinery of Dominance in Russia* (New Brunswick, NJ: Transaction Publishers, 2011), ch. 4.
29. The most recent show of force happened in 2014, when Russia seized a part of Ukraine's territory and provided weapons (along with human and financial resources) to the separatists in Eastern Ukraine.
30. R. Walmsley, *World Prison Population List*, 10th edn (London: International Centre for Prison Studies, 2013), at http://www.prisonstudies.org/sites/prisonstudies.org/files/resources/downloads/wppl_10.pdf [accessed 17 April 2014].
31. A. Wilson, *Virtual Politics: Faking Democracy in the Post-Soviet World* (New Haven, CT, and London: Yale University Press, 2005), p. 43.
32. Reporters without borders, *World Press Freedom Index 2014* (2014), at https://rsf.org/index2014/en-index2014.php [accessed 17 April 2014].
33. Oleinik, *Market as a Weapon*.
34. Many members of the Russian power elite hold advanced academic degrees. As of the end of 2011, about 40 per cent of top officials working at the Presidential Executive Office, the federal government and the government executive office had degrees equivalent to PhD or *Habilitation* (Russia historically has a two-level doctorate system, similar to that in Germany), with degrees in the social sciences being the most popular (A. Oleinik, *Knowledge and Networking: On Communication in the Social Sciences* (New Brunswick, NJ: Transaction Publishers, 2014), p. 119). However, a series of recent

scandals and revelations suggest that a significant share of these degrees were obtained in an irregular manner, as a result of plagiarizing and corruption in the other forms.

35. World Bank, World Development Indicators. Total natural resources rents are the sum of oil rents, natural gas rents, coal rents (hard and soft), mineral rents and forest rents. Oil rents are the difference between the value of oil production at world prices and total costs of production and so forth.

36. L. Fredricksen, 'The Fraser Institute Annual Survey of Mining Companies', *Applied Earth Science (Trans. Inst. Min. Metall. B)*, 111 (2002), pp. B171–6, on p. B172.

37. World Bank, World Development Indicators and Federal State Statistics Service of the Russian Federation, National Accounts: GDP annual growth rates, at http://www.gks.ru/free_doc/new_site/vvp/tab3.xls [accessed 17 April 2014].

38. World Bank, Doing Business Project, at http://www.doingbusiness.org/ [accessed 17 April 2014].

39. Oleinik, *Market as a Weapon*, p. 189.

40. R. L. Bruno, M. Bytchkova and S. Estrin, 'Institutional Determinants of New Firm Entry in Russia: A Cross-Regional Analysis', *Review of Economics and Statistics*, 95 (2013), pp. 1740–9, on p. 1748.

41. This term is commonly used in Russia to describe efforts focused on enhancing discipline within the state apparatus, to increasing state servants' compliance with orders of their superiors and to subordinate all branches of power and all authorities, including regional and municipal, to a single centre, namely, the Presidential Executive Office.

42. H. G. Broadman, 'Reducing Structural Dominance and Entry Barriers in Russian Industry', *Review of Industrial Organization*, 17 (2000), pp. 155–76, on p. 160.

43. A. Libman and L. P. Feld, 'Strategic Tax Collection and Fiscal Decentralization: The Case of Russia', *German Economic Review*, 14 (2013), pp. 449–82, on p. 463.

44. This observation applies not only to Russia, but to the other emerging markets too. The entry of foreign companies into the Chinese market requires building and maintaining networks of useful connections, *Guan-xi*. 'Developing these relationships often appeared to be the only way to open necessary doors. According to one respondent, understanding Guan-xi was more important than all the market research' (U. Elg, P. N. Ghauri and V. Tarnovskaya, 'The Role of Networks and Matching in Market Entry to Emerging Retail Markets', *International Marketing Review*, 25 (2008), pp. 674–99, on p. 685).

45. Oleinik, *Market as a Weapon*, pp. 221, 227–8.

46. B. Venard, 'Organizational Isomorphism and Corruption: An Empirical Research in Russia', *Journal of Business Ethics*, 89 (2008), pp. 59–76, on p. 69.

47. Not counting Crimea and the city of Sebastopol, whose inclusion into the Russian Federation in March 2014 is disputed and considered as illegitimate by the majority of the United Nations members.

48. V. Mau and K. Yanovskiy, 'Political and Legal Factors of Economic Growth in Russian Regions', *Post-Communist Economies*, 14 (2002), pp. 321–39; A. Libman, 'Democracy, Size of Bureaucracy, and Economic Growth: Evidence from Russian Regions', *Empirical Economics*, 43 (2012), pp. 1321–52; A. Libman, 'Natural Resources and Sub-National Economic Performance: Does Sub-National Democracy Matter?', *Energy Economics*, 37 (2013), pp. 82–99.

49. Libman and Feld, 'Strategic Tax Collection and Fiscal Decentralization'.

50. C. Castiglione, Y. Gorbunova, D. Infante and J. Smirnova, 'FDI Determinants in an Idiosyncratic Country: A Reappraisal over the Russian Regions during Transition Years', *Communist and Post-Communist Studies*, 45 (2012), pp. 1–10; S. Ledyaeva, P.

Karhunen and R. Kosonen, 'The Global Economic Crisis and Foreign Investment in Russia from the EU: Empirical Evidence from Firm-Level Data', *Eurasian Geography and Economics*, 53 (2012), pp. 772–89. The latter study uses the firm as a unit of observation and the region as a unit of analysis.

51. Bruno, Bytchkova and Estrin, 'Institutional Determinants of New Firm Entry in Russia'.
52. See Chapter 3, Section 4.
53. Ledyaeva, Karhunen and Kosonen, 'The Global Economic Crisis and Foreign Investment in Russia from the EU', p. 784.
54. Out of eighty-three subjects only seventy-nine were retained for the analysis. Chechnya was excluded due to low data reliability. Out of four autonomous districts only one, Chukotka, is the subject of the Russian Federation in its own right, whereas Yamalo-Nenets, Nenets and Khanty-Mansi districts are administratively subordinate to the other regions. Thus, the three latter districts were also excluded from the analysis. Several other scholars chose to work with similar samples of seventy-nine subjects: Mau and Yanovskiy, 'Political and Legal Factors of Economic Growth in Russian Regions', Bruno, Bytchkova and Estrin, 'Institutional Determinants of New Firm Entry in Russia'; Libman, 'Natural Resources and Sub-National Economic Performance'; Libman and Feld, 'Strategic Tax Collection and Fiscal Decentralization'.
55. Russian Federal Treasury, Otchet ob ispolnenii byudzhetov sub'ektov RF i mestnykh byudzhetov [Report on the execution of the budgets of the subjects of the Russian Federation and the local budgets], at http://www.roskazna.ru/byudzhetov-subektov-rf-i-mestnykh-byudzhetov/doc/Otch_2012.rar [accessed 18 April 2014].
56. Federal State Statistics Service of the Russian Federation, *Finansy Rossii, 2012 god* [Russian Finances, 2012], Moscow, 2012, at http://www.gks.ru/free_doc/doc_2012/fin12.rar [accessed 19 April 2014], pp. 142–3.
57. Federal State Statistics Service, *Regiony Rossii: Sotsial'no-ekonomicheskie pokazateli, 2013 god* [Regions of Russia: Socio-Economic Data, 2013], Moscow, 2013, at http://www.gks.ru/free_doc/doc_2013/region/soc-pok.rar [accessed 18 April 2014], pp. 160–1.
58. Federal State Statistic Service of the Russian Federation, Struktura and osnovnye pokazateli deyatel'nosti khozyaistvuyushchikh sub'ektov za 2012 god [Structure and key parameters of operation of economic subjects in 2012], at http://www.gks.ru/free_doc/doc_2013/bul_dr/xoz-12.rar [accessed 18 April 2014], table 55.1.
59. See Chapter 1, Section 2.
60. Peterbugskaya Politika Foundation, 13-i reiting politicheskoi vyzhivaemosti gubernatorov [13th ranking of the governors' political survival], 2013, at http://www.fpp.spb.ru/rate13.php [accessed 18 April 2014]. Before 2004, the governors of the Russian regions were elected; since then they have been appointed by the president. In these circumstances a governor's political survival refers to her chances to be reappointed for the next term. A similar ranking was produced in 2000–4 by experts of the Moscow Carnegie Center with the purpose of assessing the regional elites' strategies in a more democratic environment (see, for instance, Libman, 'Natural Resources and Sub-National Economic Performance', p. 85 for an example of its use in econometric tests).
61. M. Mann, *The Sources of Social Power: A History of Power from the Beginning to A.D. 1760*, 4 vols (Cambridge: Cambridge University Press, 1986), vol. 1, p. 2.
62. D. C. North, 'Three Approaches to the Study of Institutions', in D. C. Colander (ed.), *Neoclassical Political Economy: The Analysis of Rent-Seeking and DUP Activities* (Cambridge, MA: Ballinger, 1984), pp. 33–40, on p. 34.

63. As yet another example of the flexibility with which public choice theorists deal with key premises of neoclassical economics, I would like to cite Dennis Mueller's assessment of state representatives' goals. 'The pursuit of profits is not the perceived legitimate goal of public bureaus, and thus it is even more difficult for public bureaucrats to convert the power they have into income. The nonpecuniary goals of management become the logical objectives of the public bureaucrat' (D. C. Mueller, *Public Choice III* (Cambridge: Cambridge University Press, 2003), p. 362).

64. Libman, 'Democracy, Size of Bureaucracy, and Economic Growth', p. 1329.

65. See Chapter 3, Section 1.

66. Mueller, *Public Choice III*, p. 371.

67. Row 010, account no 20700000000000180 in the Russian system of public finance.

68. Oleinik, *Market as a Weapon*, pp. 228–9.

69. Russian Federal Treasury, Otchet ob ispolnenii konsolidirovannogo byudzheta sub'ekta RF i byudzheta territorial'nogo gosudarstvennogo vnebyudzhetnogo fonda za 2012 god [Report on the execution of the consolidated budget of the subject of the Russian Federation and the budget of the regional state social security fund], at http://www.roskazna.ru/byudzhetov-subektov-rf-i-mestnykh-byudzhetov/doc/Otch_2012.rar [accessed 18 April 2014]. The conversion rate in mid-December 2012 (US$1=RUR30.71) was used.

70. Oleinik, *Market as a Weapon*, p. 228.

71. M. Dorsch, 'Bailout for Sale? The Vote to Save Wall Street', *Public Choice*, 155 (2013), pp. 211–28, on p. 224.

72. See Chapter 2, Section 5.

73. A previous study suggests a somewhat unusual relationship between the scope of state ownership and the amount of voluntary contributions. In his dataset dated 1998, Venard found a negative association between the level of corruption and the scope of state ownership. He claims that 'in the first period of capitalism development and democratization in Russia, the intervention of government in economic activities may be necessary to spread and implement a correct institutional framework' (Venard, 'Organizational Isomorphism and Corruption', p. 72). Keeping in mind that the dependent variable refers to transfers made in an official and transparent manner, there may exist a positive association between the dependent variable and the regional government ownership. This prediction does not derive from the theory of gate keeping, however.

74. Source of information: Federal State Statistics Service, *Regiony Rossii*, pp. 376–7. This control was used, namely, in Castiglione, Gorbunova, Infante and Smirnova, 'FDI Determinants in an Idiosyncratic Country'; Libman, 'Democracy, Size of Bureaucracy, and Economic Growth'.

75. Source of information: Federal State Statistics Service, *Regiony Rossii*, pp. 401–2. This control was used in Libman and Feld, 'Strategic Tax Collection and Fiscal Decentralization'.

76. Source of information: Federal State Statistics Service, *Regiony Rossii*, pp. 718–9. My previous studies suggest that this is a powerful predictor for several macroeconomic indicators in Russia (Oleinik, *Market as a Weapon*, p. 217).

77. Source of information: Federal State Statistics Service, *Regiony Rossii*, pp. 47–8.

78. Source of information: Federal State Statistics Service, *Regiony Rossii*, pp. 309–11. This control was used in Castiglione, Gorbunova, Infante and Smirnova, 'FDI Determinants in an Idiosyncratic Country'; Ledyaeva, Karhunen and Kosonen, 'The Global Economic Crisis and Foreign Investment in Russia from the EU'.

79. Source of information: Federal State Statistics Service, *Regiony Rossii*, pp. 453–4. This control was used in Mau and Yanovskiy, 'Political and Legal Factors of Economic Growth in Russian Regions'; R. Aidis, S. Estrin and T. M. Mickiewicz, 'Size Matters: Entrepreneurial Entry and Government', *Small Business Economics*, 39 (2012), pp. 119–39; Bruno, Bytchkova and Estrin, 'Institutional Determinants of New Firm Entry in Russia'.

80. Source of information: Federal State Statistics Service, *Regiony Rossii*, pp. 372–3. This control was used in N. Fabry and S. Zeghni, 'Foreign Direct Investment in Russia: How the Investment Climate Matters', *Communist and Post-Communist Studies*, 35 (2002), pp. 289–303; Castiglione, Gorbunova, Infante and Smirnova, 'FDI Determinants in an Idiosyncratic Country' (in both cases as a dependent variable).

81. Source of information: Federal State Statistics Service, *Regiony Rossii*, pp. 691–2. This control was used, namely, in Castiglione, Gorbunova, Infante and Smirnova, 'FDI Determinants in an Idiosyncratic Country' (landlines).

82. Source of information: Federal State Statistics Service, *Regiony Rossii*, pp. 673–6. This control was used in Castiglione, Gorbunova, Infante and Smirnova, 'FDI Determinants in an Idiosyncratic Country'; Ledyaeva, Karhunen and Kosonen, 'The Global Economic Crisis and Foreign Investment in Russia from the EU'.

83. Source of information: Federal State Statistics Service of the Russian Federation, *Regiony Rossii: Osnovnye kharakteristiki sub'ektov RF, 2013 god* [Regions of Russia: Basic Characteristics of the subjects of the Russian Federation], Moscow, 2013, at http://www.gks.ru/free_doc/doc_2013/region/subject.rar [accessed 18 April 2014]. This control was used in Castiglione, Gorbunova, Infante and Smirnova, 'FDI Determinants in an Idiosyncratic Country'.

84. Source of information: Federal State Statistics Service of the Russian Federation, *Regiony Rossii: Osnovnye kharakteristiki sub'ektov RF*. This control was used in Libman, 'Democracy, Size of Bureaucracy, and Economic Growth'; Libman, 'Natural Resources and Sub-National Economic Performance'.

85. Source of information: Federal State Statistics Service of the Russian Federation, *Regiony Rossii: Osnovnye kharakteristiki sub'ektov RF*. This control was used in Castiglione, Gorbunova, Infante and Smirnova, 'FDI Determinants in an Idiosyncratic Country'; Ledyaeva, Karhunen and Kosonen, 'The Global Economic Crisis and Foreign Investment in Russia from the EU'. Both studies found that border regions and/or regions with sea ports have more open economies and attract more FDI than the other regions.

86. Libman, 'Natural Resources and Sub-National Economic Performance', p. 84. The same author uses the physical volume of oil and natural gas production as a control in Libman and Feld, 'Strategic Tax Collection and Fiscal Decentralization'.

87. Federal State Statistic Service of the Russian Federation, Struktura and osnovnye pokazateli deyatel'nosti khozyaistvuyushchikh sub'ektov, table 61. Only 1.3 per cent of this tax goes to the regional budgets, the rest goes to the federal budget (Ministry of Finance of the Russian Federation, Struktura postuplenii v konsolidirovannyi byudzhet RF [Structure of revenues of the consolidated budget of the Russian Federation], at http://info.minfin.ru/kons_doh.php [accessed 18 April 2014]), which nevertheless does not exclude using the *NDPI* as a proxy for the region's endowment in natural resources.

88. J. W. Osborne, 'Best Practices in Data Transformation: The Overlooked Effect of Minimal Values', in J. W. Osborne (ed.), *Best Practices in Quantitative Methods* (Thousand Oaks, CA: Sage, 2008), pp. 197–204.

89. Dagestan, Ingushetia, the Mari El Republic, the Tuva Republic and Chukotka autonomous districts. The city of St Petersburg reporting a negative value of other voluntary

contributions in 2012 (this may be due either to an accounting error or to the return of some previously received contributions) was added to this list.

90. $F=4.053$, $p=0.05$. It should be noted that 'the F tests used in ANOVA are fairly robust to violations of this assumption [of equality of variances], unless the numbers of scores in the groups are small and/or unequal' (R. M. Warner, *Applied Statistics: From Bivariate Through Multivariate Techniques* (Thousand Oaks, CA: Sage, 2008), p. 470).

91. A tolerance of less than 0.20 or 0.10 and/or a variance inflation factor (VIF) of 5 or 10 and above indicates a multicollinearity problem. The values of these measures for Capital funds were 0.028 and 36.091 respectively, for GRP per capita: 0.065 and 15.298, for Population: 0.2 and 4.997. An alternative solution to the problem of collinearity involves using factor analysis or principal component analysis, see, for example, Aidis, Estrin and Mickiewicz, 'Size Matters', p. 126.

92. A similar approach was adapted by P. Karhunen and S. Ledyaeva, 'Corruption Distance, Anti-Corruption Laws and International Ownership Strategies in Russia', *Journal of International Management*, 18 (2012), pp. 196–208, on p. 201; Libman and Feld, 'Strategic Tax Collection and Fiscal Decentralization', p. 468.

93. Federal State Statistics Service of the Russian Federation, *Finansy Rossii*, pp. 150–3.

94. Federal State Statistics Service of the Russian Federation, *Sostav rabotnikov, zameshchavshikh gosudarstvennye (munitsypal'nye) dolzhnosti i dolzhnosti gosudarstvennoi grazhdanskoi (munitsipal'noi) sluzhby po polu, vozrastu, stazhy raboty, obrazovaniyu* [Socio-demographic characteristics of state (municipal) employees working at state (municipal) bodies], Moscow, 2013, at http://www.gks.ru/free_doc/doc_2013/bul_dr/goskadr_13.rar [accessed 19 April 2014], vol. 2, table 7.

95. Peterbugskaya Politika Foundation, 13-i reiting politicheskoi vyzhivaemosti gubernatorov.

96. R. K. Merton, 'Bureaucratic Structure and Personality', *Social Forces*, 18 (1940), pp. 560–8, on p. 561.

97. This finding undermines Vernard's claim (see this chapter, Section 2, endnote 20) that direct government intervention in economic activities may be necessary to reduce corruption. Other voluntary contributions refer to the most transparent dimension of transactions between A and C. If the tendencies of the late 1990s described by Vernard continued up to 2012, the association between the amount of other voluntary contributions and Regional_assets would have been positive.

98. E. Babbie and L. Benaquisto, *Fundamentals of Social Research*, 1st Canadian edn (Scarborough, ON: Nelson, 2002), p. 436.

99. Oleinik, *Market as a Weapon*, pp. 166–70.

100. These manipulations did not help achieve perfection, however. Namely, the values of the two measures of collinearity for RetailPC and IncomePC approached the threshold levels (0.19, 5.4 and 0.17, 5.9 respectively).

101. It should be noted that the total amount of losses is less perfect proxy for A's interests. As discussed before, losses increase or decrease in parallel with profits. The problem of collinearity prevented the entering of net profits in these models.

102. Represented by Harberger's triangle and Tullock's quadrangle in Figure 3.2.

103. The use of a more comprehensive index of experts' evaluations of the governor's chances to remain in office produces an even messier picture. Survival refers to the mean of the two most recent assessments of the governor's entrenchment. When I used, as the dependent variable, the sum of all assessments of the current governor's entrenchment (her overall track record) subject to the square root transformation, F-statistic for the same selection of the independent and control variables as in Model 6 appeared to be

low and not statistically significant (F=1.161, p=0.328). The entry as the dependent variable of a log-transformed product of the governor's length of tenure and the mean of two most recent assessments of her entrenchment led to similar outcomes (F=0.923, p=0.534). Finally, the overall regression was not statistically significant either when I used as the dependent variable the mean of all assessments of the governor's entrenchment as opposed to the mean of two most recent assessments (F=1.617, p=0.103).

104. See the exact quote in Chapter 2, Section 4, endnote 12.

5 Access to Justice: The Rule of Lawyers

1.   M. Weber, *Economy and Society: An Outline of Interpretative Sociology*, ed. R. Guenther and C. Wittich, 2 vols (1922; New York: Bedminster Press, 1968), vol. 1, p. 54; see Chapter 2, Section 4, endnote 15 for the full citation.

2.   Judging by prison population rates (International Centre for Prison Studies 2013), the countries with the most repressive judiciaries include the US (716 at the end of 2011), Cuba (510), the Russian Federation (484), Belarus (438) and El Salvador (425); see Chapter 4, Section 2.

3.   P. Bourdieu, 'The Force of Law: Toward a Sociology of the Juridical Field' (1986), *Hastings Law Journal*, 38 (1987), pp. 805–53, on p. 838.

4.   Department of Justice of Canada, Mandate and Strategic Outcomes, at http://www.justice.gc.ca/eng/abt-apd/mandat/index.html [accessed 17 June 2013].

5.   S. P. Baumgartner, 'Does Access to Justice Improve Countries' Compliance with Human Rights Norms? – An Empirical Study', *Cornell International Law Journal*, 41 (2011), pp. 441–91, on p. 457.

6.   P. Hannaford-Agor and N. Mott, 'Research on Self-Represented Litigation: Preliminary Results and Methodological Considerations', *Justice System Journal*, 24 (2003), pp. 163–81, on p. 171.

7.   D. L. Rhode, *Access to Justice* (New York: Oxford University Press, 2004), p. 82.

8.   J. R. Commons, *Legal Foundations of Capitalism* (1924; Madison, WI: The University of Wisconsin Press, 1959), p. 141.

9.   Rhode, *Access to Justice*, p. 4.

10. R. Zorza, 'Access to Justice: The Emerging Consensus and Some Questions and Implications', *Judicature*, 94 (2011), pp. 156–67, on p. 167; for a review of the literature on the issue of costs, see K. Taylor and K. Svechnikova, *What Does it Cost to Access Justice in Canada? How Much is "Too Much"? And How Do we Know?* (Edmonton: The Canadian Forum on Civil Justice, 2010).

11. A. Paterson, L. Farmer, F. Stephen and J. Love, 'Competition and the Market for Legal Services', *Journal of Law and Society*, 15 (1988), pp. 361–73.

12. 'Jailhouse lawyers' are prison inmates with some knowledge of law who give legal advice and assistance to their fellow inmates. Sometimes this term is used more broadly. It then describes any jurist who provides legal advice to a client without signing a formal contract and being acknowledged as a 'lawyer on the record' by the court.

13. For instance, there are no restrictions as to who may represent a litigant in Russia, as per Sections 25.3 and 25.5 of the Administrative Code of the Russian Federation.

14. Rhode, *Access to Justice*, p. 74.

15. O. E. Williamson, *The Economic Institutions of Capitalism: Firms, Markets, Relational Contracting* (New York: The Free Press, 1985); on the concept of asset specificity see also Chapter 6, Section 4.

16. A. Zaheer and N. Venkatraman, 'Determinants of Electronic Integration in the Insurance Industry: An Empirical Test', *Management Science*, 40 (1994), pp. 549–66, on p. 553.

17. A wrong colour of the cover or incorrect line spacing may lead to a rejection of a court document containing otherwise valid arguments. This holds true even if departures from a prescribed format are minor (e.g. 1.8 line spacing as opposed to double line spacing).

18. An empirical finding that 'it is the type of problem not the characteristics of the person having the problem [including the level of income] that is the major predictor of lawyer seeking' (H. M. Kritzer, 'To Lawyer or Not to Lawyer:Is that the Question?', *Journal of Empirical Legal Studies*, 5 (2008), pp. 875–906, on p. 877) arguably confirms the importance of knowing particular procedural requirements. The more sophisticated the procedures set for a particular type of legal case is, the more chances there are that the litigant will seek legal advice, regardless of the amount of resources at the litigant's disposal.

19. H. Sommerlad, 'Some Reflections on the Relationship between Citizenship, Access to Justice, and the Reform of Legal Aid', *Journal of Law and Society*, 31 (2004), pp. 345–68.

20. R. Moorhead and P. Pleasence, 'Access to Justice after Universalism: Introduction', *Journal of Law and Society*, 30 (2003), pp. 1–10, on p. 2.

21. J. P. George, 'Access to Justice, Costs and Legal Aid', *American Journal of Comparative Law*, 54 (2006), pp. 293–315, on p. 312.

22. M. J. Anderson, 'Legal Education Reform, Diversity, and Access to Justice', *Rutgers Law Review*, 61 (2009), pp. 1011–36, on p. 1015.

23. See Chapter 2, Section 4.

24. T. Eggertsson, *Economic Behavior and Institutions* (Cambridge: Cambridge University Press, 1990), pp. 5–6; see also Chapter 2, Section 1.

25. Critical sociologists describe the formation of rational interests in detail by considering the example of the housing market. They assert that 'the housing market is ... *truly constructed by the state*, particularly through the financial assistance' (P. Bourdieu, *The Social Structures of the Economy*, trans. C. Turner (2000; Cambridge: Polity, 2005), p. 89; emphasis in the original).

26. Commons, *Legal Foundations of Capitalism*, p. 242; see also Bourdieu, 'The Force of Law', p. 831.

27. G. Ailon, 'What *B* Would Otherwise Do: A Critique of Conceptualizations of "Power" in Organizational Theory', *Organization*, 16 (2006), pp. 771–800, on p. 776.

28. P. Bourdieu, 'Rethinking the State: Genesis and Structure of the Bureaucratic Field', *Sociological Theory*, 12 (1994), pp. 1–18, on p. 10.

29. Bourdieu, 'The Force of Law', p. 833; emphasis in the original.

30. Weber, *Economy and Society*, vol. 1, p. 976; see also D. Matza, *Delinquency and Drift* (1964; New Brunswick, NJ: Transaction Publishers, 1990), pp. 118–19.

31. Bourdieu, 'The Force of Law', p. 817.

32. Bourdieu, 'The Force of Law', p. 808.

33. US President George W. Bush echoes this line of thought, stating in his 2004 State of the Union address that 'our agenda for jobs and growth must help small-business owners and employees with relief from needless Federal regulation and *protect them from junk and frivolous lawsuits*' (emphasis added).

34. Bourdieu, 'The Force of Law', p. 817.

35. H. De Soto, *The Other Path: The Economic Answer to Terrorism* (1989; New York: Basic Books, 2005).

36. Socioeconomics has a similar ambition to study the interplay of two motives in human behaviour, utility maximization and moral imperatives. 'Where the neoclassical as-

sumption is that people seek to maximize one utility, we assume that people pursue at least two irreducible "utilities", and have two sources of valuation: pleasure and morality' (Etzioni, A., *The Moral Dimension: Toward a New Economics* (New York: The Free Press, 1988), p. 4).

37. Commons, *Legal Foundations of Capitalism*, p. 67.

38. A. Oleinik, *Market as a Weapon: The Socio-Economic Machinery of Dominance in Russia* (New Brunswick, NJ: Transaction Publishers, 2011), pp. 145–63.

39. Weber, *Economy and Society*, vol. 1, p. 217.

40. The arguments below refer to the common law system, yet they can also be adapted to the particularities of civil law.

41. De Soto, *The Other Path*.

42. Anderson, 'Legal Education Reform, Diversity, and Access to Justice'; T. Kelly, 'Law, Culture and Access to Justice under the Palestinian National Authority', *Development and Change*, 36 (2005), pp. 865–6.

43. The case of Canada is particularly interesting. This country has two legal traditions, common law and civil law (in the province of Québec). Legal processes deriving from common law may be perceived as alien and imposed from above by supporters of the project for Québec sovereignty. For instance, the Front de Liberation du Québec Manifesto popular in the second half of the 1960s (especially at the beginning of the October 1970 crisis) labelled the judges as 'rotten' and associated them with 'the Anglo-Saxons of the Commonwealth' (the Manifesto was aired by CBC/Radio-Canada on 8 October 1970).

44. De Soto, *The Other Path*.

45. D. Beetham, *The Legitimation of Power* (Atlantic Highlands, NJ: Humanities Press International: 1991), p. 16; see also Chapter 1, Section 3.

46. Commons, *Legal Foundations of Capitalism*, p. 300; G. M. Hodgson, 'On the Institutional Foundations of Law: The Insufficiency of Custom and Private Ordering', *Journal of Economic Issues*, 43 (2009), pp. 143–66, on p. 155.

47. De Soto (De Soto, *The Other Path*) uses the term 'extralegal' to describe actors and practices that remain outside the justice system.

48. Commons, *Legal Foundations of Capitalism*, p. 355.

49. These alternatives correspond to Type I and Type II errors in statistical analysis (W. L. Newman, *Social Research Methods: Qualitative and Quantitative Approaches*, 6th edn (Boston, MA: Allyn & Bacon, 2006), p. 373); see also Chapter 7, Section 1.

50. The 'first' Coase theorem depicts such a world. It states that if transaction costs are nil, the initial distribution of property rights does not affect the value of production (C. Ménard, 'Transaction Cost Economics: From the Coase Theorem to Empirical Studies', in A. Oleinik (ed.), *The Institutional Economics of Russia's Transformation* (Aldershot: Ashgate, 2005), pp. 45–64, on pp. 46–7). In practical terms this means that the parties are able to exchange property rights without a court's intervention: the party who values a property right the most will get it sooner or later. This party will buy out the right from the other party who possessed it at the initial stage.

51. The information asymmetry increases, paradoxically, if state representatives are a party in a dispute. State representatives have an 'innate instinct for secrecy' (M. Spencer and J. Spencer, 'Coping with *Conway* v. *Rimmer* [1968] AC 910: How Civil Servants Control Access to Justice', *Journal of Law and Society*, 37 (2010), pp. 387–411): they tend to provide the court with as little information as possible.

52. As of June 2013, the *Web of Knowledge*, the most comprehensive database of scholarly publications covering the period since the start of the nineteenth century, lists thirty-four sources only on the topic of judges' motivation ('Topic=(judge* motivation), Categories=(Law OR Criminology Penology)).

53. Neoclassical economists assume that the judge maximizes utility like any other actor. For instance, the judge presumably has an interest in rendering impartial judgments because the reputation of impartiality helps increase the number of 'clients' (litigants who choose this particular judge) in the future and, consequently, the judge's income (P. Milgrom, D. C. North and B. Weingast, "The Role of Institutions in the Revival of Trade: The Law Merchant, Private Judges, and the Champaign Fairs', *Economics and Politics*, 2 (1990), pp. 1–23).

54. A.T. Turk, 'Law as a Weapon in Social Conflict', *Social Problems*, 23 (1976), pp. 276–91, on p. 276.

55. Bourdieu, 'The Force of Law', p. 814; see also Commons, *Legal Foundations of Capitalism*, p. 332. Economists tend to consider law as instrumental. Neoclassical economists see law as an instrument for achieving an optimal allocation of resources, namely in conditions of non-zero transaction costs. The 'second' Coase theorem states that, when transaction costs are positive, the initial distribution of property rights counts and the court shall intervene by allocating resources to those who value them the most (C. Ménard, 'Transaction Cost Economics', p. 47). Institutional economists consider law as a tool for social change. 'The law tends to be instrumental for the institutionalists, while for Proudhon, the law is based on morals and is an expression of justice' (S. Solari, 'The "Practical Reason" of Reformers: Proudhon vs. Institutionalism', *Journal of Economic Issues*, 46 (2012), pp. 227–40, on p. 237).

56. Commons, *Legal Foundations of Capitalism*, p. 125.

57. See also Chapter 2, Section 5.

58. Commons, *Legal Foundations of Capitalism*, p. 304.

59. A comparative analysis of the system of criminal justice shows that human rights tend to be protected if the accused are provided only with legal counsel. 'The case of the correlation between the right to counsel and a country's human rights practices is fairly robust, if not particularly strong' (Baumgartner, 'Does Access to Justice Improve Countries' Compliance with Human Rights Norms?', p. 486).

60. Bourdieu, 'The Force of Law', p. 834.

61. Commons, *Legal Foundations of Capitalism*, p. 356.

62. The search was conducted on 26 March 2013 using the *Lexis-Nexis* database.

63. Most publications, 68.1 per cent, are articles, 15.4 per cent are editorials or op-ed commentaries, 8.4 per cent are letters to the editor and 8.4 per cent are other types (announcement, book or movie review, etc.)

64. 'Described as focused on "efficiency and effectiveness rather than (on) equality and ideals", the New Labour model has been presented as a modernized social democratic version of access to justice as access to legal services, which will be more effective in countering social exclusion' (Sommerlad, 'Some Reflections on the Relationship between Citizenship, Access to Justice, and the Reform of Legal Aid', p. 362).

65. J. P. George, 'Access to Justice, Costs and Legal Aid', p. 296.

66. Rhode, *Access to Justice*, p. 3.

67. A. Oleinik, 'Mixing Quantitative and Qualitative Content Analysis: Triangulation at Work', *Quality & Quantity*, 45 (2010), pp. 859–73.

68. Bourdieu, 'The Force of Law', p. 818.

69. *GM*, 2002.
70. *NYT*, 1992.
71. *T*, 1993.
72. Bourdieu, 'Rethinking the State', p. 5; emphasis in the original.
73. *GM*, 1992.
74. *NYT*, 2010.
75. *T*, 2004.
76. *GM*, 2012.
77. *NYT*, 2004.
78. *T*, 2006.
79. *GM*, 2006.
80. *NYT*, 2004.
81. *T*, 2012.
82. *GM*, 1994.
83. *NYT*, 2010.
84. *T*, 1996.
85. Rhode, *Access to Justice*, p. 5.
86. *GM*, 2002.
87. *NYT*, 2004.
88. *T*, 2000.
89. As noted before, the code 'Financial barriers' can be added to this list.
90. *GM*, 2000.
91. *T*, 2001.
92. Sommerlad, 'Some Reflections on the Relationship between Citizenship, Access to Justice, and the Reform of Legal Aid', p. 367.
93. *GM*, 2002.
94. *NYT*, 2004.
95. *T*, 1999.
96. *GM*, 1997.
97. *T*, 2001.
98. *GM*, 2012.
99. *NYT*, 2010.
100. *T*, 2004.
101. *GM*, 1998.
102. *NYT*, 2009.
103. *T*, 2011.
104. A letter to the editor published in *The Times* in 1997.
105. Oleinik, 'Mixing Quantitative and Qualitative Content Analysis'.
106. The two-dimensional map of coding co-occurrences was produced using the techniques of multidimensional scaling. This shows the relative frequency (measured by cosine theta) of the codes co-occurring in the same paragraph. The larger the circle, the more often a particular code occurs. The closer the circles, the more often the corresponding codes co-occur in the same paragraph. The stress (distortion in the process of data reduction) is close to an acceptable level: stress of .15 or lower refers to the highest standard (H. R. Bernard, *Social Research Methods*, 2nd edn (Thousand Oaks, CA: Sage, 2013), p. 413).
107. Taylor and Svechnikova, *What Does it Cost to Access Justice in Canada?*.
108. In Figure 5.1, they are visualized by lines connecting particular codes.

109. The observed frequency of a sequence (for instance, Code A followed by Code B) was compared with its expected frequency. After converting the difference into a Z-value, one is able to calculate the probability of obtaining this particular sequence.

110. *GM*, 2002.

111. The relative frequency of the codes was cross-tabulated with the country of publication and the format of publication. Values of Student's F and their level of statistical significance informed the decision as to whether the observed differences can be deemed statistically significant.

112. Rhode, *Access to Justice*, p. 20.

113. Zorza, 'Access to Justice', p. 160.

6 An Invisible Dimension of the Visible Hand: Entry Control in Internal Labour Markets

1. O. E. Williamson, *The Economic Institutions of Capitalism: Firms, Markets, Relational Contracting* (New York: The Free Press, 1985), ch. 3.

2. R. H. Coase, 'The Nature of the Firm', *Economica*, new series 4 (1937), pp. 386–405, on p. 388. The work cited is D. H. Robertson, *Control of Industry: Cambridge Economic Handbooks IV* (London: Nisbet, 1923), p. 85.

3. M. Weber, *Economy and Society: An Outline of Interpretative Sociology*, ed. R. Guenther and C. Wittich, 2 vols (1922; New York: Bedminster Press, 1968), vol. 1, p. 943; see also the introduction to Chapter 2 in this book.

4. J. S. Coleman, *Foundations of Social Theory* (Cambridge, MA, and London: The Belknap Press of Harvard University Press, 1990), pp. 71–2.

5. H. Simon ('A Formal Theory of the Employment Relationship', *Econometrica*, 19 (1951), pp. 293–305) describes the difference between the two positions in terms of the employment contract, which applies to permanent positions, and the sale contract, which applies to temporary positions. The sale contract involves the exchange of a specified quantity of a completely specified commodity (labour) for a stated sum of money. This contract has a predetermined end-date: it expires as soon as the completely specified commodity is delivered.

6. O. E. Williamson, *Markets and Hierarchies, Analysis and Antitrust Implications: A Study in the Economics of Internal Organization* (New York: The Free Press, 1975), p. 132.

7. Weber, *Economy and Society*, vol. 1, p. 4.

8. C. I. Barnard, *The Functions of the Executive*, 30th anniversary edn (1938; Cambridge, MA: Harvard University Press, 1968), p. 4.

9. O. E. Williamson, 'Comparative Economic Organization: The Analysis of Discrete Structural Alternatives', *Administrative Science Quarterly*, 36 (1991), pp. 269–96, on p. 274.

10. Barnard, *The Functions of the Executive*, p. 23. See also Hannah Arendt's similar argument on benefits of actions 'in concert' cited in Chapter 1, Section 1, endnote 5.

11. L. Putterman, 'The Firm as Association versus the Firm as Commodity: Efficiency, Rights and Ownership', *Economics and Philosophy*, 4 (1988), pp. 243–66, on p. 246.

12. In a broad sense, hierarchy is another name for the organization: 'an integrated organization or "hierarchy" can be defined as a conscious arrangement jointly chosen by agents (or a subset of agents) to deliberately coordinate their actions on a regular basis and for specific purposes through a set of (partially) explicit agreements combining command and cooperation' (C. Ménard, 'Theory of Organizations: The Diversity of Arrangements

in a Developed Market Economy', in A. Oleinik (ed.), *The Institutional Economics of Russia's Transformation* (Aldershot: Ashgate, 2005), pp. 88–111, on p. 94). In a narrow sense, a hierarchy refers to an organization with a unitary, centralized structure.

13. Williamson, *Markets and Hierarchies, Analysis and Antitrust Implications*, ch. 8.

14. J. R. Commons, *Legal Foundations of Capitalism* (1924; Madison, WI: The University of Wisconsin Press, 1959), p. 18.

15. Barnard, *The Functions of the Executive*, pp. 172–3.

16. As argued, for example, by James Galbraith. In *The New Industrial State* (London: H. Hamilton, 1967) he emphasizes the transfer of power within the organization from the owner to representatives of the technostructure, a group of specialists in management and decision making.

17. The existence of hybrid forms makes the boundary between the organization and the market more blurred. Hybrid organizations such as long-term or relational contracts between partners, who maintain their formal autonomy, include elements of both bargaining and managerial transactions (Ménard, 'Theory of Organizations', pp. 95–6). Despite their growing popularity, hybrids refer to a particular arrangement. This arrangement complements the market and the organization rather than substituting for them.

18. M. Jensen and W. Meckling, 'Theory of the Firm: Managerial Behavior, Agency Costs and Ownership Structure', *Journal of Financial Economics*, 3 (1976), pp. 305–60, on p. 310.

19. P. B. Doeringer and M. J. Piore, *Internal Labour Markets and Manpower Analysis* (Cambridge, MA: Harvard University and Massachusetts Institute of Technology, 1970), pp. 1a–I.2; italics in the original.

20. C. Haeck and F. Verboven, 'The Internal Economics of a University: Evidence from Personnel Data', *Journal of Labour Economics*, 30 (2012), pp. 591–626, on p. 595.

21. David Kreps defines organization culture a set of rules that facilitate mutual understanding between the boss and the employees: 'it gives hierarchical inferiors an idea *ex ante* how the organization will react to circumstances as they arise' (D. Kreps, 'Corporate Culture and Economic Theory', in J. Alt and K. Shepsle (eds), *Perspectives on Positive Political Economy* (Cambridge: Cambridge University Press, 1990), pp. 90–143, on p. 126).

22. D. M. Burton, 'Revisiting Internal Labour Markets', in P. Osterman (ed.), *Economy in Society: Essays in Honor of Michael J. Piore* (Cambridge, MA: The MIT Press, 2013), pp. 11–42, on p. 14.

23. P. Osterman and D. M. Burton, 'Ports and Ladders: The Nature and Relevance of Internal Labour Markets in a Changing World', in S. Ackroyd, R. Batt, P. Thompson and P. S. Tolbert (eds), *The Oxford Handbook of Work and Organization* (Oxford: Oxford University Press, 2005), pp. 425–45, on p. 441.

24. A. Heisz, 'The Evolution of Job Stability in Canada: Trends and Comparisons to U.S. Results', *Canadian Journal of Economics*, 38 (2005), pp. 105–27, on pp. 122, 124.

25. Burton, 'Revisiting Internal Labour Markets', p. 11.

26. Doeringer and Piore, *Internal Labour Markets and Manpower Analysis*, p. I.2; italics in the original.

27. Doeringer and Piore, *Internal Labour Markets and Manpower Analysis*, p. III.26.

28. Doeringer and Piore, *Internal Labour Markets and Manpower Analysis*, pp. III.26–7.

29. Barnard, *The Functions of the Executive*, p. 89.

30. Williamson, *Markets and Hierarchies, Analysis and Antitrust implications*, p. 52.

31. S. Macdonald and C. Williams, 'The Survival of the Gatekeeper', *Research Policy*, 23 (1994), pp. 123–32, on p. 123.

32. S. Macdonald and C. Williams, 'Beyond the Boundary: An Information Perspective on the Role of the Gatekeeper in the Organization', *Journal of Product Innovation Management*, 10 (1993), pp. 417–27, on p. 425.

33. See Chapter 1, Section 2 on differences between strategic and structural components of power.

34. Barnard, *The Functions of the Executive*, p. 149; Williamson, *Markets and Hierarchies, Analysis and Antitrust implications*, p. 43; H. Ishida, Kuo-Hsien-Su and S. Spilerman, 'Models of Career Advancement in Organizations', *European Sociological Review*, 18 (2002), pp. 179–98;

35. S. L. C. Bosley, J. Arnold and L. Cohen, 'How Other People Shape our Careers: A Typology Drawn from Career Narratives', *Human Relations*, 62 (2009), pp. 1487–1520, on p. 1506.

36. Osterman and Burton, 'Ports and Ladders', p. 430.

37. Haeck and Verboven, 'The Internal Economics of a University', p. 595.

38. R. Burt, 'The Social Structure of Competition', in N. Nohria and R. Eccles (eds), *Networks and Organizations: Structure, Form, and Action* (Boston, MA: Harvard Business School Press, 1992), pp. 56–90, on p. 79.

39. The concept of power triad was introduced in Chapter 2, Section 4.

40. M. Aoki, *Economie japonaise: information, motivations et marchandage* (1989; Paris: Economica, 1991), p. 58.

41. Ishida, Kuo-Hsien-Su and Spilerman, 'Models of Career Advancement in Organizations', pp. 183–4.

42. In the Canadian case the Public Service Employment Act (S.C. 2003, c. 22, ss. 12, 13) regulate the movement of the labour force within public service organizations.

43. J. Killian and N. Eklund (eds), *Handbook of Administrative Reform: An International Perspective* (Boca Raton, FL: CRC Press, 2008).

44. Barnard, *The Functions of the Executive*, p. 256; see also Aoki, *Economie japonaise*, pp. 45, 168.

45. See Chapter 2, Section 5 and Chapter 3, Section 1.

46. C. Crossland and D. C. Hambrick, 'Differences in Managerial Discretion across Countries: How Nation-Level Institutions Affect the Degree to Which CEOs Matter', *Strategic Management Journal*, 32 (2011), pp. 797–819, on p. 797.

47. The fact that the boss may be assisted by a human resources (HR) specialist or even delegate some decisions regarding hiring to the latter does not affect the main argument as long as the boss has the final say in hiring.

48. Doeringer and Piore, *Internal Labour Markets and Manpower Analysis*, p. 5.17.

49. Barnard, *The Functions of the Executive*, p. 217.

50. Barnard, *The Functions of the Executive*, p. 42.

51. See Chapter 3, Section 1.

52. Barnard, *The Functions of the Executive*, p. 240.

53. Doeringer and Piore, *Internal Labour Markets and Manpower Analysis*, p. I.3; Osterman and Burton, 'Ports and Ladders', p. 428.

54. American Association of University Professors (AAUP), '1940 Statement of Principles on Academic Freedom and Tenure', at http://www.aaup.org/report/1940-statement-principles-academic-freedom-and-tenure [accessed 12 June 2014].

55. American Association of University Professors (AAUP), '2006 AAUP Contingent Faculty Index', p. 6, at http://www.aaup.org/sites/default/files/files/AAUPContingentFacultyIndex2006.pdf [accessed 12 June 2014].

56. C. Ménard, 'Transaction Cost Economics: From the Coase Theorem to Empirical Studies', in A. Oleinik (ed.), *The Institutional Economics of Russia's Transformation* (Aldershot: Ashgate, 2005), pp. 45–64, on pp. 54–5.

57. Doeringer and Piore, *Internal Labour Markets and Manpower Analysis*, p. II.2.

58. Williamson, *Markets and Hierarchies, Analysis and Antitrust Implications*, pp. 73–9.

59. Doeringer and Piore, *Internal Labour Markets and Manpower Analysis*, p. II.9.

60. Haeck and Verboven, 'The Internal Economics of a University', p. 593.

61. A.Oleinik, *Knowledge and Networking: On Communication in the Social Sciences* (New Brunswick, NJ: Transaction Publishers, 2014), chs 2, 6.

62. This is a positive statement arguably describing the current stage in the evolution of academia: 'the relationship between academics and their universities increasingly resembles employee–employer relationships, because rewards and sanctions are, more than before, in the hands of the managers of higher education institutions' (C. Musselin, 'How Peer Review Empowers the Academic Profession and University Managers: Changes in Relationships between the State, Universities and the Professoriate', *Research Policy*, 42 (2013), pp. 1165–73, on p. 1167). It should not be interpreted in a normative manner – however academia is organized. Neither had it applied to the universities in the past. When serving as president of Columbia University, Dwight D. Eisenhower reportedly 'referred to faculty as employees of the university, he was quickly admonished with the response, "Mr. President, faculty are not employees, they are the university"' (R. D. Howard, G. W. McLaughlin, W. E. Knight and Associates, *The Handbook of Institutional Research* (San Francisco, CA: Jossey-Bass, 2012), p. 140).

63. American Association of University Professors (AAUP), '2006 AAUP Contingent Faculty Index', p. 9.

64. Oleinik, *Knowledge and Networking*, pp. 165–7; see also Chapter 7, Section 1.

65. T. Veblen, *The Higher Learning in America: A Memorandum on the Conduct of Universities by Business Men* (1918; New York: Sagamore Press, 1957), p. 35.

66. Oleinik, *Knowledge and Networking*, ch. 5.

67. Depending on their research intensity and the relative scope of the graduate and undergraduate programmes that they offer, North American universities are conventionally classified in four groups: doctoral and research universities, Masters degree universities (comprehensive universities in Canada), Baccalaureate universities (undergraduate universities in Canada) and associate degree colleges.

68. W. Goldsmith, 'Harvard has Lowest Percentage of Tenure-Track Profs in Ivies', *Harvard Crimson*, 13 December 2006.

69. Oleinik, *Knowledge and Networking*, pp. 142–3.

70. The study of Haeck and Verboven ('The Internal Economics of a University') represents a notable exception: the researchers consulted the personnel records of all professors employed at a large European university between 1991 and 2007.

71. A search in the Web of Science database carried out on 13 June 2014 using keywords Topic: LinkedIn AND Topic: 'labour market' did not produce a single hit. When the keywords were changed for Topic: LinkedIn AND Topic: employment, the search produced a list of five articles.

72. LinkedIn Executive account holders can see all details of their second- and third-level connections. The search was conducted on 5–6 May 2014 using the following parameters: Title: professor, Company (current): 'Higher School of Economics' OR 'Memo-

rial University' OR 'University of Mississippi' OR 'Moscow State University', Location: Russia OR Canada OR United States OR Russia.

73. The number of webpages created and indexed at http://www.hse.ru/org/persons as of 27–8 May 2014.

74. The variance of Y scores should be fairly homogeneous across groups, that is, across levels of the dummy variables. For the LinkedIn data, this condition is not met for most, 6 out of 8, of the dummy variables. However, the F tests used in ANOVA are fairly robust to violations of this assumption (see Chapter 4, Section 3, endnote 44). The condition in question is met for 7 out of 8 dummy variables in the HSE official data, however.

75. As in the previous chapters, the terms 'dependent' and 'independent' are used for the sake of convenience.

76. 'There are a number of different meaningful ways to measure job stability. A common approach is to examine the average tenure of currently employed individuals' (Heisz, 'The Evolution of Job Stability in Canada', p. 109; see also Doeringer and Piore, *Internal Labour Markets and Manpower Analysis*, p. VIII.39–40).

77. Russia historically has a two-level doctorate system, similar to that in Germany (see Chapter 4, Section 2, endnote 8). The first of the two doctoral degrees, *kandidat nauk*, is largely considered to be equivalent to a PhD degree in North America, even if disagreements on this issue continue.

78. Haeck and Verboven, 'The Internal Economics of a University', p. 604.

79. Haeck and Verboven, 'The Internal Economics of a University', p. 600.

80. P. Aghion, M. Dewatripont, C.Hoxby, A.Mas-Colell and A.Sapir, 'The Governance and Performance of Universities: Evidence from Europe and the US', *Economic Policy*, 25 (2010), pp. 7–59, on p. 55.

81. Burton, 'Revisiting Internal Labour Markets', p. 12.

82. The HSE has campuses in Moscow, St Petersburg, Perm and Nizhny Novgorod.

83. See this chapter, Section 2.

84. For instance, in the Belgian university mentioned previously, females represent only 13 per cent of its full-time faculty members (Haeck and Verboven, 'The Internal Economics of a University', p. 600).

85. My previous research showed that bonuses awarded to faculty members by administrative heads in a discretionary manner represent a significant part of the former's salaries at the HSE (Oleinik, *Knowledge and Networking*, pp. 141–2).

86. Standardized and unstandardized coefficients have the following meaning. 'The b_i coefficients for each dummy-coded predictor variable may correspond to contrasts between group means or to differences between group means and the grand mean' (R. M. Warner, *Applied Statistics: From Bivariate Through Multivariate Techniques* (Thousand Oaks, CA: Sage, 2008), p. 474).

87. See Chapter 4, Section 4, endnote 2.

88. This university has an explicit policy for placing its graduates on a fast track in hiring and promotions; see Oleinik, *Knowledge and Networking*, p. 143.

89. The elaboration paradigm considers this situation as an example of specification, i.e. we have specified the conditions under which the original relationship occurs.

90. Federal State Statistics Service, *Obrazovanie v Rossii* [Education in Russia] (Moscow, 2003), table 5.15.

91. A. Chandler, *The Visible Hand: The Managerial Revolution in American Business* (Cambridge, MA: Harvard University Press, 1977).

7 Quality Control as a Weapon: Gate Keeping in Peer Review

1.   If the university refers to a particular organization in science, the term 'academia' is understood here as the institutional environment of science. In other words, the scope of academia extends beyond the boundaries of the university and the other scientific organizations (research institute, labouratory, etc.).

2.   P. Gibbs and H. J. Macy, 'Introduction: The Arena of Gatekeeping', in P. Gibbs and E. H. Blakely (eds), *Gatekeeping in BSW Programs* (New York: Columbia University Press, 2000), pp. 3–21, on p. 9.

3.   M. Lamont, *How Professors Think: Inside the Curious World of Academic Judgment* (Cambridge, MA: Harvard University Press, 2009), p. 2.

4.   W.-M. Roth 'Editorial Power/Authorial Suffering', *Research in Science Education*, 32 (2002), pp. 215–40.

5.   'Although never termed as such, peer review in the 19th and 20th centuries acted as a gatekeeper' (T. H. Gould, *Do We Still Need Peer Review? An Argument for Change* (Lanham, MA: Scarecrow Press, 2013), p. 49).

6.   'Public universities ... are concerned with providing services to meet the needs of stake-holders, including students, prospective and past students, staff, government, partners and the wider community, rather than with primarily satisfying the financial goals of shareholders' (G. D. Carnegie and J. Tuck, 'Understanding the ABC of University Governance', *Australian Journal of Public Administration*, 69 (2010), pp. 431–41, on p. 437).

7.   See, for instance, S. J. Ferris and M. McKee, 'Matching Candidates with Academic Teams: A Case for Academic Tenure', *International Journal of Law and Economics*, 25 (2005), pp. 290–310, on p. 292.

8.   P. Bourdieu, 'The Force of Law: Toward a Sociology of the Juridical Field' (1986), *Hastings Law Journal*, 38 (1987), pp. 805–53.

9.   P. Bourdieu, 'Rethinking the State: Genesis and Structure of the Bureaucratic Field', *Sociological Theory*, 12 (1994), pp. 1–18.

10.   P. Bourdieu, *The Social Structures of the Economy*, trans. C. Turner (2000; Cambridge: Polity, 2005).

11.   See A. Oleinik, *Market as a Weapon: The Socio-Economic Machinery of Dominance in Russia* (New Brunswick, NJ: Transaction Publishers, 2011), pp. 154–5 and Chapter 2, Section 4, endnote 5.

12.   D. C. North, *Structure and Change in Economic History* (New York: W. W. Norton, 1981), p. 36.

13.   R. H. Coase, 'The Nature of the Firm', *Economica*, new series, 4 (1937), pp. 386–405, on p. 390.

14.   North, *Structure and Change in Economic History*, p. 41.

15.   P. Dasgupta and P. A. David, 'Toward a New Economics of Science' (1994), in P. Mirowski and E.-M. Sent (eds), *Science Bought and Sold: Essays in the Economics of Science* (Chicago, IL: The University of Chicago Press, 2002), pp. 219–48, on p. 227; see also M. Callon, 'From Science as an Economic Activity to Socioeconomic of Scientific Research: The Dynamics of Emerged and Consolidated Techno-Economic Networks', in Mirowski and Sent (eds), *Science Bought and Sold*, pp. 277–317, on p. 286.

16.   In the words of John Commons, 'the modern concept of property has evolved from the holding of things to the control of the supply of things through controlling the transactions of persons' (J. R. Commons, *Legal Foundations of Capitalism* (1924; Madison, WI: The University of Wisconsin Press, 1959), p. 320).

17. T. Sandler, *Collective Action: Theory and Applications* (Ann Arbor, MI: The University of Michigan Press, 1992), p. 60.

18. S. F. Hamilton, D. L. Sunding and D. Zilberman, 'Public Goods and the Value of Product Quality Regulations: The Case of Food Safety', *Journal of Public Economics*, 87 (2003), pp. 799–817.

19. Social Sciences and Humanities Research Council, Memorandum of Understanding 'Roles and Responsibilities in the Management of Federal Grants and Awards' (2007), section 3.1b of Schedule 6 'Peer review', at http://www.nserc-crsng.gc.ca/nserc-crsng/policies-politiques/mouroles-protocolroles/index_eng.asp [accessed 27 June 2014].

20. G. Simmel, *The Philosophy of Money*, trans. T. Bottomore and D. Frisby (1970; London: Routledge & Kegan Paul, 1978), p. 129.

21. Simmel, *The Philosophy of Money*, p. 115.

22. 'Peer review is a mechanism ... for quality control' (D. Shatz, *Peer Review: A Critical Inquiry* (Lanham, MA: Rowman & Littlefield Publishers, 2004), p. 1); see also A. Etzioni, 'The Need for Quality Filters in Information Systems', *Science*, new series, 171 (1971), p. 133.

23. Gould, *Do We Still Need Peer Review?*, p. 35. The cited author does not explain, however, why the individual academic needs to submit her work to the judgment of a peer beforehand. I think that Simmel's argument helps to locate a missing link in Gould's reasoning.

24. Gould, *Do We Still Need Peer Review?*, p. 46.

25. For more detail on the concept of the Republic of Letters, see A. Oleinik, *Knowledge and Networking: On Communication in the Social Sciences* (New Brunswick, NJ: Transaction Publishers, 2014), pp. 165–7, and Chapter 6, Section 4.

26. M. Polanyi, 'The Republic of Science: Its Political and Economic Theory' (1969), in Mirowski and Sent (eds), *Science Bought and Sold*, pp. 465–85, on p. 471. A web of cross-references described by Polanyi has some features of the beauty contest that John Maynard Keynes used as a point of reference in his description of the stock market (see the introduction to Chapter 4, in particular endnote 4). Some consequences of this rather surprising similarity will be explored in Subsection 2.1 of this chapter (see endnote 8).

27. The geodesic triangle does not have anything in common with the power triad.

28. K. Alder, *The Measure of All Things: The Seven-Year Odyssey and Hidden Error That Transformed the World* (New York: The Free Press, 2002), p. 223.

29. For instance, triangulation in scientific research takes several forms: data triangulation (the use of data from several sources), theory triangulation (comparison of several theoretical frameworks), methodological triangulation (the application of two or more methods for processing the same data) and investigation (the involvement of two and more researchers who implement the same programme in an independent manner) triangulation. For more detail, see T. D. Jick, 'Mixing Qualitative and Quantitative Methods: Triangulation in Action', *Administrative Science Quarterly*, 24 (1979), pp. 602–11 and A. Ma and B. Norwich, 'Triangulation and Theoretical Understanding', *International Journal of Social Research Methodology*, 10 (2007), pp. 173–84.

30. Shatz, *Peer Review*, pp. 86–9.

31. Shatz, *Peer Review*, p. 16. Similar negative consequences are attributed to government regulation of product quality in the markets. 'If the government regulates product quality in a way that reduces choice, there is a loss of freedom, which is a public good itself, since it cannot be denied to any consumer and is enjoyed by all consumers simultaneously' (Hamilton, Sunding and Zilberman, 'Public Goods and the Value of Product Quality Regulations', p. 800).

32. 'The research indicates a stronger likelihood that unsuitable articles would be rejected when three reviewers were involved (instead of two), it also indicates a higher likelihood that more suitable articles would be rejected' (Gould, *Do We Still Need Peer Review?*, p. 67); see also Oleinik, *Knowledge and Networking*, pp. 91–2.

33. Austin Turk points out a similar transformation of law (A. T. Turk, 'Law as a Weapon in Social Conflict', *Social Problems*, 23 (1976), pp. 276–91). Law as a means of conflict management does not enjoy immunity against the eventual transformation into its opposite, namely a 'partisan weapon' in the hands of one party in the conflict.

34. H.A. Simon, 'Rationality as Process and as Product of Thought', *American Economic Review*, 68 (1978), pp. 1–16.

35. Academia has more than two sorts of boundaries and, correspondingly, gates. The scarcity of research funds represents a third type of boundary and separate procedures for peer review of grant applications. The study of the control of access to research funds remains outside the scope of the present chapter, however. The interested reader would do well to consult additional sources, such as Lamont, *How Professors Think* and Oleinik, *Knowledge and Networking*, pp. 85–90.

36. David Shatz makes a similar assumption in his study of peer review. When discussing peer review in academic publishing, he states that 'for the purposes of this book it will not matter ... whether review of an article is conducted by an outside referee or an editor or some in-house person or persons' (Shatz, *Peer Review*, p. 8). In the hierarchy of academic publishing, the editor has a higher rank than the author of a manuscript.

37. Ferris and McKee, 'Matching Candidates with Academic Teams', p. 291.

38. This change in the emphasis produces a conflict of interest: an academic's obligations as a network member diverge from her obligations as a citizen of the universal Republic of Letters or Republic of Science (Oleinik, *Knowledge and Networking*, ch. 3). The academic develops an 'us versus them' mentality and, consequently, a bias against members of the other networks. Shatz uses the concepts of affiliational and ideological biases in this respect. The former refers to a belief that 'as a class, members of a particular group do work that is inferior to members of other groups'. 'A referee (or editor) who antecedently holds strong views for or against an author's position' has the latter type of bias (Shatz, *Peer Review*, pp. 39, 42; emphasis in the original).

39. Ferris and McKee, 'Matching Candidates with Academic Teams', p. 300.

40. In this sense, peer review in the context of networking has features like those of the beauty contest mentioned by Keynes in his discussion of the operation of the stock market (see Section 1, endnote 15 in this chapter).

41. M. Foucault, *The Government of Self and Others: Lectures at the Collège de France, 1982–1983*, trans. G. Burchell (New York: Picador/Palgrave Macmillan, 2011), p. 183.

42. M. Foucault, *The Courage of Truth (The Government of Self and Others II): Lectures at the Collège de France, 1983–1984*, trans. G. Burchell (New York: Palgrave Macmillan, 2011), p. 61. As a matter of fact, a similar opinion was shared by many European intellectuals during the Age of Enlightenment (M. Malia, *Russia under Western Eyes: From the Bronze Horseman to the Lenin Mausoleum* (Cambridge, MA: The Belknap Press of Harvard University Press, 1999), p. 45). They believed that the education of an individual vested in power represents a better investment of their time and efforts than the education of masses.

43. C. I. Barnard, *The Functions of the Executive*, 30th anniversary edn (1938; Cambridge, MA: Harvard University Press, 1968), p. 217.

44. O. E. Williamson, 'Comparative Economic Organization: The Analysis of Discrete Structural Alternatives', *Administrative Science Quarterly*, 36 (1991), pp. 296–96, on pp. 272–5.

45. Gould, *Do We Still Need Peer Review?*, pp. 15, 94, 111.
46. Probably for this reason Foucault admits that enlightened absolutism is not a panacea after all. When Foucault provides his account of Socrates's life, he concludes: 'be it democracy or tyranny ... Socrates anyway found himself in a situation that all in all amounted to the same thing' (Foucault, *The Government of Self and Others*, p. 317).
47. The use of inverted commas can be better understood in the light of the previous discussion: even if the assessor and the assessed initially enjoy equal status in academia, the use of the strategy of gate keeping by the former helps her to enhance her relative status.
48. E. L. Boyer, *Scholarship Reconsidered: Priorities of the Professoriate* (New York: The Carnegie Foundation for the Advancement of Teaching, 1990), p. 78; see also Chapter 7, Section 3 of the present volume for more empirical detail.
49. M. S. McPherson and M. O. Shapiro, 'Tenure Issues in Higher Education', *Journal of Economic Perspectives*, 13 (1999), pp. 85–98, on p. 95; W. O. Brown, Jr, 'Faculty Participation in University Governance and the Effects on University Performance', *Journal of Economic Behavior and Organization*, 44 (2001), pp. 129–43, on p. 138; B. M. Cunningham, 'Faculty: Thy Administrator's Keeper? Some Evidence', *Economics of Education Review*, 28 (2009), pp. 444–53, on p. 445. The scarcity of primary data regarding the internal operation of academia has to be mentioned, however. For instance, the two last studies use the data collected through a 1970 survey of faculty working at American universities. No large-scale and equally comprehensive survey of American faculty has been conducted since then.
50. Gould, *Do We Still Need Peer Review?*, p. 30.
51. Gould, *Do We Still Need Peer Review?*, p. 57.
52. Shatz, *Peer Review*, p. 16.
53. Shatz, *Peer Review*, p. 151.
54. The results of the 1970 survey (see endnote 17 in this section) show that less than one-third of faculty teaching at the American universities, 28 per cent, published eleven or more articles in academic and professional journals during their careers (Boyer, *Scholarship Reconsidered*, table A-19). These academics formed the group of well-published scholars at that time.
55. P. Bourdieu and J-C. Passeron, *La reproduction: Éléments pour une théorie du système d'enseignement* (Paris: Éditions de Minuit, 1970).
56. S. J. Harnad, 'The Invisible Hand of Peer Review' (2000), in D. Shatz, *Peer Review: A Critical Inquiry* (Lanham, MA: Rowman & Littlefield Publishers, 2004), pp. 235–42, on p. 236; see also Oleinik, *Knowledge and Networking*, pp. 86–8.
57. Roth, 'Editorial Power/Authorial Suffering', p. 231.
58. Gould, *Do We Still Need Peer Review?*, p. 150.
59. Indexing is not always a purely technical task, however. This is why many publishers still ask the author to index her work instead of doing this in house. The management of large volumes of qualitative data also requires solving a number of methodological problems. One of the solutions refers to the use of advanced methods of qualitative and quantitative content analysis (A. Oleinik, 'Sbor, agregirovanie i obrabotka kachestvennykh dannykh' [Collection, aggregation and processing of qualitative data], *SOTsIS – Sotsiologicheskie Issledovaniya*, 5 (2014), pp. 121–31).
60. Gould, *Do We Still Need Peer Review?*, p. 133. *Sage Open* represents a practical attempt to move in this direction. *Sage Open* is a multi-disciplinary online depository with editors assigned (by the *Sage* administrative staff) to work with a single article only. This model does not need editors working on a continuous basis.

61. Tenure policies at many universities clearly state 'a decision not to award tenure is … in no sense a judgment of incompetence. Not all competent faculty meet the standards necessary for tenure at [a particular university], nor are all those who meet such standards automatically fitted or needed to serve the present and future needs of the University's programs' (University of Mississippi, 'Tenure Policies and Procedures' (2013), at https://secure4.olemiss.edu/umpolicyopen/GetPdfActive?pol=10647010& ver=active&file=10647010_active_20050330.pdf [accessed 29 June 2014]).

62. In some countries, for instance France, Italy, Spain and Denmark, the hiring process is controlled externally. If the government organizes a nationwide competition, then government representatives take the place of the university administration in the power triad and occupy the position of C_3 within it (P. Aghion, M. Dewatripont, C. Hoxby, A. Mas-Colell and A. Sapir, 'The Governance and Performance of Universities: Evidence from Europe and the US', *Economic Policy*, 25 (2010), pp. 7–59, on p. 55).

63. C. Musselin and F. Pigeyre, 'Les effets des mécanismes du recrutement collégial sur la discrimination: le cas des recrutements universitaires', *Sociologie du travail*, 50 (2008), pp. 48–70, on p. 57.

64. C. Musselin, 'How Peer Review Empowers the Academic Profession and University Managers: Changes in Relationships between the State, Universities and the Professoriate', *Research Policy*, 42 (2013), pp. 1165–73, on p. 1170.

65. Boyer, *Scholarship Reconsidered*, table A-8. The reader shall bear in mind, however, that this survey was carried out in 1970 and no more recent data are available.

66. R. D. Howard, G. W. McLaughlin, W. Gerald, W. E. Knight and Associates, *The Handbook of Institutional Research* (San Francisco, CA: Jossey-Bass, 2012), p. 145.

67. A discussion of grade inflation, its forms and driving forces can be found in Oleinik, *Knowledge and Networking*, ch. 7.

68. Shatz, *Peer Review*, pp. 124–32, 155.

69. Sociologists of organization recognized the importance of the issues of whistle-blowing and started to study this phenomenon relatively recently (R. Swedberg, *Principles of Economic Sociology* (Princeton, NJ: Princeton University Press, 2003), p. 97).

70. Boyer, *Scholarship Reconsidered*, p. 16.

71. P. Hutchings, M. T. Huber and A. Ciccone, *The Scholarship of Teaching and Learning Reconsidered* (San Francisco, CA: Jossey-Bass: A Wiley Imprint and Stanford, CA: The Carnegie Foundation for the Advancement of Teaching, 2011), p. 91.

72. University of Mississippi, 'Tenure Policies and Procedures'.

73. Memorial University of Newfoundland (MUN), 'Collective Agreement between MUN and MUN Faculty Association', 26 February 2010 – 31 August 2013, Section 11.07, at http://www.mun.ca/munfa/CA201013.htm [accessed 29 June 2014].

74. Memorial University of Newfoundland, 'Collective Agreement between MUN and MUN Faculty Association', section 11.26.

75. Ministry of Education of the Russian Federation, 'Polozhenie o poryadke zameshcheniya dolzhnostei naugno-pedagogicheskikh rabotnikov v vyshem uchebnom zavedenii Rossiiskoi Federatsii' enacted on 26 November 2006 [Principles of the appointment to research and teaching positions at the universities in the Russian Federation], section 4.

76. L. S. Lewis, *When Power Corrupts: Academic Governing Boards in the Shadow of Adelphi Case* (New Brunswick, NJ: Transaction Publishers, 2000), p. 11.

77. H. De Boer, J. Huisman and C. Meister-Scheytt, 'Supervision in "Modern" University Governance: Boards under Scrutiny', *Studies in Higher Education*, 35 (2010), pp. 317–33, on pp. 317–18. The supervisory body might be assisted by the internal auditor and her office, as in the MUN case.

78. T. Christensen, 'University Governance Reforms: Potential Problems of More Autonomy?', *Higher Education*, 62 (2011), pp. 503–17.
79. See Chapter 6, Section 3, note 15.
80. P. M. Kretek, Ž. Dragšić and B. M. Behm, 'Transformation of University Governance: On the Role of University Board Members', *Higher Education*, 65 (2013), pp. 39–58, on p. 40.
81. The scope of C_3's discretion tends to be particularly large at the public universities: government often fails to exercise due oversight of their senior management. Speaking figuratively, senior managers of the public universities eventually start awarding tenure to themselves. A study shows that the average tenure of presidents at public institutions is approximately five years greater than that of their private counterparts, ceteris paribus (F. G. Mixon Jr and R. W. McKenzie, 'Managerial Tenure under Private and Government Ownership: The Case of Higher Education', *Economics of Education Review*, 18 (1999), pp. 51–8, on p. 54). All four universities in my sample are public. As of July 2014, the MSU rector had served in that capacity for more than twenty-two years, the HSE rector – for more than twenty-one years.
82. See the introduction to this chapter.
83. B. S. Cole and R. G. Lewis, 'Court Cases and Judicial Opinions Related to Gatekeeping in Colleges, Universities, and Professional Schools', in P. Gibbs and E. H. Blakely (eds), *Gatekeeping in BSW Programs* (New York: Columbia University Press, 2000), pp. 212–35, on p. 214.
84. Memorial University of Newfoundland, 'Collective Agreement between MUN and MUN Faculty Association', sections 1.52, 10.08.
85. University of Mississippi, 'Tenure Policies and Procedures'.
86. File №11–27083 at the Moscow appellate court (file №2-73/13 at the Basmanny district court in the city of Moscow).
87. See also Chapter 6, Section 4 on the 'oligarchy of letters'.
88. Gould, *Do We Still Need Peer Review?*, p. 9.
89. Shatz, *Peer Review*, p. 12.
90. This proposal is considered in more detail in Oleinik, *Knowledge and Networking*, pp. 94–9.

INDEX

For Product Safety Concerns and Information please contact our EU
representative GPSR@taylorandfrancis.com Taylor & Francis Verlag GmbH,
Kaufingerstraße 24, 80331 München, Germany

Printed and bound by CPI Group (UK) Ltd, Croydon, CR0 4YY
01/05/2025
01858359-0003